Approaches to Teaching
Bechdel's *Fun Home*

THE MEMOIR IS A CONFLICTED ELEGY FOR MY EXASPERATING FATHER— SMALL TOWN BOY, SENSITIVE ARTIST, SOCIOPATH, VORACIOUS READER, PETTY TYRANT, HIGH SCHOOL TEACHER, MORTICIAN, AND HOMOSEXUAL VOLUPTUARY.

SLIGHTLY PERFECT.

EACH CHAPTER LOOKS FOR INFORMATION ABOUT HIM IN BOOKS BY SOME OF HIS FAVORITE AUTHORS. THE CHAPTER TITLES REFER TO THESE LITERARY CLUES.

ARCHIVAL MATERIAL IS WOVEN INTO THE TEXT. PHOTOS, MAPS, LETTERS, POLICE REPORTS, NEWSPAPERS, MARGINALIA,…

spared him a great deal of loneliness. He had been unfair; while his imagination and vanity had given her too much importance, his pride had given her too little. He discovered the cruel paradox by which we always deceive ourselves twice about the people we love - first to their advantage, then to their disadvantage. Today he understood that Marthe had been genuine with him - that she had been what she was, and that he owed her a good deal. It was beginning to ra̶ ̶ ̶ ̶ ̶ ̶ ̶ ̶ ̶ s of the street; t̶ ̶ ̶ ̶ ̶ ̶ ̶ ̶ ̶ ̶ ̶ aw Marthe's sudd ̶ ̶ ̶ ̶ by a burst of gratitude he could not express - in the old

…ALL OF THESE ARE DRAWN ON AS EVIDENCE.

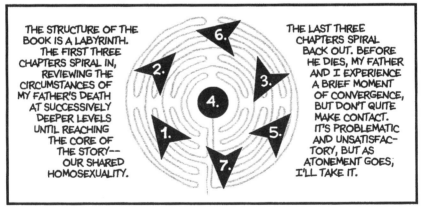

THE STRUCTURE OF THE BOOK IS A LABYRINTH. THE FIRST THREE CHAPTERS SPIRAL IN, REVIEWING THE CIRCUMSTANCES OF MY FATHER'S DEATH AT SUCCESSIVELY DEEPER LEVELS UNTIL REACHING THE CORE OF THE STORY-- OUR SHARED HOMOSEXUALITY.

THE LAST THREE CHAPTERS SPIRAL BACK OUT. BEFORE HE DIES, MY FATHER AND I EXPERIENCE A BRIEF MOMENT OF CONVERGENCE, BUT DON'T QUITE MAKE CONTACT. IT'S PROBLEMATIC AND UNSATISFAC-TORY, BUT AS ATONEMENT GOES, I'LL TAKE IT.

Courtesy of Alison Bechdel, from her 2003 book proposal for *Fun Home*.

Approaches to Teaching Bechdel's *Fun Home*

Edited by

Judith Kegan Gardiner

The Modern Language Association of America
New York   2018

© 2018 by The Modern Language Association of America
All rights reserved
Printed in the United States of America

MLA and the MODERN LANGUAGE ASSOCIATION are trademarks
owned by the Modern Language Association of America.
For information about obtaining permission to reprint material from
MLA book publications, send your request by mail (see address below) or
e-mail (permissions@mla.org).

Library of Congress Cataloging-in-Publication Data:

Names: Gardiner, Judith Kegan, editor.
Title: Approaches to teaching Bechdel's Fun home / edited by Judith Kegan Gardiner.
Description: New York : Modern Language Association of America, 2018. |
Series: Approaches to teaching world literature, ISSN 1059-1133 ; 154 |
Includes bibliographical references and index.
Identifiers: LCCN 2018026970 (print) | LCCN 2018044416 (ebook)
ISBN 9781603293600 (EPUB) | ISBN 9781603293617 (Kindle)
ISBN 9781603293587 (cloth : alk. paper) | ISBN 9781603293594 (pbk. : alk. paper)
Subjects: LCSH: Bechdel, Alison, 1960– Fun home. | Bechdel, Alison,
1960—Study and teaching. | Graphic novels—Study and teaching (Higher)
Classification: LCC PN6727.B3757 (ebook) | LCC PN6727.B3757 F863 2018 (print) |
DDC 741.5/973—dc23
LC record available at https://lccn.loc.gov/2018026970

Approaches to Teaching World Literature 154
ISSN 1059-1133

Published by The Modern Language Association of America
85 Broad Street, suite 500, New York, New York 10004-2434
www.mla.org

For Annika and Eden

CONTENTS

PREFACE

I discovered Alison Bechdel's comics in the 1980s and read with delight their witty, astute, and politically engaged running commentaries on American culture. Her series *Dykes to Watch Out For* created an imaginary lesbian community whose coherence was utopian in comparison with the fragmented rest of American society, despite the quirks of its continuing characters and the controversies in which they were involved (Gardiner, "Bechdel's *Dykes*"). Nevertheless, *Fun Home: A Family Tragicomic* came as a surprise. In the form of a unified graphic memoir, it displays the same wit and intelligence as Bechdel's earlier comics but has greater emotional depth and artistic mastery. Its web of allusions situated the memoir in multiple literary traditions and genres, both canonical and popular, and provided additional pleasure to my reading as a professor of English literature. I immediately incorporated the book into my classes. My students were responsive but had difficulty with the allusions and with the book's recursive structure. I therefore proposed to the Modern Language Association that teachers would appreciate a collection of essays exploring this book.

I hope *Approaches to Teaching Bechdel's* Fun Home provides teachers with useful and productive pedagogical strategies for a variety of courses. Crediting *Fun Home*'s literary, artistic, and cultural resonances, this volume aims to help college instructors make this sophisticated contemporary text accessible to students as an integrated whole.

Introduction
Judith Kegan Gardiner

Alison Bechdel's graphic memoir of 2006, *Fun Home: A Family Tragicomic*, tells the intertwined stories of the narrator's coming out as a young lesbian and of the troubling enigma of her father, Bruce, a closeted gay high school English teacher who died suddenly when he was hit by a truck.[1] The book's title, ironically naming the family funeral home, evokes the saddest and funniest of human experiences, death and sex, subjects whose investigation structures the memoir. Its subtitle indicates the memoir's generic plenitude and its conflation of people and texts with the themes of love, language, and the love of language. The subtitle also implies that the family, not just the book, is "tragicomic," a kind of drama in which serious, potentially fatal issues are resolved into a happy ending. But the structure of *Fun Home* is more complicated than that, as shown by Bechdel's labyrinthine diagram, reproduced as the frontispiece to this book, depicting her plan to have her memoir spiral inward to its central, unanswerable question—whether or not her father's death was a suicide—then spiral outward again to her later life as an open lesbian.

The comments in this introduction address the issues raised by teachers of *Fun Home*, who responded to a survey conducted by the Modern Language Association, and by the original essays that follow in this volume, which are organized according to sections directed to the literature classroom, to the memoir's graphic form, to the topics of psychology and sexuality, and finally to alternative classroom structures. I start by discussing the book's most striking issues, particularly with reference to its allusions, themes, and genres. Next, I comment on the challenges provoked by the book's visual form to literature instructors as well as to those in interdisciplinary classes. Then, I look at its treatment of psychology and sexuality, which make *Fun Home* exciting but also sometimes troubling for students—in women's and gender studies as well as literature courses.

Fun Home addresses issues of importance to young adults today. It can be read as an autobiography and novel of development, tracing its protagonist's engagement with literature and literature's role in helping the protagonist search for a personal identity. It crosses boundaries of genre and redefines the literary conventions of memoir, biography, autobiography, graphic memoir, and comic book as well as those of the bildungsroman and specifically of the *Künstlerroman* (novel of an artist's development). It is a book about books and reading and about how reading can change lives. Its chapters are structured around allusions to James Joyce, F. Scott Fitzgerald, Marcel Proust, Oscar Wilde, and Virginia Woolf. It can be read as a love letter to the tradition of English literature and to the importance of reading in shaping individual lives. It can also be viewed as a book about drawing that enhances the visual literacy of its viewers and their ability to navigate the multimodal format of the graphic text. This volume of essays, especially in the "Materials" section, helps teachers and students become comfortable with these diverse sources and traditions.

In *Fun Home*'s first scene Bruce Bechdel is reading *Anna Karenina*, a tragic novel that foreshadows his own death, which may or may not have been a suicide. Later in the memoir Bruce says his daughter is his only high school student worth teaching. Although Alison spurns her father's attempts to direct her reading and only skims James Joyce's *Ulysses* in college, she finds inspiration for her own young adult life from Adrienne Rich's poetry and Kate Millett's *Flying*. Alison's recollections are laden with mythological and literary allusions as well as references to history and popular culture. Sometimes these allusions help the reader decipher the psychologies of the focal characters, and often they raise philosophical questions about what one can—or cannot—know about oneself or others. In the pre-Stonewall period, people whose gender presentation or sexual orientation did not conform to the dominant society often wished to shield their personal lives from outside view. Their lives could seem to others to be characterized by secrecy, evasiveness, and lies, as well as by ironic hints and coterie connections to be enjoyed by those in the know. The love letters Bruce writes to his wife-to-be, Helen, seem to arise from his ambivalent infatuation with reading about Fitzgerald and Fitzgerald's romance with Zelda. Selections from these love letters are copied into the text of *Fun Home* near the end of the book, when the reader has already witnessed Helen Bechdel's disappointment with her marriage as well as Alison's yearning for her preoccupied parents' love and attention, which as a child she displaces by kissing her stuffed animals good night. The book's nonchronological structure thus shapes the emotional effects of Bechdel's narrative choices for its readers and rewards close attention from students. In addition, Bechdel's re-creation of her father's words superimposes her life on his, as does her equivocal insistence that she and her father are completely similar or completely different. She involves herself in this superposition of father and daughter in several ways. She draws the words of the many documents she reproduces, including maps, her childhood diaries, Bruce's letters, even his police report. She also poses and photographs herself in the position of all the characters in her memoir, using these selfies to guide her drawing and thus blending herself with her father.

Fun Home revolves around the father-daughter axis of Alison and Bruce Bechdel, though Alison's mother and brothers also feature in some episodes. The subtitle, "A Family Tragicomic," alludes to the entire family dynamic as well as to the memoir's mixed genre. The pun on *fun home* connects the funeral home that Bruce owns, where he eviscerates and embalms corpses, with the Bechdel residence, which is not much fun for his family, and with his job at the local high school, where he dissects English and American literature for students he considers intellectually dead. Student readers of the memoir may enjoy evaluating Bruce as a teacher as well as Alison's college teachers in comparison with their own pedagogical ideals. At times Bruce enlists the labor of his own children in the fun home. There they have more fun together flying imaginary airplanes to Havana than they do when isolated in the museum-like mansion Bruce has reconstructed as their home.

The text raises the issue of whether or not Bruce can be seen as a tragic hero, a question that demands full discussion of his portrayal as a tyrannical patriarch, of his secret sexual preference for young men, and of the historical period of the closet in American life (Gardiner, "Queering"). Although his death in a road accident is an established fact, his state of mind on the fatal day remains a mystery. As a literary character, he is complex. He is portrayed in Bechdel's drawings as an abusive husband towering over his family and sometimes as a supportive father playing airplane with his young daughter and, years later, seated next to her at the piano playing a duet.

The tragicomedy also has many comic aspects, both in the sense of a happy ending, since Alison emerges from family isolation to join a fulfilling lesbian community, and in the book's references to the tradition of newspaper comics like Bechdel's own series *Dykes to Watch Out For.* Bechdel's wit incorporates many sly literary allusions: for example, to Oscar Wilde's plays and to Toad of Kenneth Grahame's *Wind in the Willows.* Albert Camus's suicide and Colette's lesbian crushes allude to the situations of the memoir's central characters. After Bruce's death Alison explodes in hysterical laughter at the existential absurdity of her vibrant father's demise. Thus the theme of death and its meanings for the living are inescapable in discussions of the text, as are questions of tone for readers who may find themselves confused by the book's oscillations between apparently serious and frivolous approaches to death and sexuality.

In the few years since its publication, *Fun Home* has become widely taught in courses in literature (American literature in particular), fiction, the graphic novel, autobiography and memoir, women's literature, gay and lesbian studies, and even art history. It has won critical accolades and is already included in lists of top books of the postmillennial period. *Fun Home* has gained many testaments of popular and scholarly recognition. It was the first graphic memoir to be named *Time* magazine's Best Book of the Year, and it won the 2007 Eisner Award for Best Reality-Based Work. Bechdel won a MacArthur Fellowship ("genius" grant) in 2014. The publication of *Fun Home* followed Bechdel's two decades of comic strips in the series *Dykes to Watch Out For,* which record the history of the lesbian community in the United States, and it was followed in 2012 by Bechdel's second biographical graphic memoir, *Are You My Mother? A Comic Drama.* The "About" page of Bechdel's Web site (dykestowatchoutfor .com) describes her as "preoccupied with the overlap of the political and the personal spheres, the relationship of the self to the world outside" and explains that whereas "*Dykes to Watch Out For* was an explicitly community-based and politically engaged project," in delving into her "deeply intimate memoirs about her father's life before the gay rights movement and her mother's life before the women's movement," she turns "a microscopic lens on the internal mechanisms of oppression and liberation." *Fun Home* has been translated into French, Italian, Portuguese (in Brazil), Hungarian, Korean, and Polish, and further translations are in process.

In 2013 the musical version of *Fun Home*, adapted from Bechdel's text, with book and lyrics by Lisa Kron and music by Jeanine Tesori, opened off-Broadway at the Public Theater. In 2015 it moved to Broadway's Circle in the Square Theatre. Michael Paulson and Patrick Healy describe the musical as "a poignant and raw exploration of family, memory, sexuality, and suicide" that had "completed a long journey from the margins to the mainstream, as it won the Tony Award for best new musical" in 2015. The original cast recording of the musical is available on an audio compact disc, and video selections can be seen on the Internet. In addition, Bechdel has recorded video lectures accessible online (see my essay "The Instructor's Library" in this volume for more on lectures by and interviews with Bechdel). These resources provide rich supplements for the classroom in multiple modes and media. They also raise questions about the genre of Bechdel's memoir and highlight the unique and disparate qualities of the graphic text in comparison with the musical. In contrast to its presentation as a musical onstage, the graphic text of *Fun Home* remains more richly allusive and more ambivalent. Kron and Tesori changed the mournful and elegiac tone of Bechdel's text, playing down elements of death, suicide, and sexuality in favor of a more upbeat celebration of the themes of family and finding one's own identity. Other differences between the published graphic text and the musical are illustrative of the two forms, and, with the help of the cast recording, published libretto, and video scenes, open to student analysis. The musical has three Alison characters: child Alison, adolescent Alison, and an adult avatar of the author, Alison Bechdel. "The three Alisons correspond" to Bechdel's "own idea of herself," she has said. "I'm someone who was always writing about my life. So that, in a way, feels natural to me. . . . Then I had the realization that what the book was really about is how I learned to be an artist from my father" (A. Abbott). In the graphic text, in contrast, Bechdel's memories of her childhood and youth at different ages smoothly transition back and forth without being divided into separate characters. The adult author is present through the thoughtful words of her captions and written comments that sound in our heads as we read, but she is not pictured.

When Bechdel and her youngest brother first watched the live performance of the musical, Bechdel says they "had this amazing moment of crying together. After the cast left the stage, we just kind of sat there and held each other, which we've *never* done" (qtd. in A. Abbott). The graphic text, however, provides readers with other experiences. It encourages readers to dwell at their own pace on the illustrations, which indicate emphasis by the size of the cells: for example, the extra wide panel that shows Alison's sense that travel enlarges one's perspective and the difficulties of following in her father's footsteps when carrying his baggage at an airport during a family vacation (*Fun Home* 63). The most emphatic visual in the memoir is the double-page spread of the sleeping, almost

nude babysitter, Roy, at the center of the book, an illustration that invites the
reader to join Alison and Bruce in their erotic, perhaps guilty, contemplation
of masculine beauty (100–01). Jan Baetens and Hugo Frey, noting especially
this centerfold, claim that "the relative discreteness" of *Fun Home*'s layout is
"dramatically disrupted each time something crucial takes place in the story"
(126). But even the regularity of Bechdel's "elementary page grid" of neatly
stacked cells, in a scene of Alison and Bruce driving to a movie, is meaningful for them: "the failed 'encounter' of father and daughter, who do not quite
manage to acknowledge and accept their shared homosexuality" is indicated by
the unchanging visual grid, the immobile characters, and the thick black strip
above them, an effect echoed in the following pages as they sit together in a
dark movie theater watching *Coal Miner's Daughter*, and the daughter in the
movie tells her father she will never see him again (Baetens and Frey 126–27;
Fun Home 220–22).

The musical adds motion, a fixed time frame, melody, rhythm, and color. In
comparison, Alison's quest for truth is drawn in the memoir through an aesthetic of plainness that contrasts her character's open honesty with what she
sees as her father's more deceptive love of appearance and artifice. The memoir
and the musical also incorporate history differently. The memoir mentions historical events like President Nixon's resignation and the Stonewall Inn demon-
strations for gay liberation, while the musical employs auditory allusions of its
own—for example, comparing the unhappy Bechdel family to the happy television Partridge family by echoing its theme song. The musical has college-age
Alison buoyantly sing "I'm changing my major to Joan" in a triumphal waltz
tempo declaration of adolescent erotic pleasure that omits the graphic memoir's
anxious mythological references to a potentially frightening first sexual experience. This song provides the musical with a snappy love lyric. Bechdel says that
another song in the musical, "Ring of Keys," has already become "the national
butch anthem," thus shading the memoir's more equivocal illustration of Alison's attraction into simple celebration (Cauterucci).

Bechdel told Judith Thurman that she admires the emotional effects of the
musical and reinterprets some of her own earlier attitudes about the relation of the
lesbian community to society at large, saying whereas she previously wanted her
work considered "distinctively queer," she has since broadened her views. "I think
what gets people is the tension between the dialogue and the music," she says,
"the yearnings so painfully stifled in the former, so cathartically released when
they sing." Bechdel adds, "It's funny. When the memoir came out, I bristled at critics who qualified the struggle it describes as 'universal.' It felt like they were trying
to co-opt my identity. But it doesn't strike me that way anymore. I've come to the
conclusion that we're all queer—there is no normal" (Thurman, "Finish Line").

The Internet provides the classroom with rich possibilities to view scenes
from the musical, to hear many of Bechdel's lectures, and to watch her drawing
technique, which involves historical research, reproducing family photographs
and letters, and posing herself in the positions in which she wants to draw her

characters (Bechdel, "Alison Bechdel: Creating *Fun Home*"). Her prolific presence in lectures and interviews has many advantages for classes studying her work, but it may also heighten the tendency for students to substitute the author's retrospective words for the complexities of her graphic text and so fall into the intentional fallacy condemned by twentieth-century New Criticism—that is, the error of letting the author's statements substitute for readings of the text itself. Teachers may warn against such retrospective assessments, directing students to the subtle emotions and visual cues in the graphic text.

Depending on the course, instructors contextualize *Fun Home* in a wide number of ways. For courses in English literature, some instructors end courses with *Fun Home* after teaching Joyce's *Portrait of the Artist as a Young Man*—or even *Ulysses*, for advanced courses in modernism. Others teach *Fun Home* in courses specifically on graphic texts. Among the delights of *Fun Home* are its simple but expressive visual style and its incorporation of a wide range of reproduced visual documents, including photographs, maps, charts, police reports, and childhood diary entries. Thus the graphic medium itself is of major importance for many teachers of the memoir who resist subordinating the visual to verbal text. Several faculty members report pairing *Fun Home* with Art Spiegelman's *Maus*, another graphic memoir that is also a joint biography of an artist and the artist's parents. Like *Maus*, *Fun Home* is a portrait of a father narrated by his adult child trying to understand a traumatic moment in history. Yet the allegorical animal figures in *Maus* insist on the book's relation to the traditions of the commercial comic book at the same time that they distance the reader from the horrors of the Holocaust. The simple black-and-white drawings in Marjane Satrapi's *Persepolis* connote the political repression of the extremist Islamic regime in Iran after the popular overthrow of the shah. In comparison, the often impassive faces depicted in *Fun Home* bespeak the family's psychological repressions. *Fun Home*'s muted color palette and restrained drawing style can, in turn, be contrasted with the deliberately exaggerated, sometimes grotesque renderings of the cross-generational, semi-incestuous relationship between the autobiographical narrator of Phoebe Gloeckner's *A Child's Life* and *The Diary of a Teenage Girl* and her mother's boyfriend. These disturbing psychological associations are minimized in the movie version of Gloeckner's *Diary* featuring a pretty, fresh-faced young actress (Heller). Such generic comparisons can also be fruitful for classes studying *Fun Home* as a memoir and a musical.

If the themes of death and the literary tradition are universally acknowledged as appropriate topics for English classrooms, there is more ambivalence about the role of sexuality, despite concurrence that the subject remains of vital interest to college readers. Courses have long included the adultery plots of Nathanial Hawthorne's *The Scarlet Letter* and Edith Wharton's *Ethan Frome* and writings by gay and lesbian authors such as Oscar Wilde, Willa Cather, and James Baldwin. Controversies about the sexuality of such canonical authors as William Shakespeare and Virginia Woolf have been considered appropriate classroom subjects for decades. Some second-wave feminist books about gay men and lesbians turned the tables on homophobia, as in Rita Mae Brown's 1973 comic classic, *Rubyfruit Jungle*, where the smart, beautiful, and invincible lesbian protagonist triumphs over an array of cowardly, bigoted, and perverse heterosexual characters. Brown's approach distances itself from earlier melancholic depictions of lesbian life like Radclyffe Hall's 1928 *The Well of Loneliness*. Such historical contrasts are likely to be of interest to women's and gender studies classes as well as to literature classes. Today's texts about LGBTQ lives are more likely to ignore the coming-out plot featured in *Fun Home* in favor of more matter-of-fact acknowledgments of same-sex as well as opposite-sex attractions and of nonnormative gender presentations.

Leading up to Bechdel's thoughtful depictions of gender, sexuality, and personal identity, recent decades have seen an efflorescence of interest in these topics. *Fun Home* addresses both the protagonist's and her father's gender nonconformity and their struggles with same-sex sexual desires. Its characters are complex and do not fit cultural stereotypes. Despite Bechdel's claim that she was "butch" to her father's "nelly" (*Fun Home* 15), such apparent dichotomies constantly break down in the memoir. In *Fun Home*, sexuality and individual psychology are treated seriously, comically, psychologically, and in the context of a wide range of other discourses. The characterizations of the Bechdel family in the text are nuanced, and the text juxtaposes different forms of nonnormative gender and sexuality in ways that encourage psychological insight and ethical questioning among student readers.

While students may be familiar with Bechdel because of *Fun Home* and the musical, some students may additionally know of the so-called Bechdel test, a reference to a 1985 episode from *Dykes to Watch Out For* where one woman says to another that she won't watch a movie unless it features at least two named women characters who talk to each other about something other than a man. Bechdel credits the test to her friend Liz Wallace but also says it is a modern version of Virginia Woolf's desire, expressed in *A Room of One's Own*, for more representations of women in relation to one another rather than in relation to men. (In *Why Comics?* Hillary Chute reproduces the original comic of the Bechdel test [10].) *Fun Home* focuses on Alison's relationship with her father and downplays her relationship with her mother, though that bond comes to the fore in the episode where Helen helps Alison overcome her obsessive-compulsive preoccupations by writing down Alison's diary entries for her. Students might be asked to analyze passages in the memoir that pass the Bechdel test.

Outside the classroom, sexual identities, behaviors, and attitudes have undergone dramatic changes in the past few decades. Although public and legal acceptance of LGBTQ identities and gay marriage has greatly increased in the United States, there remains a vocal minority hostile to portrayals of sexual diversity. *Fun Home* has figured in a few censorship attempts, ostensibly to protect college students from its contents and to punish those schools where the book has been taught. In 2014 the South Carolina House of Representatives withdrew $52,000 in state funding from Charleston College, its entire budget for a summer reading program, because *Fun Home* was included in the curriculum (Kellogg). In response, Bechdel and the cast of the musical traveled to South Carolina and performed the musical to support the college (Portwood). On 12 June 2016, a single armed gunman murdered forty-nine people at the Pulse nightclub in Orlando, Florida, a bar with many gay patrons, particularly from the Hispanic community. Responding to this tragedy, Michael Cerveris, the actor playing Bruce Bechdel in the musical, organized another fund-raising trip, this time for the cast to travel to Orlando on their one day off from their Broadway schedule to perform a benefit performance for the survivors and families of victims of the massacre. The play "is a call to courageously embrace life and love and a warning of the danger of living in fear and denial. . . . Its only agenda is compassion," said Cerveris, who also commented on the emotional bond uniting the performers and the audience, the play becoming a place where people could bring their grief.

The essays collected in this book proceed in the same order as the topics covered in this introduction and address the themes highlighted in the MLA survey. The essays in "Materials" describe *Fun Home*'s sources and allusions, followed by essays in "Approaches" that group essays around teaching the literary tradition, and especially the genres of memoir and autobiography; teaching graphic aspects of the text; approaching the subjects of psychology and sexuality with students; and teaching the memoir in nontraditional educational formats. While the essays are thematically grouped, they can be read in any order, which will reveal further connections between them. The authors describe classes from first-year to advanced undergraduate in a variety of educational institutions, and they recount specific classroom exercises and assignments. The contributors are primarily based in the United States, but some are from Canada, the United Kingdom, Australia, and Denmark. Two authors, Valerie Rohy and Daniel Fogel, taught with Bechdel at the University of Vermont, where Bechdel was a professor-at-large. Many faculty members assign the videos that depict Bechdel's laborious drawing process, bringing the artist into the classroom virtually. These videos plus interviews and much more are available on Bechdel's Web site (dykestowatchoutfor.com).

This volume's "Materials" section begins with a time line, by Sarah Buchmeier, that is keyed both to historical events during the decades the memoir covers and to the corresponding pages in *Fun Home*, thus encouraging a historical approach, particularly to American society in the 1970s and 1980s. The "Materials" section also includes essays by D. Quentin Miller and Rohy that annotate the book's wide-ranging literary and theoretical references. Many students find Bechdel's extensive allusions in *Fun Home* daunting. Miller counts allusions to over sixty works of literature and mythology in the text and describes Bechdel's inclusion of them as "meticulous and precise." Rohy provides an annotated list of theoretical allusions in *Fun Home*, commenting that "Bechdel has gone everywhere first, because many of the theoretical methods one might use to interpret [*Fun Home*] are already at work inside the text." The lists of literary and theoretical references in the memoir can provide teachers with guidance for classroom assignments.

While Bechdel's literary allusions to Joyce and Fitzgerald, for example, structure the memoir and are explicitly noted in it, Rasmus Simonsen's contribution to this volume is a resource that teachers may find less obvious but nevertheless useful: a list of architectural and decorative features pictured in the drawings of the Bechdel home, features that often metonymically represent the book's characters and conflicts, especially Bruce's love of artifice in contrast with Alison's aesthetic and ethics of plainness. Julie Enszer's essay broadens the range of contexts teachers bring to *Fun Home* by describing its interlocking narratives about lesbian, gay, bisexual, and transgender history and print culture in order to encourage students to think about "how history shapes lived experiences."

Part 2, "Approaches," features essays focused on pedagogical and theoretical approaches to teaching *Fun Home*. The first group of essays addresses concerns of the literature classroom, such as the book's generic multiplicity and its themes of identity and family. Julia Watson discusses the interplay of biography, autobiography, and other genres in the text, exploring how the stories of Alison and her father both interrelate and diverge as the memoir's "domestic ethnography" proceeds. Watson encourages students to address "how Bechdel's visual self-reference implicates viewers in complexities of looking that reflect on their own desires." In a course on teaching modernism within a great-books program, Ariela Freedman examines the tensions in the text between autobiography and fiction, subjectivity and self-making. She also suggests that in "Bechdel's tussle with modernist classics, students will recognize their own academic odysseys." Susan Van Dyne, who curated the Bechdel papers in the Smith College library, uses an archival and deconstructive approach to unpack the connections between family and truth in Bechdel's evolving drafts and manuscripts for *Fun Home*, written over several years. The lists of the memoir's literary and theoretical references in Miller's and Rohy's contributions provide teachers with guidance for classroom assignments, like Soo La Kim's exercise that requires students to collaborate in research that explicates allusions and other intertexts as narrative devices "not only to tell what happened but to get at the difficult and contradictory emotional truths about what happened." Using an intersectional approach favored by many gender studies as well as literature teachers, JoAnne Ruvoli explores the constraints of the all-white Christian community where the Bechdels live in comparison with the ethnically various communities that populate Bechdel's *Dykes to Watch Out For* comics. And in a course called "Banned Books and Novel Ideas" Eric Detweiler draws on the ancient rhetorical tradition of *ethopoeia*, or imitation of the character of a proposed speaker, for an assignment in which students write a letter or monologue in the voice of Alison or Bruce Bechdel, which Detweiler describes as an "exercise in rhetorical failure rather than rhetorical mastery—one that emphasized the limits the writer encounters in attempting to speak for or as another." Concluding this group of essays, the drama theorist Sue-Ellen Case compares the graphic narrative of *Fun Home* with the musical adaptation. She invites her students to imagine how other stagings might create Bechdel's dramatic world and notes the changes in the work's reception as it moves from page to stage, "from depicting a movement in search of civil rights to one more successful in gaining them."

The next section discusses the challenges of teaching *Fun Home* as a visual text. All the essays in this section highlight the advantages of increasing students' visual literacy. Many faculty members supplement reading *Fun Home* with texts on graphic literacy, several of which are discussed in my essay, "The Instructor's Library," in this volume. In his course for first-semester undergraduates, Daniel Fogel introduces his students to narrative theory as a way to help them "grasp more fully the meaning and power of *Fun Home* in all its complex emotional and thematic dimensions." To emphasize the visual aspect of the text, Michael Chaney argues in favor of the rubric "autobiographical graphic novel," while other contributors call *Fun Home* a memoir. "How do the pictures of *Fun Home* tell truths that words alone cannot convey?" Chaney asks. Alexis Boylan argues that *Fun Home* should be seen not only "as primarily a visual text" but "more specifically, as a work of contemporary visual art production," taught in relation to other current visual artworks. The importance of photography to *Fun Home* raises its own set of questions, as David Bahr demonstrates in describing an exercise requiring his students to re-create family photographs as drawings and reimagine the stories behind them and at the same time apply their experiences of the exercise to their experience with *Fun Home*.

The following section takes on delicate and necessary questions regarding psychology, sexuality, and gender that arise in women's and gender studies courses as well as courses in literature, American studies, cultural studies, and rhetoric. The essays in this section raise epistemological and ethical questions concerning how we can know what we know about ourselves and about others, and particularly about how we can know our own and others' desires. Some essays in this section find the interpretative models of psychoanalysis useful, while others take a more historical approach or apply the theoretical lenses of contemporary feminist and queer theory and of disability and trauma studies. Audrey Bilger explores the many genres of *Fun Home* in the context of Bechdel's *Dykes to Watch Out For* as well as of psychoanalytic theories about humor, while Dana Heller uses the luncheonette scene in *Fun Home*, in which child Alison first sees a butch truck driver, to unlock the possibilities of growing up butch. Monica B. Pearl discusses gay male, rather than lesbian, identity to contextualize the character of Bruce Bechdel in the twentieth century, a discussion connecting sexuality and history with the architectural details described in Simonsen's essay. Jennifer Lemberg expands the discussion of sexual difference beyond the usual categories by comparing *Fun Home* with two memoirs about lesbians with transgender partners. Environmental contexts feature in Debra J. Rosenthal and Lydia Munnell's essay, which considers the usual queer "rural-to-urban migration story" by turning students' attention to the rural spaces of

Fun Home. Erica Galioto approaches *Fun Home* as a narrative about trauma in comparison with Bechdel's psychoanalytically focused memoir about her mother and herself, *Are You My Mother?* Cynthia Barounis invites her students to see parallels—and contrasts—between child Alison's obsessive-compulsive phase and the emergence of her lesbian self-identification. In contrast to narratives of cure and recovery, Barounis emphasizes ways "the memoir validates obsessive-compulsive behaviors," with Bechdel's elaborate drawing process included among such behaviors that have positive results, as clearly seen in the book's text before us.

The final group of essays in this book takes up issues generated by teaching in nontraditional contexts. In her online course Ellen Gil-Gómez asks students how *Fun Home* can be read as a detective comic. Also using online pedagogy, Christine Quinan has students converse with one another through blogs. Drawing on an Australian government–funded study of student reading habits, Judith Seaboyer and Jessica Gildersleeve invite students to produce brief ungraded "affective responses" to the text, an activity that facilitates self-reflection, ethical inquiry, and responsible engagement with the text. Donna Pasternak's essay on reading *Fun Home* as young adult literature recounts her experiences mentoring prospective high school teachers in relation to her belated realization that she was herself mentored by Bruce Bechdel when she was training to be a teacher, a coincidence that complicates and enriches her exploration of ethics in the classroom.

Bechdel's afterword concludes the volume, explaining the conception of *Fun Home*'s structure as a Daedalian labyrinth, which she drew as part of her 2003 book proposal (see frontispiece). Her labyrinthine spiral maze provides an opportunity for instructors to have students analyze the book's structure and its nonchronological arrangement of chapters. Students might note which characters take the spotlight in various episodes, how old the characters are in each incident, and how their crises are resolved or not. Collectively, this exercise provides the class as a whole more insight into how Bechdel builds her recursive structure; how the relationships, especially between Alison and her parents, change; and how students' reactions to the story as it proceeds are shaped by the order in which Bechdel reveals the memoir's issues. Students may discuss, for example, the effects of our knowing of Bruce Bechdel's death long before its graphic portrayal late in the memoir.

The Modern Language Association's survey of college instructors about their experiences teaching *Fun Home* was answered by over one hundred faculty members, from Brazil, Germany, and Singapore as well as from the United States. Most teachers of *Fun Home* report high student engagement and interest. Negative responses, chiefly in reaction to the book's explicit treatment of sexuality, are rare. The following summary of the survey responses is addressed to teachers curious about the classroom experiences of other faculty members teaching *Fun Home.*

Many survey respondents referred to students' unfamiliarity with *Fun Home*'s allusions and intertexts. Others connected the themes of personal and sexual identity with these allusions and with the challenges of responding to the literary genres of autobiography and memoir. For example, Leah Anderst highlights "the way that Bechdel constructs a self (her 'self' is in relation to others, is refracted through books, is non-linear)" and also notes, "When I am teaching students to write personal/autobiographical essays, Bechdel's example is great for describing the different autobiographical 'I's' and their fluidity." Kinohi Nishikawa contextualizes questions about the self and what one can know about others by teaching *Fun Home* as a mystery story. Instructors commented that students often felt personally involved in the book and identified with its characters. For example, Robin Bernstein finds that many students share the book with their parents and siblings when they are home for spring break.

Other instructors focused their responses on the experience of teaching a graphic text in an English course. In an introductory course in literary criticism, John Alberti discovered that "students are often surprised that visual texts can take more time to read than purely verbal texts (a counterintuitive experience)." In an introductory course on graphic narrative Linda Macri urged her students to consider how Bechdel uses "comics to tell a story that has very little action, that is primarily cerebral and reflective, and how [Bechdel] accomplishes that in a medium that we often associate with action."

The sexual and psychological aspects of the text attracted numerous but disparate comments. For example, one teacher in the survey said some religious students thought the book offensive, and, in contrast, a teacher of queer studies reported with surprise that "students who identify as nonbinary trans found the work too limiting in terms of how gender and desire are represented." Ronak Kapadia reported that many of his students "raised concerns about [Bechdel's] lax depiction of her father and others in terms of mental or cognitive disabilities ('autism-like,' 'OCD')." Other faculty members described some students as disturbed by or hostile to the sexual representations in the book, and these teachers were pleased when other students responded to homophobic remarks in class. One teacher suggested inviting to class representatives of campus LGBTQ organizations who could describe the availability of campus resources. A women's studies teacher, Melissa Rogers, said she opened her class with "the heterosexual questionnaire," which encourages students to question the "naturalness of sexual identity categories" (Rochlin). Several faculty reported that deflecting students' attention from sexual content to formal aspects of the text improved the class atmosphere. For example, Jesse Molesworth described his students as uncomfortable discussing the book's more graphic scenes, but stated that "[t]hese scenes must be discussed. So I typically turn the discussion to questions of form and representation." Similarly, when, in a freshman composition course, Sinduja Sathiyaseelan encountered student resistance to depictions of nudity and sexuality, she reframed the text "as a study of effective storytelling techniques and structure" and found her students "much more receptive" than when she put the book in a "social justice context." Some instructors reported that students were energized rather than alienated by the book's frankness. For instance, Edward Brunner found that "the freshmen soldiered through because they were bright-eyed at the prospect of actually talking about sexual issues openly—now they knew they weren't in high school."

NOTES

I thank the respondents to the survey on teaching *Fun Home* as well as the contributors to this volume, including my research assistant Sarah Buchmeier, who compiled the works-cited list and the index.

[1] I refer to the author as Bechdel and the represented autobiographical character as Alison.

Part One

MATERIALS

Biographical and Historical Time Line for Alison Bechdel

Sarah Buchmeier

Relevant page numbers in *Fun Home* are indicated in parentheses.

26 July 1933	Helen Augusta Fontana is born in Lock Haven, Pennsylvania, to Andrew and Rachel Fontana.
8 Apr. 1936	Bruce Allen Bechdel is born in Beech Creek, Pennsylvania, to Claude and Dorothy Bechdel. His siblings are Paul, Jane, and Eleanor (140).
1959	Bruce and Helen are married in Luzern, Switzerland (71).
10 Sept. 1960	Alison Bechdel is born in Lock Haven, Pennsylvania, to Helen and Bruce Bechdel. Her siblings are Bruce (Christian) Bechdel II and John Bechdel.
28 June 1969	Demonstrations against police harassment of gay, lesbian, transgender, and cross-dressed patrons of New York City's Stonewall Inn ignite movement for gay liberation in the United States (104).
1970	Alison Bechdel develops an obsessive-compulsive disorder (135–39, 148).
1974	President Nixon resigns following the Watergate trial (54, 171, 181).
1977–81	Bechdel attends Oberlin College (46–47, 49, 200–03, 206–10, 224).
1980	Bechdel comes out as a lesbian to her parents (58–59, 76–77, 210).
2 July 1980	Bruce Bechdel dies when hit by a truck (27–30, 50–54, 81, 89, 116–17, 124–25, 226–27, 232).
1983	Bechdel's first work is published in *Womannews*.
1983–2008	*Dykes to Watch Out For* strips published by Firebrand Books.
1985	The so-called Bechdel test is published in *Dykes to Watch Out For*.
2006	*Fun Home: A Family Tragicomic* is published.
2008	*The Essential* Dykes to Watch Out For is published.
2012	*Are You My Mother? A Comic Drama* is published.
2012	Bechdel receives a Guggenheim Fellowship and other awards.
2013	The musical adaptation of *Fun Home* opens at the Public Theater in New York City.
2014	Bechdel is awarded a MacArthur Fellowship.
26 June 2015	The United States Supreme Court legalizes gay marriage.
2015	Bechdel marries Holly Rae Taylor.
2015	*Fun Home* debuts on Broadway and wins a Tony Award for Best Musical.

The Instructor's Library

Judith Kegan Gardiner

Texts and Interviews

There is one version of Alison Bechdel's graphic memoir *Fun Home: A Family Tragicomic*. Bechdel keeps an active blog and listing of her publications, interviews, reviews, and events at her Web site (dykestowatchoutfor.com). The site's biographical section complements the time line in the present volume, which provides page numbers in *Fun Home* for personal and historical events mentioned in the text. This essay does not address the literary and theoretical sources of *Fun Home*, which are the focus of two following essays in this book. This essay briefly summarizes a number of resources that teachers may find helpful in a variety of courses: texts, interviews, and videos by Bechdel; books on teaching graphic novels; scholarship addressing comics as a genre and *Fun Home* in particular; resources for incorporating the musical adaptation of the graphic novel; and comments from instructors who have taught *Fun Home* in a variety of academic settings.

A useful text for teachers of *Fun Home* is the compilation of Bechdel's twenty-five years of cartooning, *The Essential* Dykes to Watch Out For, which follows members of an imagined lesbian community through its connections, celebrations, and breakups, all in the context of the characters' ambivalence toward United States culture as a whole. The volume includes most of Bechdel's eleven prior publications of her serial comic strip, *Dykes to Watch Out For*, with a continuing set of central characters, in particular Mo, the politically correct lesbian who voices some exaggerated versions of Bechdel's own opinions on contemporary American culture. The multicultural lesbian urban community portrayed in these comic strips contrasts with the more homogeneous semirural environment of *Fun Home*, and the single-page *Dykes* comics make good classroom comparisons with both the themes and the visual techniques of the memoir. Bechdel's Web site includes an archive of the comic strips and "cast biographies" of her characters. Bechdel's second memoir is titled *Are You My Mother? A Comic Drama*. Like *Dykes to Watch Out For*, it features relationships among women, and it also has an emphasis on psychoanalysis.

Many teachers use Bechdel's online interviews and talks to engage students. The Internet provides the classroom with rich possibilities to view scenes from the musical adaptation of *Fun Home*, to hear Bechdel's lectures, and to watch her drawing technique, which involves conducting historical research, reproducing family photographs and letters, and posing herself in the positions in which she wants to draw her characters. Particularly informative is the detailed demonstration of her quest for accuracy and her drawing technique in the five-minute video "Alison Bechdel: Creating *Fun Home: A Family Tragicomic.*" Useful interviews with Bechdel include those with Terry Gross (Bechdel, "Lesbian Cartoonist") and with Hillary L. Chute (Bechdel, Interview), published in Chute's *Outside the Box*, which includes interviews with other graphic artists that instructors might compare with Bechdel, such as Lynda Barry, Aline Kominsky-Crumb, Phoebe Gloeckner, Scott McCloud, Joe Sacco, Art Spiegelman, and Chris Ware. Bechdel's hour-long keynote lecture at the 2015 Queers and Comics Conference is available online (Bechdel, "Queers"), as is the half-hour talk with Jeanine Tesori and Lisa Kron on *Theater Talk* (Bechdel et al.). A short video clip discusses Bechdel's childhood experience with obsessive-compulsive disorder (Bechdel, "OCD"). In an interview with Adam R. Critchfield and Jack Pula, Bechdel focuses on her positive experiences with psychotherapy and her changing views about the origins of her homosexuality (Bechdel, "On Psychotherapy"). In an interview with Judith Thurman in *The New Yorker,* Bechdel shares her reactions to the musical version of *Fun Home* and her plans for a graphic book on contemporary fitness trends, including her own experiences with karate (Thurman, "Drawn").

A rich scholarly source is the Sophia Smith Collection at Smith College, which houses the Alison Bechdel papers, described by Susan Van Dyne in this volume.

Resources for Teaching Graphic Texts

Many teachers in English departments report their own and their students' pleasure in discussing the visual aspects of *Fun Home*, but they may also feel unprepared to do justice to the richness and complexity of texts that are simultaneously visual and verbal. Instructors have found Scott McCloud's books useful for basic information about comics. His graphic text, *Understanding Comics: The Invisible Art*, introduces the semiotics of the comic strip, explaining how flat and static sequential drawn art represents time, motion, and emotion as well as space. Assigned in whole or in part, this book can be used to shape classroom assignments around McCloud's concepts, such as the function of the gutters and white spaces between cartoon cells. Some instructors prefer his more recent book, *Making Comics: Storytelling Secrets of Comics, Manga, and Graphic Novels*, for its detailed explication of the representation of characters and emotions in graphic texts. Its comparisons between Western comics and Japanese manga provide a cross-cultural perspective. Additionally, Will Eisner's *Graphic Storytelling and Visual Narrative* provides rich examples of a wide range of graphic techniques. An essential text is Chute's *Why Comics?*, which puts Bechdel's work in the context of other "comics for grown-ups" (1) and devotes much of the chapter "Why Queer?" to Bechdel and to *Fun Home* (357–87). Chute describes Bechdel's career trajectory, from a college-era graphic self-portrait to the musical version of *Fun Home*, with particular attention to the "seed for the book" in the discovery of the "aesthetically beautiful and shocking" photograph of the nearly nude Roy, the Bechdels' former babysitter, which Bechdel draws as the book's "centerfold" (360, 361, 370–71).

A foundational work in the semiotics of comics is *The System of Comics* by the Belgian scholar Thierry Groensteen, who describes the "spatio-topical system" of comics through the organization of panels and white space on the page (24). Neil Cohn uses both semiotics and cognitive theory to explain the visual language of comics. Helpful books discussing the genre of graphic art are Michael Chaney's edited volume *Graphic Subjects: Critical Essays on Autobiography and Graphic Novels*, which contains several essays in a section titled "Visualizing Women's Life Writing." Julia Watson's essay "Autographic Disclosures" is placed in the context of essays about comparable works, including those by Marjane Satrapi and Phoebe Gloeckner. Jan Baetens and Hugo Frey's *The Graphic Novel: An Introduction* provides a broad historical context for graphic texts, such as those of Bechdel and Spiegelman, and describes the interplay of drawn images and verbal text in graphic narratives. Jared Gardner's "A History of the Narrative Comic Strip" narrates a short summary of comics history that may be useful for the classroom. *Crossing Boundaries in Graphic Narrative: Essays on Forms, Series, and Genres*, edited by Jake Jakaitis and James F. Wurtz, connects sequential art with more traditional literary forms. Justin Hall's anthology *No Straight Lines: Four Decades of Queer Comics* places Bechdel's work in the context of other graphic narratives with queer themes and characters.

Collections of essays on teaching comics include Lan Dong's *Teaching Comics and Graphic Narratives: Essays on Theory, Strategy, and Practice* and Matthew L. Miller's *Class, Please Open Your Comics: Essays on Teaching with Graphic Narratives*. The title of Carrye Kay Syma and Robert G. Weiner's *Graphic Novels and Comics in the Classroom: Essays on the Educational Power of Sequential Art* points to the proliferation of terminology in this growing field by using three terms—*graphic novels, comics*, and *sequential art*—variously favored by scholars in the field. Stephen Tabachnick's *Teaching the Graphic Novel* includes Japanese and Franco-Belgian as well as American examples. Chute's *Graphic Women: Life Narrative and Contemporary Comics* is appropriate for courses with a gendered approach and contains a chapter on *Fun Home* that is particularly attentive to the "repetition and regeneration" displayed in Bechdel's exactingly detailed reproductions of "an archive of family documents," including photographs, letters, diaries, and even police reports (175).

Many teachers now structure whole courses around graphic texts or include more than one graphic text in classes chiefly devoted to more conventional prose. One of the most popular texts taught alongside *Fun Home* is Spiegelman's *Maus: A Survivor's Tale*, which treats the trauma of the Holocaust as a cat-and-mouse beast fable that affects both the autobiographical American narrator and his father, a concentration camp survivor. This autobiography (of the narrator) combined with biography (of a parent) occurs in *Fun Home* as well. Another popular graphic text taught with *Fun Home* is Marjane Satrapi's *Persepolis* series, though some teachers find troubling the book's negative depiction of the Islamic revolution in Iran. In women's studies courses *Fun Home* is often taught with other women's graphic autobiographies, for example, those of Lynda Barry and Phoebe Gloeckner. Courses focused around young adult literature may choose other graphic texts for comparison with *Fun Home*: for instance, books with young male protagonists like Craig Thompson's *Blankets: A Graphic Novel*, a love story about a boy brought up in a strict, fundamentalist Christian family, and David Small's *Stitches: A Memoir*, in which an adolescent boy finding his identity also has to confront the traumas of having become gravely ill and mute.

Critical Commentary

Chute, a pioneer in the field of women's graphic literature, cotaught a course with Bechdel on comics and autobiography at the University of Chicago in 2012 and continues to publish scholarly works on the topic (*Graphic Women*; "Comics as Literature?"; "Comics Form"; *Disaster Drawn*; *Why Comics?*). Chute originally published her "Public Conversation" with Bechdel (Bechdel and Chute) in the prestigious academic journal *Critical Inquiry*; it was reprinted in Chute's *Outside the Box* (Bechdel, Interview). Scholarly commentaries on graphic texts are becoming more frequent, including in new journals like *Studies in Comics* and special sections of established periodicals like the forum "Comics and the Canon" in *Partial Answers: Journal of Literature and the History of Ideas*.

At the time of this writing, the *MLA International Bibliography* finds sixty-seven results for "Alison Bechdel" in its subject search, including several dissertations. The results include German and French as well as anglophone scholarship. About one-fifth of the essays focus on discussion of the graphic narrative as a form; psychological exploration is the next-most-popular category, while several focus on the father-daughter bond or representations of childhood or the family in *Fun Home*. Several essays are in the traditions of source studies or narratology, and others are genre studies or ecological in emphasis. The *JSTOR* archive collections provide access to scholarly essays on Bechdel and *Fun Home*, many available as full-text PDFs. For more popular responses to *Fun Home* and its author, students may find resources in general humanities or newspaper databases. As of this writing the blog *Feministing* lists forty-two results in a search for "Bechdel," several referring to the so-called Bechdel test on women's participation in films; a search for "Fun Home" on *Feministing* produces other current topics, including fan appreciation and notes on censorship controversies involving the book.

Academic critics have responded favorably to *Fun Home* since its appearance, declaring its aesthetic importance and analyzing the book from sophisticated perspectives. Ann Cvetkovich, for example, praises *Fun Home* not only in the context of graphic memoirs like *Maus* and *Persepolis* but also in terms of its ability "to redefine the connections between memory and history, private experience and public life, and individual loss and collective trauma" (126). Robyn Warhol similarly writes that *Fun Home* adds "unanticipated dimensions to currently circulating models of narrative poetics" (1). Chute champions the current "energy around comics" and claims that Bechdel's "archivally driven work . . . is innovating the field of comics and expanding the study of life narrative" ("Comics Form" 107, 116).

Publications on *Fun Home* and the inclusion of Bechdel in university literature curricula continue to increase. Monalesia Earle compares Bechdel with Toni Morrison to examine new ideas of the family in fiction, and Annette Fantasia situates Bechdel's memoir in the tradition of the Victorian bildungsroman, in which the artist's sensibilities are formed in relation to the visual and textual structures of his or her environment. Fiorenzo Iuliano sees Bechdel as rewriting Marcel Proust on love and memory, and Leah Anderst compares Bechdel's and Doris Lessing's uses of narrative empathy. Taking feminist and psychoanalytic approaches, Heike Bauer notes the importance of Bechdel's reading for the construction of her lesbian identity, while Rachel Dean-Ruzicka analyzes emotions in *Fun Home* through Freud's and Judith Butler's ideas of mourning and melancholia.

The epistemological questions posed by *Fun Home*, such as what can one know about another person's mind or motives, have evoked considerable scholarly discussion. Rebecca Scherr explores the ethics of "truth claims" in "autographic" works like *Fun Home*, asking, "do we 'buy' Bechdel's perspective because she has brought us so close to the text . . . and simultaneously 'touched' us on a deeply emotional level?" (141). Elisabeth El Refaie's monograph *Autobiographical Comics: Life Writing in Pictures* discusses the "nature of the autobiographical self and its relationship with body awareness and body image" in the "embodied selves" pictorially depicted in European and North American comics (7). Commenting on Bechdel's practice of redrawing documents in her memoir, El Refaie suggests that "[b]y filtering photographs through her own unique vision, Alison Bechdel thus seems to be drawing attention to the complex relationship between photography and the 'truth'" (165). Hélène Tison, too, connects *Fun Home*'s visual style with its emotional effects, claiming that Bechdel's redrawing of photographs like the book's centerfold of Roy the babysitter forces the reader into a position of identification with Alison. Tison says that Bechdel's drawing style suggests a "cinematographic zooming-in effect" that unifies the disparate fragments of the author's memories. Thus, the book succeeds, she claims, "in graphically offering her dead father an identity and an integrity whose lack may have played a part in his suicide" (361).

K. W. Eveleth takes a deconstructive approach to *Fun Home*, emphasizing the interconnected "visuoverbal medium" of the graphic memoir and the undecidability of the text while also disputing the interpretations of prior scholars. Warning readers not to fall into simple psychological explanations of Alison's or Bruce's character, Eveleth stresses the text's contradictions: its binaries—butch and nelly, truth and lies—blur into one another as the memoir proceeds, and "conflicting modern and postmodern conceptions of truth (one interior and essential, the other exterior and differential) collide." Eveleth continues, "the tension between what is 'real' and what is 'artificial' is both the major thematic concern of *Fun Home* and its predominant structural conceit" (103). For Eveleth, the book is "marked indelibly as a queer archive, an exploration of indeterminacy for its own sake" (105).

In discussing Bechdel's childhood period of obsessive-compulsive disorder or the all-white environment of the author's hometown, both of which are described in *Fun Home*, teachers may wish to incorporate the perspectives of disability studies (Connor et al.) or critical race theory (Twine and Warren) into their classes.

The Musical

The original cast recording of the award-winning musical based on *Fun Home* is available both on an audio compact disc (Tesori and Kron, Fun Home: *A New Broadway Musical*) and on *YouTube* as a compilation of twenty-seven recordings of the musical's songs (Tesori and Kron, Fun Home *Full Soundtrack*). The libretto, by Jeanine Tesori and Lisa Kron, is available in an inexpensive print edition (Tesori and Kron, *Fun Home* [Samuel French]).

The recordings of the musical and its libretto are rich resources for the classroom, particularly for comparisons with the graphic text. Students can consider how the music and lyrics direct and alter their attitudes toward the characters. The musical form also raises questions about the genre of Bechdel's memoir and highlights the unique qualities of the graphic text. Lisa Kron and Jeanine Tesori, respectively the librettist and composer of the musical, took part, with Bechdel, in Terry Gross's 2015 interview (Bechdel, "Lesbian Cartoonist").

For background on the history of the musical genre, helpful sources for teachers are Larry Stempel's *Showtime: A History of the Broadway Musical Theater,* John Bush Jones's *Our Musicals, Ourselves: A Social History of the American Musical Theatre,* and the collection of essays in William A. Everett and Paul R. Laird's *The Cambridge Companion to the Musical.* The Web site *Musicals 101,* compiled by John Kenrick, makes much information about musicals readily accessible.

Literary Allusions in *Fun Home*

D. Quentin Miller

Fun Home insists, almost aggressively, on the primacy of literature at its core. Bechdel's narrator explains, "I employ these allusions to [Henry] James and [F. Scott] Fitzgerald not only as descriptive devices, but because my parents are most real to me in fictional terms. And perhaps my cool aesthetic distance itself does more to convey the arctic climate of our family than any particular literary comparison" (67). These bits of wisdom are meant as aids to the reader trying to understand the proper way to approach this unusual work, but they also serve to destabilize meaning rather than to clarify it: if her parents are most real to her "in fictional terms," how is the reader supposed to understand the author's deep and meticulous search for truth that uses her own diary, photographs, and letters her parents wrote to each other, all drawn in her own hand, as evidence? The "perhaps" in the second sentence quoted above allows us to dismiss the enormous weight of allusions by suggesting that Alison's extreme bookishness is part of a distancing pattern that explains herself and her family. But perhaps not. Perhaps the allusions blur the line between fiction and reality in the same way that they blur the line between something called literature and something called graphic narrative. Bechdel's compilation in *Fun Home* of an almost impossible list of required reading stakes a claim for the importance of classic literature in the twenty-first century even as, according to a blurb at the front of the book, "the great writing of the twenty-first century may well be found in graphic novels and nonfiction" (ii).[1] *Fun Home* does not obscure its literary foundations; rather, it argues that graphic narratives have a profound obligation to showcase them. Those who teach *Fun Home* have a responsibility to point out the way the allusions deepen and enrich meaning, parallel to Alison's father's desire to communicate with her through recommending a growing list of challenging books.

Fun Home contains more literary allusions than T. S. Eliot's *The Waste Land*. By my count, excluding works of criticism and theory discussed in Valerie Rohy's essay in this volume as well as clinical books such as those by William H. Masters and Virginia E. Johnson, Dr. Benjamin Spock, and the collectively authored *Our Bodies, Ourselves, Fun Home* alludes to some sixty works of literature and mythology, and roughly half of those works are alluded to in multiple panels. Few undergraduates have read even a small fraction of the works Bechdel alludes to, and yet *Fun Home* cannot be fully appreciated if the allusions are disregarded, because Bechdel's inclusion of them is meticulous and precise.

When I show my students a list of the works of literature alluded to in *Fun Home*, they sheepishly admit that they have read relatively few of them. Our challenge is to cope with the list's demands while also understanding the different ways Bechdel uses allusion. In this regard *Fun Home* is a test case for the function of allusions, which can lead to an important discussion about literary history in a book that some may not consider literary because of its emphasis on the visual. Bechdel saturates her work with literary allusions to demonstrate the way she communicated with her parents, to chronicle her intellectual growth alongside her coming-of-age and sexual awakening, to insist on the literary merit of her "tragicomic" by lending it the gravitas of literary history, to suggest a parallel between literary interpretation and the interpretation of unspoken codes that dominated Bechdel's father's life, and to provide the reader with food for thought about the nature of the literary canon by juxtaposing accepted classics with less canonical works that facilitated her understanding of her sexual identity.

This discussion leads to a deeper understanding of the many ways allusions operate in the memoir, but it does not solve the readerly challenge of deciding between the lazy, passive response to an allusion—to skip over it—and the more rigorous response to pursue the allusion, read the original work, and conduct research, which would not be practical for all the allusions in *Fun Home*. We begin by discussing some of the recurrent allusions, especially to works that my students may not have read (even if they know they should have). In terms of frequency and depth, the six most recurrent allusions are to James Joyce's *Ulysses*, Oscar Wilde's *The Importance of Being Earnest*, Marcel Proust's *À la recherche du temps perdu*, F. Scott Fitzgerald's *The Great Gatsby*, Colette's *Earthly Paradise*, and Albert Camus's *A Happy Death*.

Through intertextual allusion, Bechdel gives readers a list of suggested reading, just as her father did for her. She admits, "I ended up in his English class, a course called 'Rites of Passage,' and I found that I liked the books Dad wanted me to read" (198). She also likes being his student; he tells her, "You're the only one in that class worth teaching," and she responds, "It's the only class I have worth taking" (199). Her hard-won admiration for her father comes partly from his passion for literature, and their literary discussions constitute some of their most earnest attempts at true communication. But in a telling panel Alison, at college, is on the phone with her father, who asks, "What are you reading? Anything good?" She warily eyes a stack of books she's been reading about homosexuality and says, "Uh . . . not really" (76). With the exception of E. M. Forster's *Maurice*, these books are not part of the literary canon. This panel highlights the division in *Fun Home* between works of undisputed literary merit, mostly by Western European or expatriate American men from the early twentieth century, and works largely outside the academic literary canon that speak to Alison's sexual awakening. In her father's question and her hesitant response there is an unarticulated distinction between literature that is good and literature that is important. Indeed, *Ulysses*, the work most frequently alluded to in *Fun Home*, seems to annoy her, and she fails to finish reading it during a college seminar devoted to it alone. At one point her character scowls at the book and utters, "What the fuck?" and in the next panel admits, "I had little patience for Joyce's divagations when my own odyssey was calling so seductively" (207). In the accompanying panel she is picking up *Lesbian Nation*, by Jill Johnston, from a stack of books.

Colette's *Earthly Paradise*, a compilation of autobiographical writings, is the hinge between good books and important books, which might be described as books for the mind and books for the body. As the work her father gave to her as a "guess" (220) about her sexuality, it is arguably the most significant recurrent allusion in the memoir, though *Ulysses* provides the most sustained series of allusions.

What follows is a list of briefly annotated literary allusions in *Fun Home*, which suggest some of the themes that are not immediately evident from the context in *Fun Home*, especially for the works to which Bechdel alludes multiple times. Parenthetical references indicate page numbers in *Fun Home*.

Albee, Edward. *The American Dream*. 1961 American play. Helen is reading it with a stranger, but Alison's observation that "this was acting" is ironic given the play's themes—the façade of the happy American family—and characters—domineering mother, emasculated father (131).

Alcott, Louisa May. *Little Women*. 1869 American novel. Theme of a family surviving hardships, girls becoming women (172).

Austen, Jane. *Pride and Prejudice*. 1813 British novel. Bruce teaches it in a high school course, and Alison responds to a question about the protagonist and the protagonist's father: "they're, like, friends" (199).

Bannon, Ann. *Women in the Shadows*. 1959 American novel. Considered pulp. Alison admits fascination with this genre (107).

Beaton, Cecil. Diaries. British; ca. 1922–74. The chronicles of a bisexual photographer, fashion designer, and socialite (205).

Broumas, Olga. *Beginning with O*. 1977 Greek American poetry. Erotic lesbian poetry (80).

Brown, Rita Mae. *Rubyfruit Jungle*. 1973 American novel. Groundbreaking in its explicit treatment of lesbian themes (205, 207).

Camus, Albert. *A Happy Death*. Written in the late 1930s, published in 1971, translated into English in 1972. The title of chapter 2 of *Fun Home*, this is the novel Bruce was reading when he died. Alison is as concerned with the parallels between Camus's early death in a car crash and her father's as she is with the themes of the novel, which address philosophical questions of obtaining personal happiness in one's life (25, 27, 28, 48, 54).

Colette. *Earthly Paradise*. 1966 French autobiography. A compilation of Colette's autobiographical writings translated into English. Arguably the most significant literary allusion in *Fun Home*, it is the book Bruce gives Alison as a way of opening up their discussion about sexuality. It also helps merge her intellectual and bodily literary interests, as she uses it to masturbate, connecting this practice—"good for a wank" (207)—to another allusion to Joyce's *Ulysses* (205, 207, 208, 220, 229).

Conrad, Joseph. *Heart of Darkness.* 1899 British novel. A brief allusion demonstrates Alison's annoyance with literary interpretation in college courses (200).

Dahl, Roald. *James and the Giant Peach.* 1961 British novel. Alison and her lover laugh at the unintended double entendre in the beloved children's book, but the allusion is also ironic in that the protagonist's parents died a premature, absurd death (81).

Drabble, Margaret. *The Waterfall.* 1969 British novel. Helen is reading it when Alison announces her menstruation. The novel deals with a disaffected, dispassionate mother who regrets her choices and has an affair (185).

Eddison, Eric. *The Worm Ouroboros.* 1922 British novel. Bruce is reading this fantasy novel after Alison and her brothers encounter a snake. The ouroboros figure is the snake that swallows its own tail, which in Alison's interpretation implies cyclicity. The figure also connotes self-destruction; Alison imagines that Bruce saw a snake when he jumped into the path of the truck (116).

Faulkner, William. *As I Lay Dying.* 1930 American novel. A text that Alison reads in college and that Bruce has passionate ideas about. Its central quest—Addie Bundren's desire to be buried in her hometown—resonates with Bruce's fate (200).

Fitzgerald, F. Scott. *The Great Gatsby.* 1925 American novel. Bruce calls it "the great American novel" and loans it to his pet students. Alison interprets it as a novel about reinventing the self and cloaking oneself with a beautiful façade to hide the less appealing aspects of one's reality. Unlike Jay Gatz, her father was a reader. Both Bruce and Fitzgerald's protagonist meet violent, premature ends when they fail to sustain their precariously divided worlds (61, 63, 64, 65, 84).

Fitzgerald, F. Scott. Stories. Bruce's fascination with Fitzgerald leads Bruce to his stories. He rattles off a number of them in a letter to Helen, but singles out "Winter Dreams," saying "he is me." The "he" is a typical Fitzgerald protagonist who chases romantic visions to remake himself. After reading a few of the stories Bruce decides to return to *Gatsby* (63).

Forbes, Esther. *Johnny Tremain.* 1943 historical novel. Helen reads this classic of children's literature to Alison to distract her from her compulsive behavior, but Alison is not able to concentrate on it (142).

Forster, E. M. *Maurice.* British novel, written in 1913, published posthumously in 1971. The novel's handling of same-sex relationships was too frank for its time. It chronicles the failure of corrective treatment for homosexuality and projects a happy ending for its male lovers. It recurs in the stacks of books Alison is reading as she explores her own same-sex desires (76, 207).

Grahame, Kenneth. *The Wind in the Willows.* 1908 Scottish novel. This children's classic provides the title for *Fun Home*'s chapter 5. Alison encounters it as a coloring book that her father appropriates, leaving her in awe of his superior artistic talents. She is particularly fascinated with the map in the book, which "bridges the symbolic and the real" (147). The chapter's correlation between beauty and death resonate with this allusion (121, 130, 146, 147).

Grass, Günter. *The Tin Drum.* 1959 German novel. Bruce reads it when he and Helen are living abroad. Its mentally ill protagonist refuses conventional middle-class life (32).

Hall, Radclyffe. *The Well of Loneliness.* 1928 British novel. A prominent lesbian novel, controversial in its time, that addresses questions of gender identification (75, 205).

Hemingway, Ernest. *The Sun Also Rises.* 1926 American novel. Alison encounters this text, admired by Bruce, in college, and she turns to him when she finds her courses too pretentious. Bruce seems more interested in biographical details and Brett Ashley as the "new woman" than he is in the novel's themes of obsessive love, weakened belief, and the moral integrity of living well (61, 200, 201).

Homer. *The Odyssey.* Ancient Greek epic poem (eighth century BCE). The Urtext for Joyce's *Ulysses.* Bechdel puns and makes metaphorical use of some of Homer's concepts, such as the odyssey itself as a metaphor for her sexual awakening (203, 213, 214, 215, 216, 221).

James, Henry. *The Portrait of a Lady.* 1881 American novel. Bechdel interprets it as a parallel text for the early years of her parents' marriage, explaining the connections thoroughly (70, 71, 72).

James, Henry. *Washington Square.* 1880 American novel. Bechdel reinforces the connection between her mother and this work, pointing out that her mother acted in an adaptation of it about a woman living with discontentment after a failed romance (66).

Joyce, James. *Dubliners.* 1914 Irish short story collection. Presented in *Fun Home* by both Bruce and by Alison's professor as mere precursors to Joyce's novels, *Dubliners* is nonetheless important, especially, as Bruce highlights, the last paragraph of "The Dead," which brings together themes of death, desire, and failed communication inherent in his own story (203, 204).

Joyce, James. *A Portrait of the Artist as a Young Man.* 1916 Irish novel. As Alison is "suffocating" from her father's exuberant literary advice, he tells her of this novel, "You damn well better identify with every page" (201). She might resent this implication partly because she is not a young man and partly because of her resistance to Joyce's deliberate obfuscation while she is seeking clarity. The title of *Fun Home*'s chapter 1 is also an allusion to the novel, indicating that she both identifies with it and retains it. The myth of Daedalus and Icarus that frames *Fun Home* is also embedded in the name of Joyce's protagonist, Stephen Dedalus (1, 201, 202, 203).

Joyce, James. *Ulysses*. 1922 Irish novel. Considered one of the masterpieces of modern literature, Joyce's novel provides Alison with a considerable challenge in college, yet it is an enduring blueprint for her interpretations of her relationship with her father. The protagonist is Leopold Bloom, who wanders around Dublin on a June day, enacting a personal mythology that parallels Homer's epic poem. Its secondary character is Stephen Dedalus from *Portrait*, and Bechdel draws frequent parallels between the novel and her relationship with Bruce, wondering "which of us was the father?" (221) after he unburdens himself of some of the secrets of his homosexual past (201, 202, 204, 206, 207, 208, 209, 210, 211, 221, 222, 226, 228, 229, 230, 231).

Kaufman, George S., and Moss Hart. *You Can't Take It with You*. 1937 American play. A comic play about a dysfunctional family. Helen stays home to act in it while Bruce takes the children to New York (189).

Kipling, Rudyard. *Just So Stories*. 1902 British stories. Tales about the origin of animal characteristics. Bruce reads these stories to Alison in one of her early positive memories of him (21).

Milford, Nancy. *Zelda*. 1970 biography. Bruce's obsession with Fitzgerald motivates him to seek out the story of Zelda, Fitzgerald's wife (84, 85).

Millett, Kate. *Flying*. 1974 autobiography. Alison is "riveted" (218) by this courageous coming-out tale, describing its author as "a latter-day Colette" (217). Bruce reads it when Alison returns to college and is fascinated by the author's openness about her sexuality. It is the first and only book that Alison brings to him (217, 218, 219, 224).

Milne, A. A. *The World of Pooh*. 1926 British children's literature. Part of Alison's revision of childhood classics (80).

Mizener, Arthur. *The Far Side of Paradise*. 1951 biography of Fitzgerald. Fitzgerald's life fascinates Bruce as much as his books do. He identifies with Fitzgerald and models himself after the frail, famous author. Alison notes that they both die at forty-four, Fitzgerald exactly three days older than her father (62, 63, 65).

Nin, Anaïs. *Delta of Venus*. 1977 American erotic stories. Nin's work provides Alison with a bridge between bodily and literary pleasures (76, 79).

Osborn, Paul. *Morning's at Seven*. 1939 American play. Helen rehearses for a production of this play by reading it into a tape recorder. Like other plays she is in, it is about individual discontentment within a family context (132).

Proust, Marcel. *À la recherche du temps perdu*. 1913–27 French novel sequence. Translated as *Remembrance of Things Past* and *In Search of Lost*

Time. The novels were important to Bruce, and Alison reads in them a number of parallels to his life: closeted homosexuality, an affinity for gardening, the power of choice, and regrets about past events. Moreover, the novels, like those by Colette and Nin, serve as another link between the high literary and the bodily in Alison's literary journey. The second volume of Proust's sequence, *In the Shadow of Young Girls in Flower,* which provides the title of the fourth chapter of *Fun Home,* dabbles with themes of female homoerotic desire. Bechdel plays with the notion of translation in her discussions of Proust (28, 87, 92, 93, 94, 97, 102, 105, 108, 109, 113, 119).

Rich, Adrienne. *Dream of a Common Language.* 1978 American poetry. The first collection by the famous feminist poet after she came out as a lesbian, it connects Alison with her lover Joan, also a poet (80).

Rule, Jane. *Desert of the Heart.* 1964 Canadian novel. One of the more literary novels about lesbian experiences that Alison reads. Perhaps not coincidentally the protagonist is a cartoonist (205).

Salinger, J. D. *The Catcher in the Rye.* 1951 American novel. A classic coming-of-age text, Bruce teaches it to Alison in his high school class, helping to form their bond (198, 199).

Sarton, May. *Mrs. Stevens Hears the Mermaids Singing.* 1965 American novel. Alison reads this early classic of the lesbian literary canon as part of her self-guided odyssey (207).

Shakespeare, William. *The Taming of the Shrew.* 1592 British drama. Alison's parents met during a college production of this play, which Alison describes as "problematic" from a feminist perspective (70). It is about a domineering husband training his wife to be obedient and parallels the worst moments of Bruce and Helen's marriage (69, 70).

Stevens, Wallace. "Sunday Morning." 1923 American poem. The title of *Fun Home*'s chapter 3 is a quotation from the poem: "that old catastrophe" refers to the crucifixion, which Bechdel bluntly states the poem is "about" (83). It is her mother's favorite poem, but there are pointed echoes of it in Bruce's life. It begins with a woman staying at home on a Sunday morning, worshiping the sensations of her domestic world while others go to church, and it ends with a contemplation about the solid logic behind worshiping the sun as a god that mingles with humanity. In another chapter a panel shows Alison and the rest of the family "off to church" while Bruce indulges in "idolatrous" sunbathing (129). The poem's famous line "death is the mother of beauty" has many valences; one is that Alison cannot see the beauty in her father's life until she has come to terms with his death (55, 82, 83, 129).

Stevenson, Robert Louis. *A Child's Garden of Verses.* 1885 British poetry. Mentioned only briefly during a card game Alison plays with her brothers and friends, this allusion reinforces the importance of childhood play, especially in the poem "Good and Bad Children" (160).

Stevenson, Robert Louis. *Dr. Jekyll and Mr. Hyde.* 1886 novel. The novel, mentioned only briefly but significantly, describes a man who lives a double life, like Bruce (160).

Styron, William. *Sophie's Choice.* 1979 American novel. A seemingly random book on the shelf of a bookstore, the allusion intensifies Helen's situation: Styron's novel frames the story of a woman full of sorrow who once was forced to make an impossible choice, though Sophie's choice is far more dramatic than Helen's (74).

Tolkien, J. R. R. *The Fellowship of the Ring.* 1954 British novel. Alison escapes into Tolkien's work of high fantasy to avoid the harsh reality of the book Bruce wants her to read, *The Catcher in the Rye* (198).

Tolstoy, Leo. *Anna Karenina.* 1878 Russian novel. On the first page of *Fun Home*, Bruce has set aside *Anna Karenina* to play with Alison. In the novel Anna commits suicide by throwing herself into the path of a train, an act eerily similar to Bruce's death. The novel's first line—"Happy families are all alike; every unhappy family is unhappy in its own way"—could be an epigraph for *Fun Home* (3).

White, E. B. *The Trumpet of the Swan.* 1970 American novel. Alison mentions this children's work in her first diary entry. It is about nonconformity and nurturing special talents, and it is fitting that Alison is wearing the tail from a Halloween costume when she reads it (140).

Wilde, Oscar. *An Ideal Husband.* 1895 Irish play. The titular phrase is first employed ironically when Bechdel questions whether an ideal husband would "have sex with teenage boys." It becomes the title of chapter 6, and Bechdel uses it to develop her comments on Wilde's life: the play was popular when Wilde was being tried for indecency (17, 151, 166). (She erroneously refers to it as *The Ideal Husband* in the last two cases.)

Wilde, Oscar. *The Importance of Being Earnest.* 1895 Irish play. The most developed of the allusions to Wilde, this play contains plenty of double entendres about the author's homosexuality, as Bechdel later realizes. Alison helps her mother rehearse for her role in it. Her mother's performance is an unmitigated triumph, but her father's arrest for his attempted seduction of a teenager recalls Wilde's situation. Bechdel borrows from Wilde a fondness for puns and an appreciation for highbrow humor (154, 155, 157, 158, 163, 164, 165, 166, 168, 181, 186).

Wilde, Oscar. *The Picture of Dorian Gray.* 1891 Irish novel. The work centers around the morality of self-indulgence, and Bechdel alludes to it to comment on the adolescent Alison's discovery of masturbation (170).

Woolf, Virginia. *The Letters of Virginia Woolf.* British correspondence, published 1975–80. The posthumously published letters of an iconic feminist thinker partially describe her same-sex relationship with Vita Sackville-West (209).

Woolf, Virginia. *Orlando*. 1928 British novel. One of the novels Alison reads while exploring her sexual identity in college. Its primary innovation is the way it breaks from traditional realism to explore androgyny and gender change without emotional baggage or psychological trauma (205).

NOTE

[1] The blurb quotes Deidre Donahue in the 29 May 2006 edition of *USA Today*.

Theoretical Allusions in *Fun Home*

Valerie Rohy

Jonathan Culler defines *theory* as any analytical work that has effects beyond its original context, particularly work that challenges "common sense" (4). Although in *Fun Home* the young Alison resists the hermeneutic methods practiced in her freshman English class—"I didn't understand why we couldn't just read the books without forcing contorted interpretations on them" (200)—that is by no means the attitude of Bechdel as an author. In fact, she concurs with Culler in construing theory broadly: the feminist axiom "the personal is political" is no less theoretical than Freud's account of the Oedipal complex. Bechdel's use of critical theory joins the largely masculine tradition of Continental philosophy with American lesbian feminism and queer theory, inviting us to speculate on the possible connections between, say, Albert Camus and Mary Daly, or between Saussure and *Our Bodies, Ourselves*. I have, in turn, construed theory broadly in the bibliography below, including nonfictional works such as Kenneth Clark's *The Nude* along with postmodern texts such as Jean Baudrillard's *Simulacra and Simulation*.

Like the literary allusions in *Fun Home*, the theoretical references appear both within the illustration panels, often in the form of books, and in the narration. The juxtaposition of image and text, which we might imagine as an inner story and an outer frame, places theory both in the place of the primary text and in the site of secondary criticism, unsettling the usual relation between literature and theory. It is not merely that theory has no preeminence over literature (it does not authoritatively answer the questions literature poses) but that theory can itself function as literature. In another neat deconstruction of supposed opposites, in *Fun Home* theory plays the parts of both subject and object, analyst and analysand.

In the annotated list that follows, an asterisk indicates the most salient reference to a text in *Fun Home*, whether a book's author, its title, or an allusion to a concept. Parenthetical references indicate page numbers in *Fun Home* unless otherwise indicated.

Abbott, Sidney, and Barbara Love. *Sappho Was a Right-On Woman:* ° *A Liberated View of Lesbianism*. In this 1972 book, the lesbian feminists Abbott and Love offer a recent history of lesbianism and a manifesto for future liberation (59). Abbott, a writer and journalist, was active in the Lavender Menace and the National Organization for Women (NOW) and was a founding member of the National Gay and Lesbian Task Force. Love also worked for lesbian recognition in NOW.

Adair, Casey, and Nancy Adair. *Word Is Out: Stories of Some of Our Lives.* ° A 1978 book based on a 1977 film of the same name, it contains transcripts of interviews with the more than two dozen gay men and lesbians who appeared in the film (75).

Atkinson, Ti-Grace (attrib.), in Anne Koedt, *Lesbianism and Feminism*. Atkinson, a feminist author and early member of NOW who later moved on to more radical groups, is credited with the phrase "Feminism is the theory, lesbianism is the practice"° (80). Alison overhears the phrase at a party, and another panel on the same page showing a book-filled bed illustrates what Bechdel calls a "fusion of word and deed."

Baudrillard, Jean. *Simulacra and Simulation*. While in ordinary usage a simulacrum° is a bad copy of something, the French philosopher and poststructural theorist suggests that the simulacrum is a representation without any grounding reality that itself takes the place of reality. The simulacrum stands in for something that does not exist; it functions as a pretense, much as Bechdel's family bonds and childhood home seem to do (17).

Booth, Wayne C. *The Rhetoric of Fiction*. Booth, a professor of English at the University of Chicago, introduces the notion of the unreliable narrator° to designate a first-person narrator who is shown to lack credibility—for example, by lying, showing bias, or being delusional. Referring to the narration in her childhood diary as unreliable, Bechdel divides her present reading self from her past writing self (184).

Camus, Albert.° "The Myth of Sisyphus." The French author and philosopher discusses alienation and the absurdity of life as well as the futile search for meaning in a meaningless world. The page Bechdel reproduces has to do with whether suicide is a reasonable response to the absurdity of life; Camus concludes that it is not (47, 48).

Clark, Kenneth.° *The Nude: A Study in Ideal Form*. Clark, a British art historian, curator, and BBC producer, published twenty books addressing such subjects as John Ruskin, Leonardo da Vinci, Rembrandt, and William Blake. His book on nude figures in art, both male and female, combines Bruce Bechdel's aesthetic and erotic interests (15, 99).

Daly, Mary. *Gyn/Ecology:° The Metaethics of Radical Feminism*. An American radical feminist theorist and theologian, Daly is best known for imagining in this work a feminist spiritual alternative to androcentric organized religion. The text was widely read, although it was criticized for its totalizing view of womanhood, which excludes transgender women and marginalizes women of color (80).

Derrida, Jacques. *Dissemination*. The collapse of apparently opposite terms that Bechdel associates with Proust—"the two ways are revealed to converge—and have always converged"° (102)—also exemplifies the deconstructive theory of which Derrida, a French critic and philosopher, was the preeminent figure. Deconstruction questions such ostensibly opposing terms as speech and writing, inside and outside. "'Writing' and 'speech' can . . . no longer be simply opposed, but neither have they become identical. Rather, the very notion of their 'identities' is put in question," Barbara Johnson explains in the introduction to Derrida's *Dissemination* (xiii). Throughout *Fun Home* Bechdel complicates the seemingly obvious binary oppositions with which the text begins—Spartan/Athenian, modern/ Victorian, butch/nelly, utilitarian/aesthete (15)—changing places with her father and showing their interconnectedness.

Freud, Sigmund.° *The Standard Edition of the Complete Psychological Works of Sigmund Freud.* The Austrian founder of psychoanalysis introduced the idea of the unconscious, placed sexuality (broadly construed) at the center of psychic life, and invented the therapeutic "talking cure." Psychoanalytic clinical practice is the basis for the *New Yorker* cartoon Alison imagines (153). Playing on several meanings of inversion, Bechdel later refers to her relationship with her father as an "inverted Oedipal complex"° (230).

Jay, Karla, and Allen Young. *The Gay Report:° Lesbians and Gay Men Speak Out about Sexual Experiences and Lifestyles.* This 1979 book presents the results of what it claims is the first survey of gay men's and lesbians' sexuality and ways of life, based on more than 5,000 respondents. The many books scattered about Alison's college dorm room show how deeply reading informs her identity as a lesbian, as if to magnify the prominence of the word *lesbian* in her dictionary and its presence in the library's card catalog (76).

Jay, Karla, and Allen Young, editors. *Out of the Closets:° Voices of Gay Liberation.* This collection of essays about gay and lesbian experiences and politics was originally published in 1972. Bechdel gives the book's title as *Out of the Closets and Into the Streets,* which was in fact the title of one of the book's chapters, taken from a popular slogan (76).

Johnston, Jill. *Lesbian Nation:° The Feminist Solution.* Here Johnston argues for radical lesbian separatism from men and male-dominated culture and regards heterosexual woman as collaborating with their oppressors (207). Like the other texts in lesbian-feminist literature and theory pictured in Alison's dorm room, this work suggests the range and intensity of her reading. Johnson was also among the many radical feminists advocating matriarchy° in the 1970s; Alison's lover Joan similarly identifies as a "matriarchist" (80).

Jung, Carl.° *The Archetypes and the Collective Unconscious.* A Swiss psychoanalyst who was originally a protégé of Freud's, Jung promotes the idea of the collective unconscious, in which all people share archetypal images,° such as the snake that Bechdel interprets as phallic (116). Later, Alison's professor's remark on "natural transformation"° refers to Jung's theory of the process, usually in dreams, of integrating the self with a greater other self in a form of rebirth (200).

Krafft-Ebing, Richard von. *Psychopathia Sexualis*. The Victorian sexologist Krafft-Ebing popularized the term *sexual inversion*,° from which Alison, by way of Proust, gleans the word "inverts,"° an "antiquated clinical term" for homosexuals (97). Sexual inversion implies congenital, not acquired, homosexuality, and a concomitant gender disturbance: in this theory, a lesbian is a woman who has a man's (heterosexual) desire for women and adopts other masculine attributes. Bechdel's gloss, "a person whose gender expression is at odds with his or her sex" (97), describes the boyish young Alison but could also be said of transgender people, whether straight or gay.

Kristeva, Julia. "Bakhtine, le mot, le dialogue, et le roman." A French feminist theorist, Kristeva invents the term *intertextuality*° to describe the ways the meanings of texts depend on a network of other texts through such mechanisms as allusion, parody, and genre. What Bechdel calls "intertextual progression" (207) is illustrated by the piles of books on gender and sexuality that Alison consumes in college.

Kübler-Ross, Elisabeth. *On Death and Dying*. This influential book outlines five emotional stages that Kübler-Ross argues are experienced during mourning—in addition to the denial and anger° Bechdel mentions, the stages include bargaining, depression, and acceptance (50).

Martin, Del, and Phyllis Lyon. *Lesbian/Woman*.° This early work of lesbian feminism promotes lesbian relationships as a progressive political choice and as a liberation from traditional gender roles (75). Of all the works in lesbian-feminist theory in *Fun Home*, it is appropriate that this, among the first published, is also the first book Alison buys.

Masters, William H., and Virginia E. Johnson. *Homosexuality in Perspective*.° Masters and Johnson researched human sexuality at Washington University in St. Louis beginning in the 1950s. In the 1960s and 1970s, they led a program designed to convert homosexuals to heterosexuality, a practice that is now considered both harmful and doomed to fail (75).

Our Bodies, Ourselves.° The Boston Women's Health Collective produced this book in 1971 to educate women about health issues, improve their ability to advocate for better care, and broach sensitive topics such as sexuality and abortion (76).

Plato. *Theaetetus*. Epistemology is the philosophical study of knowledge: How do we know what we think we know? Are our perceptions, memories, and conclusions reliable? Plato's dialogue examines what constitutes true knowledge, much as the "epistemological crisis"° around Alison's diary suggests that nothing can be known with certainty (141). This radical uncertainty, however, does not obviate Alison's need to record what may or may not be accurate accounts of her days.

Queer.° The word *queer*, whose many definitions Bechdel considers (57), has long been an epithet directed against LGBT people, but beginning in the early 1990s it was also reclaimed as a term of defiance and solidarity by the activist group Queer Nation, formed in New York in 1990 ("Queer Nation") and by the academic practice of *queer theory*, a term coined by Teresa de Lauretis in a 1991 essay of the same name.

Ruskin, John.° *The Stones of Venice.* Originally published in 1851–53 by the preeminent British art critic of the Victorian period, the book—which Alison's father reads in bed—chronicles the history of Venetian architecture and argues for the supremacy of Gothic over Renaissance styles (19). Ruskin's sexuality continues to be debated and his aesthetic sense was an influence on Oscar Wilde, among others.

Russell, Bertrand.° *Principles of Mathematics.* The British philosopher and mathematician offers Russell's paradox (1901) as a critique of Georg Cantor's set theory. Bechdel cites one popular version of the paradox, "Who barbers the barber?," an example of logical contradiction (51). This conundrum follows from her discussion of the absurdity of life and death in the preceding pages.

Saussure, Ferdinand de. *Course in General Linguistics.* This book, published posthumously in 1916 by Saussure's students, earned him the title "father of modern linguistics." In it he defines a linguistic sign as an arbitrary relation between a signifier and a signified, whose connection is not their essential sameness but their difference from other possible pairings. Thus the signifier and signified are bound never to coincide completely. The "rift between signifier and signified"° haunts Alison when it seems her diary can never be adequate to the events it records, another version of the "epistemological crisis" signaled by her notation "I think" (141, 142).

Shilts, Randy. *And the Band Played On:° Politics, People, and the AIDS Epidemic.* The first widely read history of the HIV-AIDS crisis in the 1980s, this book was criticized by the gay community for a number of reasons, not least Shilts's depiction of a gay man he calls "patient zero," who is alleged to have knowingly spread the virus. The Bechdel family's presence at the bicentennial celebrations in New York, festivities discussed by Shilts, figures how close her father came to the HIV-AIDS crisis, which might, Bechdel suggests, have imposed a different tragic ending on his life (195).

Spock, Benjamin.° *Baby and Child Care.* Spock, an American pediatrician, published multiple editions of his best-selling book starting in 1946 (138). He is known for engaging with psychoanalysis and promoting more permissive parenting.

Tripp, Clarence Arthur. *The Homosexual Matrix.°* A psychologist who worked with Alfred Kinsey, Tripp contends that sexual orientation is socially constructed rather than innate and attempts to explain sexual differences between men and women in evolutionary terms (205).

Vida, Ginny, editor. *Our Right To Love:° A Lesbian Resource Book.* This collection of essays and interviews on lesbian life and culture includes such topics as health, activism, and the law, as well as a list of lesbian organizations (207).

Wimsatt, W. K., and Monroe Beardsley. "The Intentional Fallacy."° This influential 1946 essay by two literary critics argues that the author's intended meaning is not the sole or even the primary meaning of a literary text, which may have plural and conflicting messages. Alison's class discussion of symbolism in literature raises the question of authorial intent when a skeptical classmate asks, "You mean, like . . . Hemingway did that on purpose?" (200).

There is an axiom: "Everywhere I go in my mind, I meet Plato coming back." The critical theorist reading *Fun Home* is likely to have a similar sense that Bechdel has gone everywhere first, because many of the theoretical methods one might use to interpret it are already at work inside the text, including queer theory and feminism, linguistics, existentialism, and deconstruction. *Fun Home* not only outlines many readers' possible hermeneutic strategies but also constitutes a work of theory itself, offering a new way of understanding the world. To acknowledge this is merely to begin an infinitely rich conversation among the text, the many thinkers to whom Bechdel alludes, and the many readers of *Fun Home*.

Interior and Exterior Design in *Fun Home*

Rasmus R. Simonsen

The concept of closure is foundational to understanding graphic narratives. According to Scott McCloud, the "gutter"—the blank space between panels—forms "the very heart of comics" (*Understanding Comics* 66), since it is what allows the reader to make sense of comics: the gutter provides closure to the reader, or, put another way, the reader adds the missing meaning that the gutter stands for. Closure, says McCloud, is the grammar of comics, the presupposed set of rules that allows us to comprehend the visual storytelling (67). But closure isn't exclusively a property of the reading subject. In fact, I argue that *Fun Home* provides a rich example of how closure also happens between objects in and across individual panels. This form of closure, in other words, is interobjective, and to some extent excludes the subjectivity of the reader.

When scholars consider the role of objects in *Fun Home*, it is usually to say something about their rhetorical capacity to illuminate the intersubjective tensions of the Bechdel household. Ariela Freedman's contribution in this volume provides an example of how Bruce's "imposition of aesthetic dominance is inseparable from his claustrophobic and oppressive control of his family." To elaborate, Freedman quotes Bechdel resentfully describing in the memoir "the way my father treated his furniture like children, and his children like furniture" (14). The metonymic tension between Bruce's aesthetics and his parenting is spelled out clearly here. The pieces of furniture are in fact like impeccable stepsiblings: "My brothers and I couldn't compete with the astral lamps and girandoles and Hepplewhite suite chairs. They were perfect" (14). Bruce's interior decorating produces bad feelings in Alison and her brothers, which in turn translate into an affective relationality that takes place not only among the Bechdel children and their ornamental counterparts but also among the objects themselves. Sylvia Lavin writes of bad objects that they are not material as such: "a bad object is a representation, a psychic image that is used to hold and contain all bad things, bad feelings—indeed badness itself" (50). However, the novel's things and spaces—interior and exterior—cannot be reduced to placeholders for the dysfunction of the Bechdel family; they exist within, across, and outside the space-time of the novel.

In teaching *Fun Home*, I have focused on locating with students the novel's interobjective associations that consequently allow for the intersubjective narrative tensions to come into relief. Doing so creates a solid foundation for students to analyze the often complex metonymic links between objects, subjects, and plot points, which are integral to making sense of the novel. I borrow the term *interobjectivity* from Timothy Morton, who, in *Hyperobjects*, writes that "[t]he sum total of all the sampling events by which an object inscribes itself on other objects is a history, in both senses of that wonderfully ambivalent Greek term—

since 'history' can mean both events and recording" (87). In this essay, events refer to the actual scenes that play out primarily among Bechdel, her father, and the objects and spaces of the family home. During these events, feelings are recorded onto the objects—such as, for example, when young Alison is made to polish, clean, and move the many different furniture and decorative objects— tasks she utterly loathes (16). Monotony and complexity are the hallmarks of interior design, Clive Edwards suggests. Decorative objects have more than an aesthetic function; they help us understand the built environment through their "patterning, the defining of edges, borders, rims and surfaces, and the creation of focal points in space" (183). In *Fun Home* the understanding of the interior environment of the house is frustrated by Bruce's eccentric design decisions. Bechdel notes early in the novel how "mirrors, distracting bronzes, [and] multiple doorways" (20) make it difficult for visitors to navigate the interior spaces. Nevertheless, to avoid reducing the materiality and historicity of the objects to the function of affective containers for Bechdel's shifting emotions directed toward her father, this annotated essay clears a space for the objects themselves to provide instructors and students with a resource for recording the different historical and material realities that interact within the space of the novel, as these all conjugate and expand on its multivalent spatiality.

According to Morton, objects belong exclusively to "the aesthetic dimension," which is "a region of traces and footprints" (*Realist Magic* 18). This means that the nonaesthetic function of interior design objects that Edwards describes would nonetheless belong to the objective history of the novel, in Morton's understanding of the term. In fact, we could say that Bechdel's book is a collection of mediated traces: each object depicted—from the photo of Roy to the statue of Don Quixote to the velvet curtains of the library—has in a sense been curated by Bechdel, put into circulation to attempt a coherent depiction of her father's secret. Despite all this evidence, the portrait of her father remains a mystery. Morton reminds us in *Hyperobjects* that "[m]ystery comes from the Greek *muein* (to close)" (170), and the aesthetic space of the Bechdel house, and consequently the novel, is fundamental to the closing off of Bruce's identity. This is to say that the interobjective patterns—the juxtaposition of furniture and decorative objects of different periods and styles—create a mesh of associations, a semiotic and ontological sheen, that makes it impossible, or even trivial, to make sense of Bruce's life according to certain dichotomies, such as those of homo/hetero or private/public suggested in the novel (102). The operation of interobjective closure puts the lie to such dichotomies, inviting a reading of historical and material complexity.

In his afterword to a special issue of *Critical Inquiry* dedicated to the theme of comics and media, W. J. T. Mitchell invokes Art Spiegelman's term *co-mix* to highlight the hybrid genre of comic art. Mitchell lists the following *co-* words as particularly pertinent to the comics form: "coordination, cooptation, coincidence, collision, cooperation" (260). Each can be used to describe different elements and passages of *Fun Home*. In the context of the list of design and architectural objects offered in the second half of this essay, readers might do well to focus on "coordination" and "collision." As apparent opposites, the two nevertheless are conjoined to form the awkward aesthetics of the book's architecture. In "The Architecture of Comics," Catherine Labio calls the Bechdel family home "the grid upon which Bechdel revisits and constructs her past" (338). Labio comments on one of the most poignant panels of the novel to facilitate her reading of the "fragile and dual nature of [the father and daughter's] bond" (339). The page's top panel shows Alison writing in the library next to her father, and the bottom panel gives the reader an external view of the scene through two large windows, the curtains forming the shape of the tip of a felt pen (*Fun Home* 86). Astutely, Labio reads architectural elements, such as shutters and columns, as having the function of hyphens that both separate and connect father and daughter (339). As a series of interobjective events— between the pages of Alison's notebook and those of the biography of Zelda Fitzgerald that Bruce is reading; between the various objects of the interior panel; between the interior and exterior of the house; between the metonymically suggestive curtain shapes and the writing tools that might have produced the words we are reading, or the ones young Alison is writing, or the ones Bruce is reading—this single page in the novel provides a richly textured example of how objects can coordinate our reading of the novel and also facilitate points of collision between different objective and subjective fields within the same space of meaning making.

The annotated list below attends to the textures of the Bechdel family home, with special attention to the Gothic style of the house and the furniture of its interiors. I have indicated the time period and production context, whenever possible, for each item. In this way, I hope to show *Fun Home* as a multilayered work of temporal and spatial complexity, in which surfaces often seek to hide or disguise rather than reveal realities, just as Bruce Bechdel seeks both to hide and to embellish the appearance of his life. The layout of the Bechdel home provides a frame for the many mythological and literary allusions of the book, and the house itself—renovated by Bruce, the "Daedalus of decor" (6)—appears as an amalgamation of various architectural styles and design traditions. This list, then, will help illustrate how studying the designerly connotations of the memoir can help students gain an understanding of how material culture impacts the production and reception of graphic narratives. For the more significant items, I provide a short analytical insight regarding the implications of the novel's treatment of interior and exterior design to help instructors and students frame their reading of the novel's interobjective elements.

The origin of much of the furniture and architectural details of the objects listed here cannot be verified because the drawn objects are often missing defining details that would provide unambiguous verification. Neither is the list exhaustive, as I have focused on the more salient ornamental architectural elements and furnishings of the Bechdel home. The drawings contain many more mundane objects that do not significantly affect the book's mood, texture, or narrative. Except where otherwise noted, parenthetical references indicate page numbers in *Fun Home*.

Architecture

Doors. Double front doors with six panels (5).

Gothic Revival. The Bechdel residence (not the funeral home) was built in 1867 in the Gothic Revival style (8). This nineteenth-century trend in American architecture was a variation on the Tudor, Elizabethan, or English cottage modes (Sweeting 46). In England, the term *Gothic* had been brought into common use by John Evelyn (1620–1706), who described it as a "Fantastical and Licentious Manner of building" (qtd. in Murray and Murray 244). Only in the eighteenth century was the Gothic deemed superior to the classical style, and Gothic aesthetics underwent a revival. In antebellum America, Alexander Jackson Davis (1803–92) and his partner, Ithiel Town (1784–1844), were the primary residential builders in the style. Later in the nineteenth century, the prominent architect Andrew Jackson Downing popularized the Gothic style further. His book *Cottage Residences* formalized the style, which was characterized by "intricate vergeboards, pointed windows, a steeply pitched roof, and gables ornamented with finials" (Sweeting 46)—all of which are found on the exterior of the Bechdel home (9). The ornamental component of Gothic Revival was supposed to reference the "true Christianity of medieval forms" (Packard 268), and the style was often used for churches. The vergeboards (ornamental roof features) of the Bechdel house feature scroll-sawn cut-outs that correspond nicely to Downing's design 7 (Downing 141–42; cf. *Fun Home* 9, bottom). The same pattern is repeated in the modillions (ornamental brackets) of the front porch supports (9, top right). A specific feature of Gothic Revival style in the Bechdel home is an abundance of irregular outlines and angles. The "asymmetrical yet interconnected forms" of houses in this style "allow a sense of dynamic movement to prevail" (Sweeting, 48, 49). Early in the memoir, what Sweeting refers to as "romantic otherness" (49) finds particular expression in the form of "a tiny scale model of [Alison's] father's more fully developed self-loathing" as a closeted gay man (*Fun Home* 20). The mix of furniture from different periods adds to the confused interiority of the Bechdel house. In short, the house's interior is a vast metaphor on the precarious nature of Bruce's relationship to his family and his sexuality.

Poche. *Poche* (French for "pocket") refers to the space or material between walls (appearing as negative space on the blueprint). This potential space allows the architect to carve out a niche, or pocket—the reason for which depends on an exchange between object and surrounding space. *Poche* is similar to what in graphic narrative theory is called the gutter. In *Fun Home* the gutters influence the negative connotation of queerness as both "athwart" and "to thwart" (57). The book's gutters can then be read as *poche*, in order to think about queerness as being never completely concealed or disclosed. What is more, queerness in *Fun Home* is highly interobjective, most clearly expressed in the associative links between ornamental features and materials in the home, particularly in the library (the queerest of spaces): flocked wallpaper, gilded accents, velvet curtains, and the Don Quixote and Mephistopheles statue lamps (60). This gathering of objects appears only three pages after the close-up of the dictionary entry for *queer.*

Porch. Suggestive of the Tuscan order, the simplest of the classical orders, displaying a complete entablature consisting of a cornice, frieze, and architrave. The entablature sits upon the support columns: two complete ones in front (*Fun Home* 5, top left), a folded one on either side of the porch, and a half one on either side closest to the house (8, bottom left; 9, top right). The two front supports do not correspond to the form of classical columns that were directly connected to the main walls of a temple. The pattern of the supports is a form of interlace (12, bottom right).

Roof. Cross-gabled with intricate vergeboards and a drop pendant shaped as a cross, which is interwoven with the vergeboards (8; 9, bottom).

Windows. The front of the house displays five four-over-four pane windows. At the center of each gable sits a simple four-pane window with a pointed arch (8, 9). Each window of the house has a sill. The frames appear to be patterned with molding (8, bottom right).

Furniture and Ornament

Astral lamps. A kind of Argand lamp, invented by the Swiss chemist Aimé Argand in 1783. This type of oil burner combined a long chimney with a cylindrical shape, making it a highly effective object of illumination; additionally, it was more smoke-free than other lamp designs at the time. In nineteenth-century America it became one of the most popular objects of illumination for the middle classes (Metropolitan Museum). Astral lamps appear almost as frequently in *Fun Home* as Tiffany lamps (12, 14, 15, 16, 17).

Cabriole chair. Likely a George Hepplewhite design, featuring a stuffed rounded shield back and tapered legs, the primary feature of the cabriole style, which mimics the shape of an animal leg (6). The material would be mahogany. Joseph Aronson remarks that Hepplewhite's style was indistinguishable from that of Thomas Shearer, another prominent Georgian era cabinetmaker (iv). Both artisans followed in the steps of Thomas Chippendale, the foremost furniture designer of the English rococo style. Hepplewhite, Shearer, and Chippendale are known as the "trisyllabic triad" of furniture design in the eighteenth century (Aronson vi). In America, Hepplewhite designs are associated with the Federal style, although American furniture of this period (1780–1820) rejected English designs by using, for example, straight instead of curved legs. Bechdel specifically mentions the "perfect" Hepplewhite suite chairs with their ornamental floral pattern, with which the Bechdel children "couldn't compete" (*Fun Home* 14; chairs on 21).

Chairs, other. The library chair featured on pp. 82–86 of *Fun Home* appears to be a bérgère-style chair, the design of which originated in the Louis XV period but is still manufactured. This pattern coheres with the rest of the rococo furniture in the Bechdel home, like the sofa (6, bottom); it is likely that much of the rococo-style pieces were made by such nineteenth-century American cabinetmakers as John Henry Belter or Charles A. Baudouine, out of New York (Metropolitan Museum). The Gothic-style hall chair (15, bottom right), which Alison finds "hard to dust" (15), resembles two pieces in the Winterthur Museum collection that were made between 1845 and 1855, most likely in New York. The material is oak.

Couch. One-ended, in the stylistic vein of so-called Old English furniture made popular in the latter half of the nineteenth century, by, among others, the Tottenham Court Road furniture dealer James Shoolbred (Gere 126; Shoolbred), a royal appointee who appealed to middle-class tastes. Eschewing the more extravagant furniture styles of the various revival design movements, Old English aesthetics signaled a return to practical forms, appealing to "individuality, flexibility and informality in the home" (Long 33). The Bechdel couch corresponds to this new domestic ideal (*Fun Home* 14, 17), the heart of which was the drawing room, where "fancy reigns supreme, and our spirits find free scope, unfettered by the weightier cares of life" (Cooper 11).

Gas chandelier. The object of an argument between Bruce and Helen Bechdel (13–14). Most likely late Victorian. This kind of chandelier was popular before the era of electricity.

Library desk. It is a "leather-topped mahogany and brass second-empire desk" (60), which places its manufacture in late-nineteenth-century France. The British design historian Penny Sparke points out that ornament traditionally has the utilitarian function of linking objects within an interior space and creating a structure for the subsequent interpretation of that space (125). The library of the Bechdel home, in particular, exemplifies this insight: each piece of furniture or ornament seems to relate to Bruce's closeted queerness; each object is a metonym of the absent referent that is his sexuality (*Fun Home* 60). The interplay between the Don Quixote and the Mephistopheles statuettes might be said to represent the whole of how the father sees his queerness, as futile and wicked: his choices of ornament ironically display this otherwise (poorly) veiled part of him. The pride he takes in the family home sublimates the shame of his sexuality, and it is this affective duality that the interior ornaments of the house implicitly reveal.

Mirrors. The mirror, or looking glass, that Alison helps her father position (14, bottom) is strikingly similar to a mahogany piece on display in the Winterthur Museum that features the same kind of curved ornamentation. This mirror is in the style of those made popular by Paul Cermenati and John Bernarda, who were partners in Salem, Massachusetts, in 1807–08 (Zimmerman and Butler 128).

Tiffany lamp. The Tiffany lamp is the most frequent of the ornamental lamps that appear in *Fun Home* (18, 65, 86, 60, 61, 65, 82, 83, 84). It is named for the stained-glass designer Louis Comfort Tiffany (1848–1933), whose studio produced the first lamps of this kind.

Walnut bookcase. Unlike the chairs, this is probably not a Georgian-era piece, as the favored wood of this period was mahogany. It resembles the popular New England late-Victorian factory-made furniture that features Italianate ornamentation (for example, the finials, or top ornaments, at each end of the bookcase), but its simple lines are characteristic of the neo-Grecian style. However, the rectangular cornice exhibits carved details (a single, perhaps Roman, eagle) typical of pre-Revolutionary grandiose furniture that was often based on the rococo style of Chippendale (*Fun Home* 60–61, 64, 82–86; cf. Bates and Fairbanks 184, 191).

Reading *Fun Home* Historically: LGBTQ History and Print Culture

Julie R. Enszer

What ideas are you playing with right now that may define your work for the next three decades? This question ends my class discussions on Alison Bechdel's *Fun Home*. Bechdel began drawing the characters of *Dykes to Watch Out For*, her iconic comic strip, in her early twenties. Many of the events of *Fun Home* happened while she was in college, and her college reading provided inspiration for her creative work. *Fun Home* offers students an opportunity to think about their own entry into creative production and about how history shapes lived experiences.

Fun Home offers historical and personal narratives about LGBTQ history and print culture. It slyly operates as an introduction to LGBTQ history; the text narrates a history of the LGBTQ community, beginning in Germany in the 1880s with sexology, including World War II and the postwar era, and concluding with the author's own coming out in the early 1980s. Bechdel, at her most subversive and her most deliciously allusive, explores intellectual history, particularly intellectual history grounded in canonical Western literature, and gestures provocatively to two conclusions: the significance of lesbians and gay men in intellectual history and the importance of expanding the canon of intellectual history to include feminist and lesbian writers and artists. *Fun Home* as autobiography explores Bechdel's life history as an artist and through that story narrates a history of lesbian-feminist print culture. Finally, Bechdel synthesizes all these histories with three historically imbued metaphors that anchor the book and argue for greater recognition of lesbians.

LGBTQ History in the United States and Europe

In *Fun Home* Bechdel narrates a history of gay and lesbian liberation beginning in the 1880s and extending through the 1980s. From Germany to Pennsylvania to New York, the Bechdel family's stories suggest possibilities lost and found for gay identity.

Bruce Bechdel served in the United States military, and Bruce and Helen, as a young married couple, lived in West Germany, an experience described as "expatriate splendor" (32). Germany was a location of early research and ideological support for gay people. In 1884, Richard von Krafft-Ebing, a nineteenth-century sexologist, asserted that homosexuality was neither deviant nor the result of a mental illness; Magnus Hirschfeld, a doctor who advocated equal rights for gay and lesbian people, worked to decriminalize homosexuality in Germany and abroad in the 1920s and 1930s. Although both Krafft-Ebing and Hirschfeld died before Bruce and Helen lived in Germany, Bechdel aligns her father's service with this intellectual history and transnational LGBTQ history.

Bruce returned from Germany to Pennsylvania to run the family business. Bechdel's drawing of the three square miles where her father spent most of his life (30, 126–27, 140, 146) raises interesting questions with regard to John D'Emilio's history of gay identity development in the United States in the middle of the twentieth century, in which migration from one's place of origin created the possibility of gay identity. After World War II, young men migrated to cities, particularly port cities like New York, San Francisco, and Los Angeles. D'Emilio argues that this movement to cities and away from families of origin allowed the development of gay and lesbian identities because people were free to organize their lives in new ways. Bruce Bechdel, however, married a woman, foreclosing that possibility.

Alan Turing's story relates intimately to *Fun Home*. Turing, whose life was popularized in the 2014 film *The Imitation Game* (Tyldum), is known as a father of modern computers and as a national hero in Great Britain for breaking the Nazis' so-called Enigma code and thus shortening World War II. Turing was gay and was subjected to chemical castration and aversion therapy to "correct" his homosexual behavior. He committed suicide in 1954 at the age of forty-one as a result. Turing's story is one of many tragedies of gay men and lesbians subjected to inhumane medical and psychological procedures after World War II. Bechdel's reflections on the possibility of her father's death as a suicide echoes Turing's life and death (196).

For gay and lesbian people, life in the 1950s in the United States was not unlike Turing's experience in Great Britain. Gay and lesbian people were harassed, stigmatized, and marginalized. The few representations of lesbians were in pulp novels, printed cheaply and mass-marketed. Pulps included lesbian stories such as *Odd Girl Out* and *Women in the Shadows*, both by Ann Bannon. Pulps portrayed lesbian love affairs, but the lesbian characters always met with tragic ends, indicating the impossibility of their attaining happiness. Bechdel read pulp novels from the 1950s, learning about bar raids and the harassment of lesbians and gay men. In *Fun Home* she refers to the requirement of that era for gay men and lesbians to wear at least three pieces of gender-conforming clothes to avoid suspicion or arrest. Bechdel, who wanted to wear boys' clothes, wonders if she would have been compliant with this regulation and how she would have survived this social control (107). This history contrasts with her experiences coming out as a lesbian a generation later and highlights the limited choices that her father had for his life.

In June of 1969 at a small New York City bar called the Stonewall Inn, a group of lesbians, gay men, transgender people, and cross-dressers rebelled against harassment by the police. Bechdel realizes that she and her family were in New York just a few weeks after this watershed gay-rights event and wonders, "Might not a lingering vibration, a quantum particle of rebellion, still have hung in the humectant air?" (104). The family visited New York again in 1976 for the bicentennial, when Bechdel was fifteen years old. She reflects on the stylized masculinity of gay male culture in the 1970s and remembers family visits to the ballet and the musical *A Chorus Line* (190). As Randy Shilts documents in *And the Band Played On*, 1976 was probably the year that HIV was introduced to the United States. Bechdel, recalling her father's activity during the bicentennial celebration, notes that had her father not died in the truck accident he might have contracted HIV and died from AIDS (195). She unites the narrative of her family with a broader narrative of gay and lesbian liberation and the AIDS epidemic of the 1980s.

Intellectual History

Intellectual history is the history of how ideas are transmitted, modified, reconstituted, and reevaluated throughout time; canonical Western literature is an important element of these stories of ideas. While intellectual history often focuses on the achievements of white men, Bechdel contests the exclusive privilege of this arena to them. For instance, the semester that she is supposed to read James Joyce's *Ulysses*, she finds herself entranced with Colette, a French writer known for her honest and frank portrayals of women's sexuality (205); Virginia Woolf, a British writer who challenged women's exclusion from education (209); and Jill Johnston, a columnist at the *Village Voice* during the 1970s who became a voice of radical lesbian feminism (207). Bechdel rejects *Ulysses* in favor of decidedly queer and feminist intellectual concerns, which she portrays as vitally linked and in dialogue with one another.

The myth of Daedalus and Icarus opens Bechdel's exploration of her relationship with her father, which she further explicates through *Ulysses* and other high-literary texts by Leo Tolstoy, Ernest Hemingway, F. Scott Fitzgerald, Marcel Proust, Edward Albee, and other works by Joyce. Bechdel understands her mother through a similarly allusive intellectual history. Various scenes highlight her mother acting in plays, including Shakespeare's *Taming of the Shrew; The Heiress*, based on Henry James's novel *Washington Square*; and Oscar Wilde's *An Ideal Husband*. Bechdel's mother is both literally and metaphorically an actor in the intellectual history assembled in *Fun Home*.

Books and plays provide guiding metaphors, connections, and analogies for Bechdel's exploration of her family history. The circular structure of the text echoes the call-and-response of literary culture. A series of central stories in the book—Bechdel's coming out, her father's amorous relationships with younger men, his death—return multiple times. Each time, Bechdel retells the stories with new facts or new literary referents. Literature, broadly construed, operates similarly; Joyce retells Homer's *Odyssey* in *Ulysses*, Kate Millett reworks Colette's sexual aristocrats with impoverished artists in *Flying*. Borrowing, sharing, and retelling characterizes intellectual history and literature, and Bechdel places herself, as an open lesbian, and her father, as a closeted gay or bisexual man, firmly in this tradition. Her text asserts that intellectual history and canonical literature include queer lives and queer people and that queer stories are vital to these narratives.

Engagement with feminist texts complements Bechdel's breathtaking proficiency with canonical texts. *Fun Home* narrates an intellectual history of feminism—and particularly of lesbian feminism, feminism concerned with integrating lesbian identity with the feminist movement. The first book she reads about people who "had completely cast aside their own qualms [about homosexuality]" includes an interview with the lesbian poet and bon vivant Elsa Gidlow (74). Throughout *Fun Home*, Bechdel turns to books to understand her sexuality. These books include texts rediscovered by feminist literary critics, like Virginia Woolf's *Orlando* and Radclyffe Hall's *The Well of Loneliness*. They also include popular books published about lesbian feminism, such as *Our Right to Love*, by Ginny Vida, and *Lesbian/Woman*, by Del Martin and Phyllis Lyons, as well as sexology texts such as *Homosexualities*, by William H. Masters and Virginia E. Johnson. Finally, popular novels like Rita Mae Brown's *Rubyfruit Jungle*, Jane Rule's *Desert of the Heart*, and May Sarton's *Mrs. Stevens Hears the Mermaids Singing* constitute an important part of Bechdel's reading. Her engagement with feminist texts situates these books as part of not only a feminist and queer canon but also the larger canon of Western literature.

Bechdel's genealogy includes works of high culture that her father suggests for her to read as well as emergent works from the women's liberation movement in the United States. She relates her and her father's experiences as gay people to broader classical narratives that are not always inclusive of gay and lesbian people. She thus challenges intellectual history to include her history and her experiences with feminist and lesbian intellectual work. Ultimately, this dazzling graphic novel modifies intellectual history, broadening it from the province of white men to include the work of lesbians and feminists.

The Life of an Artist and Histories of Lesbian-Feminist Print Culture

Fun Home spent two weeks on *The New York Times* best-sellers' list during the summer of 2006, and *Entertainment Weekly*, *Time*, and *Publisher's Weekly* recognized it as a best book of the year. The musical adaptation won multiple Tony awards. Commercial success for a book by an open lesbian would have been unthinkable twenty years earlier, particularly a book with frank depictions of cunnilingus and meditations on a relationship between an adult man and a male teenager. What changed?

Lesbian-feminist print culture, a broad series of publishing, organizing, and community activities initiated by lesbian feminists beginning in 1969 and extending to today, provided a platform for Bechdel's work and helped to create a context for her commercial success. Bechdel began publishing her comic strips in *Womannews*, a New York–based feminist newspaper, and they became known and loved in feminist, lesbian, and LGBTQ communities. As the comic strip developed into *Dykes to Watch Out For*, Bechdel syndicated it herself, mailing the artwork to lesbian, gay, feminist, and progressive newspapers around the United States. By the early 1990s the success of the comic strip allowed her to stop working a day job. During the 1990s and early 2000s, Bechdel published the weekly strip and nine collections of *Dykes* with Firebrand Books, building an audience for her quirky cast of lesbians in partnership with her book publisher, Nancy Bereano. Feminist bookstores connected Bechdel and Firebrand Books with a market of eager readers. Collectively, this lesbian-feminist literary ecosystem created the means for Bechdel to support her artwork through sales of comic strips, books, and calendars. This vibrant, dedicated audience both sustained Bechdel's work and advanced a broader movement for greater social acceptance for lesbians, gay men, and bisexual people, creating a context for *Fun Home* and Bechdel's subsequent accolades, including the 2014 MacArthur Fellowship.

Metaphors and Their Histories; or, Three Cs of Fun Home: Cadaver, Centerfold, Cunnilingus

Three central images metaphorically anchor Bechdel's historical narratives: the cadaver, the centerfold, and cunnilingus. These images explore twinned representations of human bodies and sexuality and through allusions explore histories of gender and sexuality. Young Alison describes her first encounter with a dead body as a "dark red cave," a visual analogy to female genitalia, foreshadowing her incipient lesbianism (44). The image of the cave returns in the second telling of Alison's sexual encounter with Joan, when she analogizes Joan's genitalia to Polyphemus's cave in Homer's *Odyssey* (214). Through the cadaver and its metaphor of a cave, Bechdel links the erotic and the necrotic, asking readers to question how erotic expressions are linked to death.

The centerfold contains three elements: the photograph, voiceover comments, and the hand (100–01). The photograph of Roy, who is bathed in sunlight and lying on a bed in his underwear, evokes paintings of women in classical art as well as of centerfolds in pornographic magazines. Bechdel's voiceover comments invite readers to imagine multiple modes of image interpretation. The hand, approximately twice the size of the reader's hand holding the page, implicates readers as viewers of art and pornography. All—Bruce, Alison, readers— are implicated in seeing the underage Roy as a sexual object. This image invites students to grapple with the ethics of sex between older adults and younger adults, the construction of pornography, and links between homosexuality and pornography. It also highlights different historical constructions of what is permitted and what is forbidden sexually.

Scenes of cunnilingus appear twice in *Fun Home*. The first scene is built around childhood stories, expressing innocent jubilation in relation to Alison's discovery of lesbianism (80–81). The second scene uses the *Odyssey* to express the enormity of Bechdel's discovery of lesbianism (214). This scene develops from small single panels to a combined panel four times larger. Bechdel describes herself with Joan as "facing a 'being of colossal strength and ferocity, to whom the law of man and God meant nothing'" (214). The earlier scene portrays physical intimacy and intimates cunnilingus; the later scene shows Alison "in true heroic fashion" moving "toward the thing I feared" with a direct representation of cunnilingus, replete with pubic hair. Bechdel writes, "Yet while Odysseus schemed desperately to escape Polyphemus's cave, I found that I was quite content to stay here forever" (214). Alison, one-eyed like the Cyclops, understands Polyphemus's cave as a lesbian home. Through cunnilingus, Bechdel finds herself and embraces life by refuting sexual shame, "in itself a kind of death" (228).

Like the histories of Bechdel's *Fun Home*, the question with which this essay begins does not suggest a linear narrative between creative work in college and future commercial success, public recognition, or being called a genius. Rather, it gestures toward the idea that critical ideas, essential questions, and crucial nodes of inquiry defined early in students' intellectual lives can shape their creative work for years to come. For Bechdel, early obsessions offer one window into thinking about the intellectual and material conditions of a working artist.

Part Two

APPROACHES

"Our Selves Were All We Had":
Parsing the Autobiographical in *Fun Home*

Julia Watson

Auto, from the Greek *autos*, a reflexive third-person pronoun that can denote "self," is a prefix that resonates throughout *Fun Home* as visual and verbal practice. The map of Bruce Bechdel's sites of birth, adult life, death, and burial in Beech Creek, Pennsylvania, is drawn as a "solipsistic circle of self, from auto-didact to autocrat to autocide," this last a wry pun (140). The phrase could be an epitaph summing up young Alison's view of her father's life as an egomaniacal project. And yet, in the complexly self-referential world of *Fun Home*, the auto-biographical is not a solipsistic exercise. Rather, the genre of the autonomous individual's reflections is reworked through multiple forms of graphic and verbal self-reference to encompass a brilliant repertoire of ways to tell and show personal stories about becoming an artist, asserting a queer identity, and making a self.

The autobiographical status of *Fun Home*, which may seem its most obvious feature, is, however, elusive to parse. We begin with the crucial distinction between acts performed by the flesh-and-blood Bechdel in producing the text, which critics term biographical paratexts, and the autobiographical references that engage us on its pages as representations of Alison's experience. We cannot occupy her body or share her felt experience—readers are on the reception end of the process. Yet students struggle with the question of what makes *Fun Home* an "autographic," in Gillian Whitlock's term, because its assemblage of artifacts, reproduced exactly and beautifully to the scale of the comic box, is so persuasively "real" and referential (966). An autobiographical story, however, is more than self-written biography, the chronological recitation of the events of a life. It is not a transparent reciting of the facts of one's experience but an interpretation at specific moments in time.[1] In courses my goal is to persuade students that *Fun Home* is not a transparent window on the flesh-and-blood Bechdel's life but a sustained act of self-reflection in time by a subject who defines her place in her family, genealogy, and historical moment through acts of auto-graphing in the text's drawings and layers of narrative. In this sense it exceeds the minimal terms of the "autobiographical pact" that Philippe Lejeune defined for written narrative: "What defines autobiography for the one who is reading is above all a contract of identity that is sealed by the proper name" (19). Instead, I offer students the definition that Sidonie Smith and I use: "Life narratives, through the memories they construct, are records of acts of interpretation by subjects inescapably in historical time and in relation to their own ever-moving pasts" (*Reading* 30). Relationality, not one-to-one correlation, is the focus.

Further, the "I" of graphic memoir as a visual-verbal presentation of self needs to be theorized with students, who often lack language to describe its autobiographical dimensions. We consider *Fun Home*'s drawn artifacts from the family archive—photographs, letters, diaries and journals, maps, obituaries—not just as reproductions of records. Rather, they are prompts to our acts of interpretation of a past that looks different from the different vantage points of young Alison at various ages, and certainly from the point of view of the mature cartoonist whose self was constructed at their intersection in making the text.[2] This discussion of the autobiographical, while most productive in courses on life narrative, is useful generally in thinking about the relation of an artist's autobiographical impulses to the creation of a self-reflexive graphic story. Bechdel did not invent the form of graphic memoir; the stunning works of other women artist-autobiographers such as Charlotte Salomon, Lynda Barry, and Phoebe Gloeckner have preceded her. But Bechdel's intense focus on the relation between making the comic and articulating her concept of self in relation to family experience makes *Fun Home* a self-theorizing autographic. In class we consider, over four days or two weeks, what autobiography, a form many scholars prefer to call life narrative, is and isn't, and explore its uses in the frames, pages, and selected chapters of *Fun Home*, practicing what I have elsewhere called a "reflexive and recursive reading practice" ("Autographic Disclosures" 28).

Beginning to Read Autobiographically

We first discuss some distinctions about autobiographical storytelling. We distinguish the memoir from fictional forms such as the novel. Memoir is referential in drawing on material from the maker's life history, but often uses fictional techniques such as dialogue, foreshadowing, and metaphor. *Fun Home*'s blend of autobiographical detail drawn from personal archives and modes of storytelling employed in their interpretation is within a long-standing practice of innovative life writing for which scholars have coined numerous neologisms.[3] A memorable example in the field of comics studies is Lynda Barry's use of the term *autobiofictionalography* to characterize her graphic memoir, *One Hundred Demons*. In the memoir's introduction Barry's persona asks, "Is it autobiography if parts of it are not true? Is it fiction if parts of it are?," tersely alluding to the conundrum of how life narrative both asserts and troubles the notion of personal truth (7). A similar mixture of archival documentation and artistic innovation occurs in such comics pathbreakers as Art Spiegelman's *Maus*, with its hybrid animal characters, and Marjane Satrapi's *Persepolis I*, in Marji's conversations with God. As Tim O'Brien suggests in *The Things They Carried*, "A thing may happen and be a total lie; another thing may not happen and be truer than the truth" (83). Bechdel's temporally complex narration and her redrawing of graphic forms from photography and illustration problematize the notion that truth inheres in surface evidence. In gesturing toward the contradictions of lived experience and the partiality of memory, her notion of truth, like that in Barry's, Spiegelman's, and Satrapi's work, situates the autobiographical in comics as a medium uniquely combining multiple media to circumvent the usual connotations of fiction.

We distinguish between the narrating I telling the story, to whom we refer as the "I-now" and call "Bechdel," and the narrated I whose experiential past is being related, to whom we refer as the "I-then" and call "Alison"; we may distinguish further among child, adolescent, and teenager. The adult narrating I has been characterized by Hillary L. Chute as a *"visual voice"* because Bechdel "recollectively frames the narrative's events" differently, "mobilizing a tacit conversation across media between different versions of self" (*Graphic Women* 5).

We observe how Bechdel's voiceover narration is placed in text boxes at the top of or above the cartoon box or in the tags with arrows that gloss some drawings. Alison, by contrast, speaks or thinks primarily within dialogue bubbles.

Initially students choose a specific frame or two from the day's reading, write a description of what they observe, and discuss, first in small groups, the differences they observe between the perspectives of the narrated and narrating I's. I also announce a choice of writing assignments that includes, as an alternative to a critical essay, creating a graphic memoir excerpt à la Bechdel and writing an analysis that explains the student's choices with reference to *Fun Home*. For example, a student could opt to change the gender of the protagonist and rethink the identities and sexualities of other characters accordingly.

Genres of Autobiographical Storytelling

Since students often think there is only one way to tell a life story, we identify some of the autobiographical genres used in *Fun Home* and discuss their storytelling possibilities. *Fun Home* is of course a confession, that core autobiographical genre since Augustine and Rousseau. It discloses a wide range of family secrets, from Alison's father's transgressions and her mother's suppressed ambitions to its merciless focus on Alison's own quirks. Because these disclosures, embedded in an intimate family story, may strike some students—particularly those from non-Western countries—as shocking or inappropriate, it is helpful to ask if such secrets are being flaunted or, conversely, puzzled over as signs of another history concealed in the conventional family archive and album.

As a narrative of childhood and family *Fun Home* is a bildungsroman, or coming-of-age story. While that form is traditionally about consolidating an identity through encounters with characters representing beliefs and values of the social milieu, the protagonists in many female and postcolonial bildungsromans invert these norms in experiencing their outsider status. In *Fun Home* many of the encounters that educate Alison are with books, across the divide between canonical texts of Euro-American literary modernism and a countercanon of gay and lesbian coming-out stories of sexual difference and political struggle. Contrasting the sources and processes of Alison's education with those of her parents, or indeed those of students' own, can be a good essay topic.

As a story of discovering an artistic vocation, *Fun Home* is also a *Künstlerroman* about developing not just one's craft but one's vision. The narrator alludes to several mentors and invokes their life stories, both those of her artistic parents and of famous writers, including some—Oscar Wilde, Radclyffe Hall—whose sexual identities led to lifelong struggles and social persecution.

As a story of grief and mourning, *Fun Home* is an autothanatography, a quest through grief and mourning for reconciliation with a dead beloved.

Fun Home can be read through other story templates—for example, as a feminist narrative of thinking back through our mothers, neatly reversed to foreground the narrator's father's life.

Relational Life Stories

Fun Home's focus is not on the isolated self; it is inescapably a family story, as its subtitle, "A Family Tragicomic," announces. Alison's experience is embedded within a domestic ethnography of the family's past history, including her father's family's immigrant genealogy. These collective tales are interwoven into what is called a relational autobiography, defined by Paul John Eakin as "the autobiography of the self and the biography *and* the autobiography of the other" (58), the other who may be known so intimately that a narrator can tell the person's story from inside the life. As students often have collective family experiences that are illuminating for thinking relationally, we focus on the following ideas.

Alison, the narrated I of *Fun Home*, is embedded in multiple relationships—primarily familial ones but also those with friends, lovers, and the biographical lives of modernist authors—that gradually enable her to articulate an identity in relation to others, particularly with her father, whose status as an "invert," a term she adopts from Proust, she shares (97). We make a list of the books drawn or mentioned, focusing on writers' lives as possible trajectories for Alison's own or her parents' self-definition.

Fun Home is also a genealogical story of self in relation to a family lineage. Chapter 2 tracks the origin story of the Bechdel family in rural Pennsylvania, as young Alison and her siblings repeatedly beg "Grammy," Bruce's mother, to tell how three-year-old Bruce was stuck in a planting field and had to be rescued and put in the oven. The reminiscence, with its metaphorics of sinking into the earth, both situates the German immigrant family as deeply located in rural life and foreshadows Bruce's burial. Although by mid-century the family's wider experience and cultural aspirations and the parents' professions as high school English teachers have made them "artistic [and] autistic" outsiders, the question of heritage haunts *Fun Home* (139). Students are intrigued by how likeness, the persistence of personality traits over generations, may inform their own sense of self. They sometimes conduct an interview with someone of their parents' generation to ask about how social and sexual norms were different when they were growing up.

Visual Embodiment and Self-Inscription

Intriguingly, of her multistage process of sketching images on tracing paper before beginning to ink them, Bechdel told interviewer Judith Thurman, "I don't start drawing until I've finished the storytelling" (Thurman, "Drawn"). *Fun Home*'s multiple graphic stories not only enhance but can be in tension with its verbal narrative. A helpful point of entry to *Fun Home* is to ask how Bechdel's inked line drawings of the material detail of her family's past represent visual embodiment, both in her production process and in our reception. I introduce the following points.

Chute's discussion of how Bechdel made photographs of herself enacting the position of each character as a guide to drawing them fascinates students (*Graphic Women* 20). In reflecting on the labor this practice requires, we explore how Bechdel's literal embodiment of all the characters is a way of inhabiting them, feeling them from the inside. I observe, however, that the interview is one of the biographical paratexts revealed after publication, and the Polaroid photographs not something we experience while reading the text. Similarly, the sketches of family photographs on each chapter's title page provoke stimulating discussion, but are part of the production process, not our reception. These aspects of making *Fun Home* do resonate, however, particularly with students in the visual arts. Jessica Naples, an MFA photography student in my graduate seminar, insightfully pointed out Bechdel's use of a "hatching technique" to create the "tonal effects" of photographic images. Bechdel does not just "reproduce" but "re-enliven[s]" the images, "making the past active in the present and mediated through the hand of the maker" as a relational link to her father (3).

I ask students to look for further evidence of how Bechdel embeds the materiality of her family history graphically in another mode of familial inscription, drawing documents. These include her parents' courtship correspondence and documents attesting to their lived reality, such as her mother's passport photos (71, 72) and the police report for her father's arrest for buying alcohol for a minor (161). Bechdel has discussed her concern with exactly replicating the design and colors of green chrysanthemums of the wallpaper of the funeral home on *Fun Home*'s flyleaves, although she could find only five of its eleven shades of green (Chute, "Interview" 1008). We consider what this obsession with accuracy, in someone who confesses to obsessive-compulsive tendencies, suggests about her desire to not just replicate the past but make its representation as authentic as memory permits, creating a storehouse not only of memories but of their affects, an "archive of feelings" in Ann Cvetkovich's sense (120).

Authenticity and Truth Claims

Students often ask whether Bechdel's artful replication is authentic. That is, what kinds of truth claims is she making, and are these verifiable? While *Fun Home*'s precise reproduction of artifacts and documents seems to be transparent evidence, a slice of life, I try to trouble the assumption that these details constitute the autobiographical. Bechdel's documentation of the real, however accurate, is unverifiable for most of us, as we cannot inhabit that now-vanished reality.[4] Rather, we focus on the ways in which *Fun Home* stages self-representation as an engagement with subjectivity and ask, How do the claims to authentic reproduction in *Fun Home*'s paratexts serve as a mode of rhetorical persuasion to ground a story posing difficult, unresolvable questions—such as whether Bruce's death was a suicide, or the reality of Alison and Bruce's deep, unspoken bond? In this light Bechdel's careful attention to material detail and historical events such as Stonewall and Watergate makes us more likely to trust the unverifiable truth claims she makes about her father, family, and self.

With graduate students I extend this point into a larger discussion of the concept of "metrics of authenticity," which Sidonie Smith and I have developed ("Witness").[5] We inquire into the relation of documentary evidence to the subjective truth of experience in what Bechdel calls the pursuit of "erotic truth" that gradually unfolds in *Fun Home* (230). What is at stake autobiographically in *Fun Home* is less Bechdel's stunning skill in authentic reproduction than how that network of material realities supports her view of sensibility and sexuality across genders and generations. This intimate, speculative knowledge, fraught with uncertainty, was largely unspeakable during her father's lifetime.

Diary Keeping and Autobiographical Discourse

The narrating I characterizes her adolescent self by noting "my own compulsive propensity to autobiography" in relation to her father's "auto-driven" life
(140). A key aspect is the role played by *Fun Home*'s citation of autobiographical documents. Chapter 5, "The Canary-Colored Caravan of Death," includes
several drawn pages of Alison's adolescent diary and describes her process of
diary keeping. But we discover that the chapter's brief *Künstlerroman* of her
development as an artist is a wry fable about the inadequacy of conventional
practices of life narration to her quest for an embodied and visually convincing
mode of self-presentation.

We note that chapter 5's frame story, its beginning and ending, recollects a
moment of father and daughter looking together at a sunset, a point to which we
later return. The chapter's core story is about how Alison doesn't—and does—
become an artist. Her seven-year-old avatar is introduced as a poem writer and
illustrator whose first halting effort at a poem drawing is thwarted when her
father "improves" it by immediately improvising a second stanza. At that point
Alison abandons both writing poetry and using color, two fundamental artistic
tools (130). The narrative then shifts to Alison's later childhood years, when
her obsessive-compulsive tendencies, autographed in close and often hilarious
detail, prompt her parents to suggest that she regulate her behavior by writing a
diary. Diary keeping becomes a family project: her father dictates its first lines
on a Ray Burial Vault wall calendar given to her for the purpose, and for two
months her mother takes dictation for it because Alison's obsessive-compulsive
habits are making the diary entries illegible. But keeping a diary is a comic
failure, as Alison's compulsiveness and sense of isolation render her unable to
confide personal disclosures in words. What cannot be written in a conventional, chronological way, however, becomes a potential space for generating a
different kind of autobiographical inscription.

The birth of Alison's consciousness of her subjectivity brings on a crisis, the
inability to narrate herself. Bechdel goes on to describe how, in the diary, young
Alison compulsively begins writing "I think" after virtually every event of daily
life she records because, as the narrator wryly observes, "All I could speak for
was my own perceptions, and perhaps not even those" (141). Yet the chronicle
of external events in her diary discloses nothing about the internal struggles the
adult narrator now acknowledges. Instead, young Alison translates her compul-
sion to mark all her perceptions as subjective into an abstract "curvy circumflex" (142). She obsessively overwrites the laconic diary passages chronicling
daily events with large *V*'s, inscriptions "bound in the strange alchemy of word
and image" that are suggestively sexual in a way she cannot yet decode (Gardner, "Autography's Biography" 5) but "assert her agency and her perspective as
primary" (Pearl 292). This fable about the development of an autobiographical
artist in a family that cultivates creative solitude suggests how the children were

nurtured in understanding life as a process of self-making: "Our selves were all we had" (*Fun Home* 139).

In chapter 5 Bechdel, the theoretically sophisticated narrating I, also offers us a metatext for thinking about the space of the autobiographical when the narrating I glosses the signifier-signified gap of subjective perception that the circumflex signals as "the troubling gap between word and meaning" (143). That is, the space of subjectivity is a blank or in-between to be inscribed—for the child Alison most satisfyingly by maps, topographies that "bridge the symbolic and the real" (147). Indeed, these chartings, particularly in the *Wind in the Willows* coloring book, anticipate the multimodal form of autobiographical comics that *Fun Home* exemplifies and suggest how drawing comics enables Bechdel to spatialize her experience of perceptual subjectivity as a "landscape" (146), a graphic "representation of time as space on the page," which Chute and Marianne DeKoven identify as a hallmark of comics (769). At the same time the act of diary keeping, which was supposed to counteract young Alison's obsessively ritualized behavior, becomes the place where she records, day by day, the compulsions that she will abandon. Ironically, for Alison diary writing is a practice not of discovery but of imitation and ventriloquism, and the diary a place to record life detail in the service of its own erasure. And Bechdel's sly story about the origin of her autobiographical consciousness in a youthful inability to keep a conventional diary suggests the origin of Alison's resistance to being bound by the strictures of the word and linear chronology. In a later class I extend the discussion of diary keeping to Bechdel's visual citation of it throughout chapter 6 to track "the degree of synchronicity" between national and family events (154). The narrator observes that the emotions an older Alison expressed were "an utter falsehood" (183) and her "narration had . . . become altogether unreliable" (184), so much so that the diary is finally full of blank pages (186).

After exploring the diary episode, we return to the frame story of chapter 5, noting that it seems to end where it began, with the poignant moment of a silhouetted Bruce and Alison gazing at a magnificently colorful sunset two days before his death. Their heads, shown from behind in the opening sequence (124), are magnified, by the last image, as silhouetted bodies framed by a fence grille, as in a film still, with Alison leaning toward her father (150), suggesting that the chapter has deepened her memory of powerfully felt experience. We also note how the end of the chapter casts us back to its beginning, a spiral of return in recursive storytelling. That is, the narrator resists telling Alison's life as a linear chronology in favor of an associative mode of organization that moves among visualized moments of memory.

Where does chapter 5, with its tale about Alison's inability to translate her self-perceptions into orderly diary keeping, fit into the autobiographical repertoire of *Fun Home*? It takes an astute autobiographer to tell a story of her failed attempt at the form, within a chapter on creativity and the birth of self-consciousness, in a memoir charting new graphic avenues for the possibilities of autobiographical storytelling. We conclude by thinking about how the virtuosity of *Fun Home* is linked to its riffing on conventional forms of life narrative and its experiments in new autographic ways to tell stories of intensely felt yet inchoate private experience.

Self-Portraiture and Self-Referential Acts

In *Fun Home*, relational portraits of Alison together with someone or something often take the place of the solo self-portraits favored by many autobiographical artists. In lieu of solo self-portraits Bechdel at times refers to the tradition in painted self-portraiture of focusing on the artist's hand as an autosignature.

I ask students to look for frames as dual self-portraits that emphasize physical or gestural resemblance between young Alison and her father. Some of these images are relational, showing their resemblance as evidence of a deep psychic affinity. At the same time the drawings often dramatize the power differential between them—across genders, generations, and styles. In the top frame on page 86, for example, father and daughter, with strikingly similar profiles, share space companionably. Crucially, however, the bottom frame locates their resemblance in how each occupies a solitary space, with vertical walls and curtains isolating them and emphasizing their introspective natures. Taken together, the images suggest a paradox of father-daughter likeness: they are similar in insisting on their separateness from others, related in their parallel lack of relationship. We could see this as a negative self-definition linked to their characteristic "inversions of one another" in dress and self-presentation (98). Another dual portrait, the bottom right frame of page 189, links the mature father and his fifteen-year-old daughter not just through facial resemblance but also by the similar affect of their unsmiling gazes framed like a portrait in front of the Empire State Building under a black sky. Students can find other examples of relational self-portraits that show Alison's link to her father as both bond and bind.

Famously, Bechdel includes a hand, twice life-size and holding a drawn photo, in a two-page spread often called *Fun Home*'s centerfold. It is accompanied by eight text boxes in which the narrating I reflects on her memory of the family babysitter, Roy, the sleeping, near-naked teenager in the photo. Her comments position her as both witness to and spectator of her father's secret homosexual life and acknowledge her identification with his "awe" of the beautiful body that evoked his desire (101). But we need to also consider the artist's hand holding the photo and remind students that the hand we see is a representation drawn by an invisible hand. I introduce M. C. Escher's lithograph "Drawing Hands," which captures a conundrum of self-portraiture: the hands we see drawing each other must have been made by a third, unseen, flesh-and-blood hand that viewers cannot access; even when staging its own making, a self-portrait is a representation. We also note how the hand holding the photo can be aligned with our own hand. I ask students what is at stake for viewers in this ambiguous moment of both empathic and voyeuristic viewing of one of *Fun Home*'s autobiographical secrets. We then turn to the end of chapter 4, which shows three life-size representations of a hand holding juxtaposed photos of Bruce and Alison (120). These images also suggest how Bechdel's visual self-reference implicates viewers in complexities of looking that reflect on their own desires.

"Reverse Narration" and Fun Home's *Last Page as Autobiographical Act*

Discussing self-portraiture shifts our thinking about the autobiographical from biographical data or documents of a life to a relation between self-representations and their maker that invite our engagement in her story. More generally, we consider how Alison's disparate self-perceptions in various boxes and panels track moments in the emergence of a self that can be glimpsed only retrospectively and intersubjectively. As Kierkegaard observed, "Life can only be understood backwards, but it must be lived forwards" (A 164). In this, we anticipate Bechdel's gloss in the last page's text box about "the tricky reverse narration that impels our entwined stories" (232) and sums up *Fun Home*'s reliance on recursive telling—in contrast to the forward thrust of biography that retells a life chronologically—to link self and other in an autobiographical story.

Because students struggle with the question of how the last page of *Fun Home* conveys the sense of an ending, I create a model for reading autobiographically, against the sequence of boxes and pages, by connecting them thematically and visually. *Fun Home*'s last page is perhaps its most dazzling example of how two temporalities confront each other, as the narrated I's memories of an objective past moment are posed against the narrating I's subjective interpretation of its significance for the self she has become. *Fun Home* sets up its last page by reiterating throughout chapter 7, with subtle variations in point of view and scale, a drawn series of father-daughter bodily postures that echo the Daedalus-Icarus relationship threaded throughout the text from its first page.

We turn first to the drawn family photograph for chapter 7's title page, which depicts Bruce in the water and young Alison on the diving board (187). Both have arms outstretched, she to balance herself in her dive, he to clasp her falling body. Their positions are repeated, with significant reversals, in several frames of the chapter. The last sequence (230–31) is two near-exactly reversed drawings showing Alison aloft on her father's shoulders in a swimming pool while her mother sits poolside reading a newspaper. In the last few frames Alison mounts a diving board and prepares to dive. This recollected moment of relationship with her father suggests it could be both an affectionate physical connection and an emotionally supportive mentorship. We work through how these images are linked to the narrating I's text boxes, a meditation on erotic truth juxtaposing James Joyce's treatment of *Ulysses* as his child with his disastrous neglect of his own children and linking that reflection to an ambiguous fragment of a letter from Bruce to Alison alluding to his bisexuality after she had come out to her parents. The fragment hints at how, despite having imposed feminine expectations on his daughter rather than having helpfully guided her, he too rebelled against heterosexual norms. This richly textured memory sequence sets up the last page as both a paradoxical pair of frames and a recursive gesture typical of *Fun Home*'s storytelling practices.

The final page startlingly juxtaposes two images, with overlaid text boxes, that propose different conclusions to the father-daughter relationship and thereby to the autobiographical story of how Alison became the narrator and artist of her own life. The top frame is a head-on close-up of the Sunbeam bread truck, observable only from the point of view of the victim. The frame's text—"He did hurtle into the sea, of course"—underscores Bruce's literal death. As our eyes leap over the gutter to the bottom frame, which flashes back to the earlier moment of swimming in the pool, the narrator's retrospective, redemptive judgment is juxtaposed with the finality of death: " . . . he was there to catch me when I leapt" (232). Our discussion of *Fun Home*'s "tricky reverse narration" focuses on how the viewer's recursive to-and-fro between these images is related to a self emerging across the leap into space of Alison's dive. And we think about the significance of the gutter in comics, of what Chute has called "its *constitutive* absence . . . a space that refuses to resolve the interplay of elements of absence and presence" (*Disaster* 35).

Bechdel cannot narrate Alison's story of coming into consciousness as an artist and a subject without at every point connecting it to her father's repressed story, which is teased out—and postulated—from her experience of rejection in the quest to affiliate with her father. I ask students to contrast the objective fact of Bruce's violent death, likely by suicide, with the subjective possibilities afforded Alison by his legacy of talents and desires. Then we ask how a concept of subjective truth might enable diverse possibilities to coexist. That is, at the end of *Fun Home*, do we have a definite answer about Bruce's end and Alison's beginning? Or, alternatively, are we left with better questions? As we end our discussion, I encourage students to voice those questions.

NOTES

[1] As Joan W. Scott asserts, what we call "experience" is "an interpretation *and* is in need of interpretation" (69).

[2] Sidonie Smith theorizes how "narrative performativity constitutes interiority" (109).

[3] See "Autobiography, variants" (in Smith and Watson, *Reading Autobiography* 258) for a fuller list.

[4] The numerous documents on Bechdel's Web site—blog, sketches and cartoons, autobiography course taught, and more—are also paratexts.

[5] We discuss the metrics, including tropes, story templates, and subject positions, that narratives of testimony and trauma employ as evidence of their credibility in a time of suspicion about hoax stories.

Teaching *Fun Home,* Teaching Modernism

Ariela Freedman

Alison Bechdel's *Fun Home: A Family Tragicomic* is the most literary of graphic memoirs.[1] The book is sprinkled with references to literary classics both explicit and subtle, which at once excite students' recognition, respond to their knowledge base, open them up to new books and ideas, and turn them toward novel interpretive possibilities. Bechdel depicts her struggle as a student with the complexities of James Joyce's *Ulysses* alongside her own odyssey of reading, both a battle for authority with parents and teachers and a profound voyage of personal discovery. In Bechdel's tussle with modernist classics, students will recognize their own academic odysseys.

Bechdel's web of references performs many functions: they are the legacy of a house of readers, an appropriation of the compulsory reading lists inflicted on her by her parents and teachers, and a rewriting of literary texts that work as both complement and counternarrative to her own story. Books serve as props, traps, deferrals, masturbatory aids, portals of discovery. Bechdel uses various strategies to integrate texts and authors in her memoir, from physical citation to slippery paraphrase to biographical speculation. She also frequently incorporates sections of the books she cites as physical objects, painstakingly replicating font styles, page numbers, and bindings. These texts are often seamlessly woven into her narrative but at other points are included as foreign objects, grafted onto the story rather than fully assimilated. As Bechdel tracks out from the content of the plays and novels she quotes to the life stories of their writers, she authorizes her own foray into autobiographical narrative, implicitly claiming that the life and the work are part of the same tangled web of discourse. As her story spirals through layers of meaning, she models interpretation as a perpetually unfinished activity, a quest without a solid object and a journey without an end point.

I teach *Fun Home* in a class called Comics and the Canon.[2] My liberal arts students have read as part of a core curriculum many of the texts Bechdel cites and can appreciate her subtle acts of rewriting and reclamation. The book encourages them to circle back to their earlier readings and highlights the recursive encounter of text with text, the rippling rings of homage and rewriting. Their range of reference might be unusually broad, but all students come to the text with different reference points and are encouraged to share moments of recognition and resonance as well as to identify moments of ironic citation, reversal, and subversion. Bechdel claims Joyce just as Joyce claimed Homer; both Bechdel and Joyce at once dethrone and affirm the importance of their predecessors. Joyce's *Ulysses* is a facilitating model for this act of literary reclamation and reinvention, since it is both the boldest such act of literary appropriation and one prominent in Bechdel's own narrative structure.

How does one teach the references in *Fun Home* without reducing the book to a series of mechanical clues and citations, without turning it into compulsory reading, and most important, without silencing the students? Letting the students take the book personally is an effective answer to these questions. Fiction, and particularly literary modernism, is a lens for examining autobiographical experience, or, to borrow Marcel Proust's words, "Every reader is, while he is reading, the reader of himself." Students can be encouraged to explore in Bechdel's work Proust's idea that "the recognition of the reader in his own self of what the book says is the proof of its veracity" (3: 949).[3]

Modernism is an elusive aesthetic, institutional, and historical category, perhaps more accurately described in the plural as *modernisms*, following Peter Nicholls's thesis in the book of that title. For Nicholls, modernism is not a "monolithic ideological formation" (vii) but a shifting constellation of aesthetic values, experiments, relationships, and groups. As Lawrence Rainey warns, modernism "is endowed with authority so monumental that the reader is tempted to overlook the very experience of encountering modernist works" (xix). At once a set of aesthetic qualities—reflexivity, opacity, ambiguity, impersonality—and a series of names to conjure with—Joyce, T. S. Eliot, Proust, Virginia Woolf, Samuel Beckett, F. Scott Fitzgerald—modernism is often preceded by its reputation of difficulty, intransigence, and exclusivity.

Certainly, Bechdel grapples with all this as she struggles with the silencing influence of the modernist icons imposed on her—as her mother's character cuttingly observes in Bechdel's later memoir, *Are You My Mother?*, "Wallace Stevens wrote transcendent poetry, and he never used the word 'I'" (200). When Bechdel shifts from *Ulysses* to the lesser-known stories of Harriet Shaw Weaver and Sylvia Beach, she challenges the clichéd narrative of the modernist genius as self-created and self-sustaining, instead portraying Joyce's masterpiece as the product of collaboration, interdependence, and finally, exploitation, as Shaw and Weaver are written out of the book's history. While Bechdel layers her representation of modernism with her critique of the authoritarianism and exclusions associated with its most iconic figure, she never loses sight of what Rainey calls "the sheer wildness" and "irredeemable opacity at the heart of modernist works" (xix). Joyce is her muse and her foil, and her relationship with him is intimate, damning, respectful, subversive, and shrewd.

The first reference to modernism in the book is to another writer who had both a filial and rebellious attitude toward Joyce, the late modernist Samuel Beckett. Bechdel's subtitle, *A Family Tragicomic*, cleverly channels Beckett's *Waiting for Godot: A Tragicomedy*, revising it for the medium of comics. Beckett's mix of dolor and humor confused critics, who tended to choose either the tragedy or the comedy: the play's American premiere called *Waiting for Godot* "the laugh sensation of two continents" (Brady 93), while influential existential critics of the 1960s like Martin Esslin saw mostly sorrow and only bitter laughter (46–62). Bechdel's book also vacillates between moments of sorrow and laughter, what Joyce calls the "jocoserious" (*Ulysses* 791), but its narrative framework soon abandons Beckett for Joyce himself, Beckett's mentor and teacher. Joyce bookends Bechdel's narrative, and Bechdel frames her story through Joyce's bildungsroman, *A Portrait of the Artist as a Young Man*, and his epic, *Ulysses*. Students can be prompted to explore the tension between the linear trajectory of the coming-of-age narrative and the circular structure of epic in Bechdel's graphic memoir.

The first section of the book is titled "Old Father, Old Artificer" and cites the famous final line of Joyce in *A Portrait of the Artist*: "Old father, old artificer, stand me now and ever in good stead" (253). It refers to what Mulligan will later call Stephen's "absurd name" in *Ulysses* (2), Dedalus, and celebrates Stephen's culminating revelation of his artistic mission. It is also more properly a beginning than an ending: invocations start epics, rather than conclude them, and Joyce's last line in *Portrait* can serve as the first line of the epic continuation of the story in *Ulysses*. When Bechdel takes Joyce's last line for her first chapter title, she redoubles the tricky temporality of Joyce's narrative structure, and when she borrows his borrowing of the Daedalus myth from Ovid, she adds another knot to the interpretive twist of the text.

Bechdel continues the Daedalus theme, commencing her story with a typically overdetermined reference to the "Icarian games" of floor acrobatics (3). The image she draws is one of both flying and falling, as the young Alison balances over her father's body. To further darken the foreshadowing of her father's death, a face-down copy of *Anna Karenina* lies beside her father's body. Bechdel's reference is suspended in the reflecting mirrors that multiply and complicate the meanings of the text. Initially Alison is the child Icarus, raised above her father in false flight. But later her father is both Icarus and Daedalus, both doomed son and maniacal inventor. Her fear of her father begins to saturate her interpretive imagination, merging the two stories; when she describes Daedalus's indifference to the human of his projects, her panel shows her father striking her brother in anger and frustration as they set up the Christmas tree. These layers of meaning fall into a kind of interpretive regress, partially anchored by the counterpoint of the concrete, simple physical action of the panels. In the book her father's death is an unfinished loss, an unassimilated trauma. This means that the project of interpreting it, of understanding it, must also remain unfinished. Bechdel draws literary reference toward the autobiographical project like dust toward a vacuum; her loss pulls everything she knows toward it.

While the authors most frequently cited—Joyce, Proust, Ernest Hemingway, Fitzgerald, Beckett, even Henry James and Oscar Wilde—fall loosely into the category of modernism, modernism is itself a tricky, layered label in Bechdel's book. In the first chapter Alison defines herself as "modern" against her father's "Victorian" (15). What she means by modern is closer to Le Corbusier's notion of modernist architecture as "a machine for living" (151)—functional, unadorned, efficient—than to the baroque and reflexive modernism of modernist literature. Her taste is a reaction against her father's fussy and perfectionist love of elaborate antique interiors. Her father is a tyrant of taste, and his imposition of aesthetic dominance is inseparable from his claustrophobic and oppressive control of his family. Bechdel describes resenting "the way my father treated his furniture like children, his children like furniture" as she remembers being directed to hold still while hanging a mirror on the wall (14). As the young Alison strains to lift the mirror, the face the mirror reflects belongs to her father. Just so, the entire house is a reflection of his taste and his desire for control. A reflection and also a deflection; Bechdel names "mirrors, distracting bronzes, multiple doorways" that made their house at once mirror and labyrinth (20). Bechdel writes that in response to this adornment and clutter she developed a "decided preference for the unadorned and purely functional" (14). Her aesthetic manifesto becomes an ethical one; if bric-a-brac and clutter were "embellishments in the worst sense" that "obscured function," then they are of a piece with her father's living a lie. Her turn to function and the unadorned is also a turn to honesty. The clean lines of modern design promise a life lived in the open.

This is a place to test Bechdel's claim to distinctiveness and her bid for autonomy. Does her art really employ the unadorned, the uncluttered? Students can be encouraged to look at not only what Bechdel is saying but also what she is doing. On the one hand, her art employs wide white gutters, an even and controlled grid, simplified faces for the characters, and a clean palette of black, white, and field gray. Indeed, where this is clutter, it belongs to her father; the most elaborate panels depict the crowded interiors of her childhood home. On the other hand, her writing weaves a story as labyrinthine and mirrored as her family history. In that sense there is a clear distinction between what Bechdel says and what she draws, the metatextual palimpsest of her elliptical prose in tension with her symmetrical boxes, stripped-down style, and solid line.

Bechdel cannot free the aesthetic enterprise from the practice of artifice any more than she can free herself from her father's legacy. If her drawing style is relatively austere, her writing is elaborate, and all its murmuring hesitation serves to shadow and complicate the simplicity of her imagined aesthetic revolution. But more than that, plainspokenness can also be a way of hiding. Bechdel admits as much when she writes, "[W]hen the subject of my parents came up in conversation I would relate the information in a flat, matter-of-fact tone" (45). Her unadorned honesty is, in fact, a mode of concealment, a way to paradoxically repress her grief through the revelation of her loss. Though Bechdel's is a highly crafted book about the lie of artifice, she acknowledges that plainness is no less a style. While she associates her father primarily with concealment, frankness is also a strategy she learns from him, through his blunt and shocking presentation of the cadavers in the funeral home when she is just a child. His exposure of the cadaver foreshadows her own later betrayal when she lays the secrets of her father's dead body bare. Bechdel's anxieties about the ethical implications of autobiography are more explicit in *Are You My Mother?*, but even in *Fun Home*—through the stories of Shaw and Weaver, through her many moments of doubt and self-questioning—Bechdel shadows artistic creation with the cost it exacts from one's circle of friends and loved ones.

If modernism in architecture signals plainness, function, and honesty, then literary modernism signals complication, artifice, and mask. Bechdel wonders if "affectation can be so thoroughgoing, so authentic in its details, that it stops being pretense and becomes, for all practical purposes, real" (60)? What if the man becomes the mask? Her father's strong identification with Fitzgerald starts to inflect his prose, which in his letters home becomes "lush with Fitzgeraldesque sentiment" (63). Bechdel compares her father to Fitzgerald's most famous creation, Jay Gatsby, whose "self-willed metamorphosis from farm boy to prince is in many ways identical to my father's" (63). The layering of fact and fiction, life and art, man and mask, mean that it is impossible to attain an unadorned honesty, a truth without art. Bechdel acknowledges a necessary artifice when she confesses her own fictive imagination: "I employ these allusions to James and Fitzgerald not only as descriptive devices, but because my parents are most real to me in fictional terms." She then adds, "And perhaps my cool aesthetic distance itself does more to convey the arctic climate of our family than any particular literary comparison" (67). The final phrase is the telling one, as Bechdel moves from citation to creation in a reflexive turn toward her own work. By referring to her own style, she trumps her literary models and makes particular claims for her contribution.

The impact of literary influences in the book is complicated by the way they are positioned in the family economy of love and debt. When Alison grows close to her father through their shared love of modernist literature, that fellowship becomes claustrophobic as he tries to control and guide her reading. But a few scenes in the book point us to the world of cartooning and of word and image, a world invisible to her father. When Alison comes across *The Addams Family* she recognizes her own family in the "occult and wordless cartoon" (34). Later she meets an artist in the Village who shows her his sequential illustrations for a Pinocchio filmstrip. An arrow in the panel points out her "marker envy" (191), an envy of an identity as well as of a vocation; she assumes the animator lives openly with his male partner and through him gets a glimpse of her future career and identity.

Reading *Fun Home* can be freeing for students precisely because it is so irreverent. Bechdel rebels against her father's love of the modernists, neglecting her course on Joyce for the contemporary feminist and lesbian literature that fills her nightstand and her bed. Her new canon is the word become flesh. But Bechdel models something much more subtle than irreverence, especially in her final chapter, as Joyce returns as a key element of her plot of failed reconciliation. She reads her father's death and her father's last letters like an undergraduate reads a text for interpretive cues, highlighting his letter right beside the page of *Ulysses* it seems to cite (230). *Fun Home* is Bechdel's act of rapprochement, her rewriting of modernism on her own terms and in comic form.

Bechdel also offers an object lesson in how not to teach *Fun Home* in her satiric portrait of a university class on *Ulysses*. When Bechdel describes her teacher, Mr. Avery, as "the wise windbag, Nestor" she at once undermines his authority and echoes Joyce's own repurposing of the Nestor episode. "I still found literary criticism to be a suspect activity," Bechdel writes, in a sentence that should give any critic of her work pause (206). In the classroom she sits quietly while a young man pontificates, an echo of her silence in the face of her father's interpretive dominance. Nonetheless, her encounter with modernist literature is profound, broadened by her own reading lists, motivated by passion rather than duty, and mediated through her retroactive reclamation of the very work that once slowed her narrative odyssey.

Even as literature is for Bechdel a gateway for understanding her lesbian identity and relationship with her father, *Fun Home* can be a gateway to comics for literature students. Every door of egress is also a door of ingress, Bechdel reminds us, quoting the section of *Ulysses* in which Bloom and Stephen enter Bloom's home and the cat leaves through the open door (209). Literary reference in *Fun Home* also serves as both egress and ingress—a way out toward literary interpretation and analysis, a way in to comics studies and intermedial representation. Subtly written and explicitly literary, *Fun Home* provides a useful entry point for students who might be initially put off by the crudeness of Robert Crumb, the faux-naiveté of Lynda Barry.

Bechdel's writing is accessible for students trained in the careful reading she amply rewards, but too great a focus on her writing can be a trap: students need to be reminded to study the pictures and to understand *Fun Home* not only as a tissue of reference but as a literary memoir in the comics medium. Images gloss, complicate, contradict, and underline the extradiagetic narrative, in the gutterless white space between the panels, which marks them as outside the time of the narrative. Like Proust, Bechdel layers the perspective of a child with the retrospective of an adult, but with a visual aid to border these layers of experience. In order to encourage students to have a personal stake in comics and to assimilate the importance of the visual in the comics medium, I assign a comics exercise modeled after Bechdel's own project. I ask students to illustrate or gloss canonical literature in comics form, and I emphasize that I am judging not skill but creativity, ingenuity, and the ability to use word and image in concert. The exercise trains students in strategies of representation and concretely demonstrates that illustration is always an act of interpretation.

I first taught *Fun Home* in 2012, which was a tumultuous year for university students in Montreal. Strikes against austerity paralyzed the university and divided students against one another in an enterprise that at times seemed idealistic, at other times quixotic. In one of my favorite results of this assignment, my student Laura Fraticelli illustrated this quixotic idealism, showing the skyscrapers of downtown Montreal turned into windmills, Quixote mounted on horseback in front of a mass of protestors. The scene is far removed from Beech Creek, Pennsylvania, and the story has little to do with Bechdel's narrative, but the comic cleverly echoes Bechdel's linked signature of life and fiction, reading and writing. Following Bechdel's example, Laura took her reading personally and, even better, was able to draw it into her own experience. Like an eager student, Bechdel learned to read her life through literature. But in order to write that life through graphic narrative, she needed to grapple with a strong act of artistic revision. Teaching *Fun Home* can encourage students to do the same.

NOTES

[1] For a more detailed discussion of the citations of James Joyce in *Fun Home*, see my article "Drawing on Modernism in Alison Bechdel's *Fun Home*." Bechdel goes into considerable detail about her literary influences in her interview with Hillary Chute in *Modern Fiction Studies* (Chute, "Interview"), and Chute elaborates on these trajectories in "Gothic Revival" and in *Graphic Women* (175–218). For the influence of literary modernism in *Fun Home*, see especially Watson; Iuliano.

[2] I thank all the students in Comics and the Canon.

[3] I cite C. K. Scott Moncrieff and Terence Kilmartin's translation of *Remembrance of Things Past* published by Random House in 1981.

Entering the Archives:
Reading *Fun Home* Backward

Susan Van Dyne

I use the *Fun Home* archives in my course The Cultural Work of Memoir, an undergraduate seminar in women's studies and English. We study literary memoirs by queer women and men, beginning with Audre Lorde's *Zami* and ending with Bechdel's *Fun Home*. The course asks how memoir as an expressive act creates livable, legible public spaces for queer lives in the consciousness of readers, drawing on the premise that life writing is a "means of 'passing on' a past that may have been obscured in order to activate its potential for reshaping a future of and for other subjects" (Smith and Watson, *Reading Autobiography* 20–21).[1] Students produce frequent analytical responses to our readings and create substantial memoir portfolios. Our assignment in the archives brings together their analysis of narrative strategies in the memoirs we read and their work as aspiring creative nonfiction writers. We spend the last of four two-hour seminar sessions in the archives looking at the drafts. Students enter the archives familiar with Bechdel's themes, practiced in the close reading of scenes, and intrigued by the interaction of the retrospective narration with the younger self drawn in images. As scholars do, they read backward, sifting the past of the book, its contradictions and omissions, to piece together how the book they know came to be.

The Alison Bechdel papers span the author's professional career as a cartoonist and graphic memoirist from 1985 to about 2011. Although most of the collection is unprocessed as of this writing, researchers may have on-site access to the papers at the Sophia Smith Collection at Smith College in Northampton, Massachusetts.[2] Highlights of the collection are a 1988 strip, *Servants to the Cause*, and the long-running *Dykes to Watch Out For*. Of the original multipage sketches for the strips in the collection from 1982 to 2002, those covering 1984 to 1988, about 135 sketches, have been cataloged. During processing of the remaining original drawings, access is restricted. Notes for character development, clippings, articles, and ideas for the strip as well as edited and annotated strips enable researchers to track Bechdel's creative process: every month for over twenty years the author generated two strips of ten to twelve panels each. Reviews, interviews, press releases, correspondence about the syndication of the strip, the publication of the *Dykes* books, and financial records offer insight into the distribution and audience for the strip and its tie-ins. Correspondence with other cartoonists shows the professional context in which Bechdel worked. Later acquisitions include proofs for *Are You My Mother?* and letters to her mother, Helen Bechdel, describing early plans for the book.

The archives for *Fun Home*, which comprise 3.5 linear feet of the (ongoing) 26.75 linear feet of the entire collection, represent a convergence of new technologies with Bechdel's artistic practice. She composes multiple prose drafts on her computer, then creates and edits her graphic layout using *Adobe Illustrator*, a process she demonstrates on *YouTube* (Bechdel, "Alison Bechdel: Creating *Fun Home*"). Many of her drawings depend on reference shots taken with a digital camera or found through *Google* searches. Much of this material remains on Bechdel's personal computer. The drafts at Smith preserve moments when she pauses to print out and edit by hand. Early computer drafts might have been "totally chaotic; either too much stuff there or not fleshed out enough," she comments, but when some sort of clarity emerged, "I had to see the physical thing, and I had to make written notes, I couldn't do that sort of thinking on the screen" (Bechdel, Personal interview).[3] Bechdel is a careful archivist of her process, dating many of her drafts and grouping others in rough chronological order. As she edited, she received feedback on printed layout drafts from readers: Harriet Malinowitz, a teacher at Long Island University; Amy Rubin, her partner from 1992 to 2006; Sydelle Kramer, her agent; and Deanne Umbrey, her editor at Houghton Mifflin. Her sketches for *Fun Home*, acquired in May 2015, are drawn on tracing paper to correspond with panels in layout format. These early roughs are refined and tightened in a second stage, and, after inking, the pencil drawings are erased. Of the "hundreds and hundreds" of reference shots she used, some are preserved in the archives (Bechdel, Personal interview). A compelling sequence among the sketches documents her translation of an underlit 3.5-square-inch glossy snapshot into the riveting centerfold of Roy the babysitter. On a digitally enhanced and enlarged 13-by-11-inch reproduction, she outlined the boy, swallowed in shadows and in his underwear. On 17-by-13.75-inch sheets of tracing paper, she transferred the lines to begin the intricate crosshatching that will produce a three-dimensional Roy in his languid pose. "It's like a metaphor for the whole book," she remembers; "that's all I have and I have to create something with hard outlines from it" (Bechdel, Personal interview).

My goal in using the archives with my class is to enlarge the scope of their understanding of how a book is made. I choose manageable samples to make the backstory of the book's creation visible through Bechdel's earliest inchoate fragments, multiple prose drafts, her efforts to see the shape of the narrative, feedback from readers, and proposals to publishers, emphasizing the process of constant revision that links all these. In commenting on documents my students analyzed in this essay, I've highlighted key resources in the *Fun Home* archives and insights that might be drawn from them. My hope is to provide teachers with examples that could enhance their teaching even if they are unable to visit the archives. Archival research is messy, disorienting, and labor-intensive for veteran researchers and especially so for students. Reading archives requires seemingly contradictory methods, an unflagging attention to detail, and a willingness to speculate, to imagine oneself in the occasion that produced an archival document. Researchers need to be patient when they don't find what they had hoped for and at the same time ready to be redirected by what they do discover.

For students, working in the archives can feel like falling down a rabbit hole. To make the task manageable and meaningful, I flag items that have raised productive questions for my own research. I offer the following suggestions for working with drafts:

> identify the source precisely, including any titles or dates;
> describe the type of document (correspondence, brainstorming notes, prose draft, outline, layout format draft);
> try to determine what problem Bechdel seems to be working on and if there are any patterns in her annotations or edits;
> identify and reread the corresponding incident or section in *Fun Home* to study any differences in the archival object.

Following our two-hour class visit, students spend at least two more hours in the archives before posting online a 500-word mini-essay analyzing what they found and how it helps them think about an aspect of the published memoir. Below I sample the work of five students: Julia Greider, Kyle Kaplan, April Dunlop, Aqdas Aftab, and Lili Siegel. I've arranged my students' topics to correspond roughly with the evolution of the book, from its psychological underpinnings to the turning point of creating a book proposal that led to a $100,000 contract with Houghton Mifflin in 2003 (Bechdel, Personal interview).

In 1999, her first year of work on the book, Bechdel frequently mined her journals for incidents to write about. "Chopin," one of the earliest fragments planned for chapter 3, "That Old Catastrophe," identifies anecdotes—her first poem, her father taking over her coloring book, her mother playing the piano—that eventually became part of chapter 5 (129–34). Early in Bechdel's seven-year process, materials often migrated from one chapter to another, yet even in these embryonic notes central themes of the book are recognizable. The draft emerged from her journal entry on a recent therapy session. Greider analyzed the therapy note, which she described as "Bechdel's birth as an artist," and Bechdel's choosing to make cartoons, in Bechdel's words, "not so much because it was who I was but because it was who they weren't" ("Chopin" 5 [15 July 1999]). Bechdel articulates the painful paradox of her artistic legacy from her parents: "What saved each of us was our creativity, our redemption through that laserlike focus on what we were good at . . . superseding our relationships to each other which were not as dependable. The real reason I didn't pursue any of my parents' interests was because they stood for all the attention I wasn't getting" (2). Through the lens of this quotation, Graider reread Bechdel's childhood mispronunciation of Chopin, which Greider had initially "interpreted as a funny moment meant to amuse the reader and show the age of the child narrator," and noticed that Bechdel explicitly links each incident about her parents' superior artistic talents to "embarrassment" and "severe, pointless, causeless mortification" for the child (19 July 1999). Although the published version is wryly comic, Greider found that "humiliation" is central in the draft and suggested Bechdel "seems to have planned to call the chapter 'Chopin' because this moment was so emblematic of this time in her life."

Kaplan focused on Bechdel's e-mail exchange with Harriet Malinowitz. Early in 2001, two years into the project, Bechdel solicited Malinowitz, who had enthusiastically reviewed her seventh *Dykes* book but whom she hadn't met, as a paid reader for her drafts. Malinowitz and Bechdel exchanged lengthy e-mails, printouts of which are found in the archives, about the advice Bechdel was seeking and what Malinowitz proposed to comment on. Most interesting among Malinowitz's categories of "practical," "content-ful," and "psychological (your feelings about writing this)" is the last. She frankly questions Bechdel's self-doubt: "It's easy to see that self-deprecation is something you more than merely dabble in . . . but if we're going to have this editorial relationship, you also have to be honest about what you think is really good—dare I say great?—about your work and about yourself as an artist" (Malinowitz to Bechdel [10 February 2001]). When Bechdel reports to Malinowitz that her mother has been "remarkably understanding" about the project, with the "perhaps predictable effect of silencing me more than her disapproval would" (Bechdel to Malinowitz [8 February 2001]), Harriet probes, "[D]id her would-be disapproval provide a necessary tension that you worked from?" (Malinowitz to Bechdel [10 February 2001]). Given Bechdel's habit of self-critique throughout early drafts, Malinowitz's frank approval of the work and searching questions made her a sympathetic reader. Bechdel also solicited feedback from her partner, Amy Rubin, and preserved layout drafts with their suggestions. Both Malinowitz and Rubin offered help with Bechdel's psychic blocks as well as editorial suggestions.

Kaplan admitted, "I didn't know what to make of the e-mails, essays, reviews, and syllabus I found. . . . I didn't understand that archived material can be read like any other story, even if it doesn't look like one." She puzzled over Bechdel's e-mail planning her first meeting with Malinowitz. The message's subject line is "Agenda," but Bechdel repeatedly asks Harriet not to read the agenda she includes, writing, "it's just my notes, not ready for your perusal really" (Bechdel to Malinowitz [3 March 2001]). Kaplan entered into the story behind the e-mail, speculating how Bechdel and Malinowitz's relationship was "professional enough to send her an agenda, but also casual enough for Bechdel to express insecurity." Reading the exchanges between the author and her reader, Kaplan asked how feedback from a reader differs from an editor's. Dunlop read e-mail exchanges with Bechdel's agent, whose feedback emphasized strategies to persuade professional readers at mainstream publishers, who, unlike Malinowitz and Rubin, had little experience with queer or graphic material.

Outlines appear regularly in the archives and represent an intermediate stage in the evolution of a chapter, a checklist of incidents to be included, arrived at through previous drafts. Because chapter 3 originally contained materials later moved to chapters 5 and 7, and sections omitted entirely from the published book, Bechdel's frequent outlines document strikingly different directions. In comparing "Catastrophe outline. 11/2/01" with the published chapter 3, Aftab considered how books function differently for father and daughter—"she uses literature as a way to come out rather than to stay in . . . while her father uses books as a means to withdraw and betray"—and suggested that "perhaps *this* is the real 'catastrophe.'" In the single-page outline, which has six headings and thirty-one subheadings, Aftab noticed only one reference to Bechdel's coming out, although in the final version the author's sexual self-discovery is central (57–59, 74–81). Outlines are not rigid schema but part of Bechdel's discovery process, as evident in two items from "Catastrophe outline. 11/2/01":

> C. Brief mention of my own coming out
> 1. jeepers, no! the fact that my coming out was so literary, so cerebral deserves going into here. . . .
> E. Dad reading *Flying* when I left it behind that spring! Omigod! This is so great, the looping circuit of book-giving structures the chapter.

These insights prompted further macro-reorganizing and revision that continued until May 2003 when Bechdel reframed chapter 3 with the dictionary definition of *queer*.

When the shape of the project was most in flux, Bechdel created single-page graphic outlines to help her imagine the architecture of the narrative and to sort which memories and insights belonged in each chapter. She saved eight of these between spring 2001 and spring 2002 that track the evolution of the book from ten chapters conceived as "essays," planned in roughly chronological order, to the eventual seven chapters of the final version, organized more thematically. These graphic outlines chart the addition of her father's books and family photos and the growing resonance of her story: "it's also about situating my father and me in the context of queer history. Wilde, Colette, Millet . . . closet vs. out, activism vs. aestheticism" (10 December 2001). But her breakthrough in conceptualizing the book came in summer 2003 when her agent urged her to draw a proposal for publishers in comic book format. Reading the six-page graphic proposal, Siegel found that Bechdel's explanations were not what she expected. In the proposal, dated November 2003, Bechdel describes the structure of the book as a "labyrinth" descending to chapter 4, "the core of the story—our shared homosexuality" (3).[4] Siegel had thought that "the father's death would have been the central thing that permeated back out into everything else" but reconsidered that perhaps "shared homosexuality shows a connection whereas death is a rupture or betrayal." She puzzled most over Bechdel's description of the last three chapters that spiral back out to the conversation with her father in the car in chapter 7: "My father and I experience a brief moment of convergence, but don't quite make contact. It's problematic and unsatisfactory, but as atonement goes, I'll take it" (3). Siegel struggled with Bechdel's term *atonement*, which seemed contradictory: "He never even came close to atoning for his treatment of those young boys and being queer was not something he needed to atone for—at least not to his queer daughter." In rereading chapter 4 for clues about Bechdel's choice to focus on atonement, she returned to Bechdel's equally unexpected comment at finding the photo of the babysitter: "Why am I not properly outraged?" (100). Siegel proposed a link between the episodes in chapters 4 and 7: "perhaps this touch of empathy that she is so unsettled by [in ch. 4] allows her to read empathy in his fragmented admissions [in ch. 7] more generously than she might otherwise."

My students' work in the archives deepened their understanding of the craft as much as the story of *Fun Home*. As writers, they were inspired by Bechdel's capacity for deep revision; as archival researchers, they experienced the pleasures of unexpected connections that are central to Bechdel's creative process.

NOTES

[1] This essay cites the 2001 edition of Smith and Watson's *Reading Autobiography*. An expanded edition was published in 2010.

[2] First citations to items in this unprocessed collection include brief document name and date. Further citations to the same document include page number.

[3] My interview with Bechdel, conducted on 27 May 2015, is not part of the archival collection.

[4] See the frontispiece of this book for a page from Bechdel's book proposal showing the structure of *Fun Home* as a labyrinth.

Self and Identity: A Group Assignment on Intertextuality in *Fun Home*

Soo La Kim

I teach Alison Bechdel's *Fun Home* in an honors section of a multidisciplinary seminar course required of all first-year students at Columbia College Chicago, a private arts and media college with a liberal arts core curriculum. The discussion-based course introduces students to college-level critical thinking and emphasizes creative assignments and reflective writing. We begin with a focus on questions of self, identity, and community, such as, Who are we? How do we see ourselves? How do others see us? How do we represent ourselves to others? I chose *Fun Home* as the primary text for this first unit because Bechdel's memoir addresses questions of identity in a way that immediately engages most readers while also rewarding closer reading and rereading.

In this context, an emphasis on the memoir's intertextuality pushes students to read in a different way. That is, in puzzling out why Bechdel embeds so many other texts in her narrative, students move beyond plot or easy symbolism toward attention to the complex layering of themes, the representation of competing perspectives, and the way Bechdel uses other stories as interpretive lenses to make sense of her own. I've found that students pick up on the omnipresence of intertexts in their online responses before I explicitly bring it up. Some students are attuned to the ways Bechdel uses specific allusions, like the Daedalus and Icarus myth or *It's a Wonderful Life*, as narrative devices, not only to tell what happened but also to get at the difficult and contradictory emotional truths about what happened. Others experience the intertexts as interfering with the clarity and accessibility of the main story or wonder why Bechdel's memoir is so thick with allusions: what's she trying to accomplish? This range of responses is fertile ground for planting the seeds of a deeper inquiry into the content, function, and effects of these intertexts. A potential barrier to student engagement, then, can be an opportunity to draw students more deeply into the story and themes of *Fun Home*. Ultimately, I want students to recognize intertextuality as a feature of texts of all kinds, not just Bechdel's. This essential aspect of *Fun Home* emphasizes the idea that all cultural products have precedents and models from which they borrow and to which they pay homage.

We spend three eighty-minute class sessions discussing *Fun Home* in its entirety, and students post to online forums between sessions; students have another week to complete outside class the collaborative assignment on intertextuality described below, which we discuss in a follow-up class session. The assignment description I provide is brief:

> *Fun Home* begins with a reference to the Greek myth of Daedalus and Icarus, the first of many references or allusions to other texts and authors

that add various layers of meaning to Bechdel's story. In this collaborative research project, we'll explore the many intertexts (references to texts within a text)[1] and figure out how they influence our understanding of the main text, *Fun Home*.

When I introduce the assignment, I divide students into four groups of four and assign each group a major intertext or author: the Daedalus and Icarus myth, F. Scott Fitzgerald, James Joyce, and Marcel Proust. In addition to their assigned intertext, each group must also find three intertexts on their own. The actual research requirements are minimal—they simply need to find a good summary of the text in question and some information about the author—and though students must cite all sources, I do not require scholarly ones. The heart of the assignment is explaining the significance of a given intertext to *Fun Home*. Each group writes and posts its entries to the encyclopedia feature of the course's online learning management system, making the work shareable with the rest of the class. The writing portion of the assignment asks students to do four things:

> summarize what the intertext is (author, date of original publication, brief description of plot, any relevant historical or biographical details);
>
> explain the context in which the intertext appears in *Fun Home* (here I stress the importance of taking good notes in class);
>
> explain the role of the intertext in the narrative and interpret the significance of the intertext—the metaphorical possibilities, tropes, themes, or meanings the intertext introduces into *Fun Home*;
>
> include any relevant images or multimedia sources that enhance this analysis of the intertext as well as a works-cited list.

In the class session after the entries are posted, we discuss students' discoveries, reinforcing certain themes we'd discussed previously while highlighting new insights. One way to keep discussion student-centered is to organize a kind of round-robin format, in which two members of each group rotate from group to group, while two members stay put, each pair responsible for explaining their findings to the other pairs in ten-minute segments.

The group assignment on intertextuality has multiple learning goals. As noted above, I want students to understand intertextuality as an integral part of cultural productions of all kinds. It's especially important for the arts and media students I teach to understand that the raw materials of any creative artifact are often drawn from what's come before. Creativity or originality doesn't happen in a vacuum, and I want them to begin reflecting on and expanding their own media consumption as part of their creative process. I also want them to gain some access to the cultural capital that is such a formative influence on Bechdel's identity and that she deploys with both irony and deep affection. Even if they never read *In Search of Lost Time* or *Ulysses*, I want them to have some sense of the cultural significance of these works. To reinforce this connection between their own creative interests and the liberal arts core curriculum that introduces students to cultural histories and canons that may be new to them, I follow this assignment with one in which students write about two "intertexts" of their own lives and post to the online encyclopedia (a minimal research component asks them to find out something about their intertext they don't already know).[2]

For me, the most important value of a group assignment like this one is that students cocreate the knowledge of the classroom through their research and writing rather than passively receive it from the instructor as the class's sole authority.[3] Rather than hearing a lecture about the interconnections among *The Importance of Being Earnest*, Oscar Wilde's biography, and the various roles Bechdel's parents play both onstage and in their marriage, students can discover those connections and articulate them in their own words. Imperfect or incomplete as these articulations may be, students are more likely to remember the insights they've come to on their own and shared with their peers. I have been pleased with the range and depth of my students' responses as they tease out the multiple, often paradoxical, connections between the narrative and the texts Bechdel refers to throughout. For example, Leah Gaynor recognized that Bruce Bechdel is both Daedalus—"Bruce created his own physical labyrinth, his glorious house filled to the brim with decor and grandeur"—and also the Minotaur, trapped in his house and threatening those trapped with him. Gaynor continued, "Bruce himself was the Minotaur. He hid his emptiness and his darker, unsympathetic self within his carefully constructed walls that would torment and terrorize all of whom are inside the maze. On the outside, the labyrinth is breathtaking, but once inside, it's easy to get trapped and stuck. Then one must face the Minotaur." Students in the Fitzgerald group noted that "Bechdel views herself as a kind of Nick Carraway to her father's story. . . . Both use ornate, lush language that doesn't at all match up with their speech in real life. And furthermore, they view their objects of fascination— Mr. Bechdel and Gatsby, respectively—with simultaneous awe and bafflement that shapes their worldview." Here, students identify the craftedness of narrative voice and the conflicted nature of both Bechdel's and Carraway's narrative points of view.

Keeping the research requirements fairly loose and letting students choose the three minor intertexts allow for more diversity of content, driven by student interest and their level of motivation. For example, one student watched a film version of *Ulysses* because she felt reading synopses of the work was inadequate. Another discovered the so-called Bechdel test on her own and was excited to share it with the rest of the class. And one group wrote about the "Icarian Games" mentioned in *Fun Home*'s opening panels (3), an ancient circus act of human juggling usually performed by family members; the group included a video link of a contemporary performance, noting that despite the imperfect ways the Bechdel family performed their familial roles, the images that bookend the memoir represent trust between father and daughter (in a way that departs from and rewrites the myth, I might add).[4]

Finally, the group assignment is premised on the value of collaborative learning, which is as important as the focus on intertextuality. When I introduce the assignment we discuss what makes for effective group work. I leave it up to the groups to determine how to divide up the work and encourage them to use an online forum to exchange ideas and drafts. At the conclusion of the assignment students complete a confidential form assessing their own performance and those of their group members in terms of work (quality and quantity), group communication, and the collaborative process. Cocreating the knowledge of the classroom is a collaboration not just among student peers but also between my students and me. The flexibility in the curriculum means I can solicit and be guided by my students' questions, examples, and interests even as I direct their attention to texts and ideas that are new to them. Intertextuality itself highlights the connectedness among authors and their cultural interlocuters and nicely thematizes the broadly collaborative nature of most creative and intellectual enterprises.

Bechdel's identities (familial, sexual, artistic) are inextricably tied to the texts through which she reads and tries to understand her parents, herself, and her past. The "fictional terms" through which her parents become most real to her, her memoir suggests, are also the terms through which we become real to ourselves (67). A consideration of *Fun Home*'s intertextuality as a function of identity formation thus allows us to reflect on identity as an interpretive act, as something both textual and contextual, pieced together from the stories we collect along the way. I hope that idea is both reassuring and empowering to my first-year students as they embark on their college careers.

NOTES

[1] I don't make a distinction between reference and intertext, and I use the concept of intertextuality fairly loosely, because my main goal is to draw students' attention to the ways Bechdel interweaves other authors and texts into her own in both written and visual form. At the same time, by assigning a major intertext to each group, I ensure that students are exploring significant thematic threads.

[2] Students write about specific bands and songs, films, television shows, books, paintings, video games, and Disney World. One student, Cassandra Selsor, wrote about the rainbow flag, symbol of the LGBTQ community, and how, as a bullied, unpopular, yet defiant middle school student, she sported rainbow-flag jewelry in an effort to both shock her tormentors and feel a connection with those outside the heteronormative mainstream. She ended her response with a series of questions about the limits of such an alliance, exactly the kind of questions about identity and identification I want students to ponder: "Still, is it a bad thing when people identify with something they can never truly understand? Are my feelings politically incorrect? [Andrew] Solomon from *Far from the Tree* remarks that people with different horizontal identities can understand each other, but at what point does someone who is not directly affected by that identity overstep their bounds?" (An excerpt from Solomon's introduction was assigned earlier in the course.)

[3]My approach to teaching has been deeply influenced by my training in the writing programs at Harvard and Princeton, which emphasize writing as a mode of thinking, a way to grapple with and organize complex ideas into compelling arguments. Within this framework, I incorporate low-stakes writing assignments as a tool for discussion and deeper thinking. More recently I've deepened and expanded my approach to student-centered pedagogy through my work at the Center for Innovation in Teaching Excellence at Columbia College Chicago, where we stress classroom community-building as a pedagogical practice and promote different models of collaborative learning. This assignment aims to incorporate these related goals and values.

[4]This initial exploration of intertexts can be expanded in multiple ways or serve as a prelude to independent research projects if instructors have more time to devote to *Fun Home*. Bechdel's memoir has several courses' worth of reading lists embedded in its pages, and one could productively design entire literature curricula (modern American literature, queer literature, hero and antihero) around *Fun Home* and its antecedents.

Interethnic Space in *Fun Home* and *Dykes to Watch Out For*

JoAnne Ruvoli

> Bechdel's comics autobiography *Fun Home* (2006)
> has brought her much greater general attention than
> *Dykes* ever did, but make no mistake—the strip is her
> masterpiece.
>
> —Ray Olson, *Booklist*

Alison Bechdel's serial comic, *Dykes to Watch Out For*, ran in alternative news-papers for over twenty years but has not attracted as much critical attention as her graphic memoirs.[1] Presenting to students excerpts of the over five hundred episodes of *Dykes* can powerfully illustrate the artist's sustained creative pro-duction and the long career that preceded *Fun Home*. While artists such as Lynda Barry, Nicole Hollander, and Lynn Johnston have produced excellent serial work over a similar time span, Bechdel's *Dykes* has a consistent quality to the storytelling and an intricately detailed set of characters that is unrivaled. In studying *Dykes*, students see the evolution of Bechdel's writing and draw-ing style and find many connections to *Fun Home* and *Are You My Mother?*[2] More important, *Dykes* can help frame a discussion about ethnicity and race in *Fun Home*.

Bechdel's *Fun Home* can be read against the fictional, multiethnic cityscape of *Dykes* to suggest connections between the constraints of the insular Pennsyl-vania town of Alison's childhood and the opportunities for interethnic alliances in the larger city. Bechdel's portrait of Beech Creek in *Fun Home* is mapped out across a mile and a half where her parents, Bruce and Helen, raise their three children. With brief escapes to New York and Europe, the family is tethered to the overwhelmingly white, heteronormative, and religious town. The Bechdel family's past is characterized by a typical American migration history. In *Are You My Mother?* Bechdel documents the immigration history of her maternal grandfather from southern Austria to Pennsylvania. As a young woman, Helen identifies culturally as Italian American, but her marriage and education mask her ethnicity (84).[3] In a life trajectory similar to Bruce's, Helen escapes small-town life to go to college, have a theater internship in Cleveland, and work in New York City, but ultimately chooses traditional marriage and childrearing.[4]

In Beech Creek, the couple retreats into literature, home restoration, and community theater, and Bechdel sparingly shows the turbulent national events of the 1960s and 1970s in the background images of newspapers and television screens. The insularity of their lives is intensely dramatized in the 2015 staging of the musical adaptation of *Fun Home* at the Circle in the Square Theater: the memory landscape of the stage is restricted to house and dorm room interiors, with brief moments that take place inside the New York apartment that the family visits and inside the car where Alison talks to Bruce for the last time. When the play represents Bruce's fatal encounter with the truck, the scene is made even more dramatic because of its rare representation of outside space. The 1970s era is portrayed through the costumes as well as the musical styles of two upbeat songs, "Come to the Fun Home" and "Raincoat of Love." Instead of the televised Nixon resignation depicted in the book, the musical shows a sitcom in the style of the *Brady Bunch* on the television.

In contrast to the characters in *Fun Home*, Bechdel's *Dykes* characters form a community fully immersed in the political and cultural context of the 1980s through the 2000s—what Judith Kegan Gardiner has described as "largely independent of and adversial to the political culture of Reagan's America" ("Bechdel's *Dykes*" 83). From marches for equality to protests against war, climate change, and corporate exploitation of the environment, Bechdel illustrates the political activism of Mo, Clarice, Sparrow, and Lois as well as the community-building of Jezanna, Ginger, and Sydney. The community is implicitly multiethnic and multiracial, and explicitly so only when ethnic and racial identities become strategies for resistance. For example, in "Suburban Subversion," a white woman mistakes Clarice, an African American lawyer, for her son's nanny when Clarice is at a park without her partner; when the Latina accountant Toni hears Clarice tell the story, she replies, "Dammit. Let's move here to spite them" (*Dykes* 191). Constructing what Susan Stanford Friedman has defined as "intersubjective spaces of self-other interactions" (141), Bechdel reduces the scale of influence that allows dominant American culture to limit characters in *Dykes's* cityscapes. Instead of representing these characters as constrained by the dominant institutions of religion, whiteness, and heteronormativity that define the small town of *Fun Home's* Beech Creek, in *Dykes* the interethnic space complicates relationships and depicts a fluidity that allows its characters to engage with national, racial, ethnic, and sexual identities in ways that are not available to Bruce's and Helen's generation. As Becky Thompson reminds readers, *Dykes* and Bechdel came of age during the multiracial lesbian-feminist movement, where the Stonewall uprising produced a "groundswell for a big vision, a color-, class-, gender-, sexuality-friendly movement, ways of loving and being that could buck up against patriarchy and racism and heterosexism at the same time" (530). While distinctly conveying the varied story space of *Dykes*, Bechdel's rendering of the strip's diversity calls attention to the narrative choices made in *Fun Home*.

In comparison with *Fun Home's* more conventional community, the *Dykes* characters experience more political and sexual freedom in their urban setting. The comparative method helps students examine whiteness in *Fun Home* characters and how it relates to the constraints experienced by the Bechdels in Beech Creek, resulting in self-censorship in the face of the threat of community gossip. In a course focused on introducing English majors to literary study and critical methodology, my students examined Bechdel's *Fun Home* alongside

Lorraine Hansberry's *A Raisin in the Sun*, Tina De Rosa's *Paper Fish*, and Jack Kerouac's *On the Road*.[5] Supplemental texts consisted of a poetry anthology and an introductory handbook of critical theories.[6] Students read and discussed each text in three rounds of one week each over the course of the semester: the first round investigated each text through the course's overarching theme of home, the second round applied the critical approaches to each text, and the third round addressed how to hone students' academic research and writing skills in a comparative final paper. *Fun Home* works especially well when students discuss introductory thematic questions of the idea of home in the first round of class activities. Using critical methods of New Criticism, reader-response theory, structuralist and deconstructive criticism, genre and popular culture theory, psychological criticism, and criticism focused on gender and feminism in the second round provided many insights into both the limits and strengths of using specific approaches to analyze the graphic memoir. For the third round, students accessed a large body of critical scholarship and popular writing available on Bechdel's work to learn how to use library resources, to practice research strategies, and to develop keyword searching necessary to support literary analysis and undergraduate critical writing. By investigating this set of texts together multiple times over the course of the semester, the racial and ethnic spaces of *A Raisin in the Sun*, *Paper Fish*, and *On the Road* provoked an examination of the ethnic and racial construction of space in *Fun Home*. Bechdel depicts a seemingly nonethnic, nonracial landscape in *Fun Home*'s major setting of Beech Creek, but supplementing the discussion with excerpts from *Dykes* allowed students to compare and question the interethnic and multiracial features of both texts.

One of the most difficult tasks is to discuss the topics of ethnicity and race with students who are not accustomed to comprehending depictions of white characters and white communities as racial or ethnic. Short but impactful essays like "White Privilege and Male Privilege," by Peggy McIntosh, and "Making Systems of Privilege Visible," by Stephanie M. Wildman (with Adrienne D. Davis), are helpful, but applying their ideas to texts can be awkward. Before discussing racial and ethnic issues in *Fun Home*, the class had explored them in *A Raisin in the Sun*, *Paper Fish*, and *On The Road*, and my goals for the *Fun Home* discussion were similar: to investigate how power relations are constructed, supported, controlled, constrained, or transgressed in the texts though the ethnic and racial characterizations of individuals, situations, and locations. The settings of Hansberry's and De Rosa's texts are segregated African American and Italian American Chicago neighborhoods where characters are discouraged and discriminated against when they try to move beyond the neighborhood boundaries.[7] Kerouac's more privileged white male characters move through big cities and small towns unconstrained by ethnic and racial boundaries.

Fun Home offers insightful parallels and differences with each of the other texts. In *A Raisin in the Sun*, the rebellious daughter's search for self-identity in part triggers transformational possibilities for the rest of the African American family members, who face blatant discrimination and potential violence if they move into their newly purchased house in a white neighborhood. While the Youngers ultimately face their challengers, in *Fun Home* Bruce dies before reacting to Helen's demand for a divorce, a request that, similar to the situation the Youngers find themselves in, would test his beliefs and security. The Italian American family in *Paper Fish* struggles with its shame of one developmentally challenged daughter and another who runs away to try to escape the family's problems. The novel provides an ethnic context to underscore Helen's prolonged silence in *Fun Home*, as well as the role that gossip and shame plays in insular communities, be they urban ethnic neighborhoods or rural small towns. Finally, *On the Road*, with its representation of Sal and Dean's intensely masculine relationship, illustrates the cultural attitudes of the late 1950s and underlines the difficulties that Bruce may have encountered as a young adult in that era. Students compared intersectional conflicts between region, sexuality, race, and ethnicity in the other texts with how Bechdel illustrates these power dynamics differently in *Dykes* and *Fun Home* in relation to politics and location.

In the third round of discussion, near the end of the semester when students were working on their comparative final papers, I used class time to practice strategies for comparison, using the authors' poems, interviews, or other excerpts to contrast with the Hansberry, De Rosa, and Kerouac texts. For *Fun Home*, students in small groups of three and four examined photocopies of over twenty individual one-page strips from *Dykes*.[8] I chose strips that focused on the politics and locations that I wanted students to examine, specifically ones that illustrated crowded urban scenes or scenes of political activism. Very few strips depict characters who are all of the same race or ethnicity. Selections included "On the Road" (17), "Crisis Management" (59), "Dancing in the Streets" (63), "Gulf Ball" (68), "Mo Zone" (83), "Seeing Pink" (156), "The Ties That Chafe" (157), "Suburban Subversion" (191), "A Just War? Or Just a War?" (221), and "Real World" (267), the last of which is Bechdel's textless response to the September 11 attacks and shows how each of the core characters responded to the news. Since students had little knowledge of the recurring characters and storylines or of the specific politics of the era, the activity tested students' abilities to read, observe, and interpret images that I had tried to encourage throughout the semester. The visual details in *Dykes* throw into relief the absence of ethnic and racial diversity and the limited contemporary political commentary depicted in *Fun Home*. As with the other third-round, in-class activities, the exercise demonstrated the benefits and drawbacks of comparative analysis and how gaps or absence in texts can be incorporated into critical discussions.

The small-group members discussed their observations of common characteristics in their sample strips, then created two-column lists to compare *Fun Home* and *Dykes*. What follows is a list that compiles the groups' notes.[9]

Fun Home	*Dykes to Watch Out For*
About Bechdel, memoir	About various characters, fiction
Plot is deep, continuous, vertical	Plot consists of surface vignettes, horizontal
Exploring sexuality	Established sexuality
Rites of passage	Less self-reflection
Outside narration	Current events
Small town	Big city
Literary references	Pop culture references
More politically correct	More controversial topics
Midwest homophobic stereotypes	More racial, sexual, gender diversity
Intricate details	Intricate details
Time	Space
Bolded words	More bold words and heavy text
Color wash	Dark crosshatching for hard topics
Softer facial expressions	Extreme facial expressions
Artifacts and objects in background	Artifacts and objects in background
Truth of the father	Truth of the world

As the students reported their small-group observations and I tallied them on the blackboard, we reviewed the ongoing, semester-long discussion about the problems of setting up binary oppositions. I often use this exercise as a limited but sometimes useful way of forcing analysis and debate in small-group activities, but I ask students to complicate their thinking in follow-up assignments.

Narrowing the discussion to locations and politics, I asked the groups to find renderings of street scenes, political events, or ethnic and racial diversity in *Fun Home* that compared with the moments in the *Dykes* strips. Students found that the New York street scenes in *Fun Home* (104, 107, 190) displayed the ethnic and racial diversity of the *Dykes* strips. Alison's university "gay union" meetings, where the narrator encounters direct political activism, also include a diverse set of individuals; one African American woman even speaks to Alison (76, 79). The renderings were so subtle compared with the bold features of *Dykes* that students disagreed about their significance. As subtle as these depictions are in *Fun Home*, New York City is the one place where Bruce experienced relative sexual freedom from the constraints of Beech Creek society, as did Alison when she lived in New York after college graduation.

Students debated two other depictions of nonwhite ethnicity in *Fun Home*. The first is Bechdel's depiction of the family babysitter, Roy, who Alison discovers was Bruce's lover (94, 95, 101–05). The drawing of Roy's curly black hair matches that of Clarice, the African American lawyer from *Dykes*. Although Roy's ethnicity is not stated in *Fun Home*, in the Broadway musical the character is played by Joel Perez, a Latino actor. The second is Bechdel's depiction of the Drs. Gryglewicz, who once asked Bruce and Helen to "engage in group sex" (167). In addition to the ambiguous ethnicity of the couple's last name, the two are distinct because they lived "in town" (160). In both cases the nonwhite ethnic markers are connected to the characters' alternative sexuality and location. The presence of interethnic and multiracial interactions in New York, at Alison's university, and in Beech Creek signals Friedman's "intersubjective spaces of self-other interactions," where participants have access to self-defining strategies of resistance and to moments freed from the constraints of the dominant society that ideologically constructs the ethnic, racial, and sexual other.

Using *Dykes* to reflect on *Fun Home* highlights many potential points of discussion that reading the graphic memoir alone may overlook. The diverse ensemble cast of the long-running strip illustrates the conflicts and alliances that continuously form and reform over time, where small communities include different points of views, be they generational, racial or ethnic, sexual or gender-based, or ideologically political. There are difficulties in comparing a fictional comic strip with a nonfictional memoir, but the two texts do talk to each other, and it could be argued that without the long apprenticeship of *Dykes*, *Fun Home* would have been a much different text. Bechdel's memoir struggles with the acts of remembering the past and understanding its impact on the present. The telescoping of time in the text's multiple frames reveals the role that space, especially that of her parents' home, played in her childhood. The *Dykes* weekly strip moves mainly through the present, as characters debate, change, and continue forward in time. Bechdel's representation of the interethnic relationships between the African American, Latino, Asian American, and white characters in *Dykes to Watch Out For* contrasts with the restrictions, insularity, and apolitical nature of Beech Creek in *Fun Home*. The interethnic diversity of Bechdel's city spaces illuminates the discussion of how small-town homogeneity can restrict individuals and police the dominant society's constraints.

NOTES

Editor's note: We observe with sadness the sudden death of JoAnne Ruvoli in 2018 when the present volume was being prepared for publication.

[1] Unless otherwise noted, quotations of the strip are from Bechdel, *The Essential Dykes to Watch Out For*, cited hereafter as *Dykes*. The newspaper series started as single-panel comics in 1983 and evolved into multipanel strips that followed a core group of fictional characters. A complete listing of publications of *Dykes to Watch Out For* is available at Bechdel's Web site (dykestowatchoutfor.com/dtwof-books).

[2] For many more points of comparison between *Fun Home* and *Dykes* beyond the interethnic and pedagogical scope of this essay, see Judith Kegan Gardiner's "Queering Genre."

[3] When I asked Bechdel in an e-mail message in 2006 about the Italian cultural codes that Helen follows in *Fun Home*, Bechdel responded that Helen's family is Italian (Bechdel, "Re: quick question"). In her later life, Helen wrote a newspaper column where she describes herself as "second-generation Italian American" and discusses the Italian immigrant mining community where she grew up ("Remembering" and "County

Home"). Mary Jo Bona has written about Helen's Italian ethnicity as undergoing a kind of erasure.

[4]See my review of *Are You My Mother?* for more on Helen's exceptionalism.

[5]I've used *Fun Home* in two similar courses that were introductions to critical methods; first in 2007 on the large, urban campus of the University of Illinois at Chicago. There were no critical studies of *Fun Home* yet available, so students had a blank slate to test their critical skills on the graphic memoir. In 2015 I revised the course and taught it at Ball State University, a smaller, public, liberal arts university in east-central Indiana, with a much less ethnically diverse student demographic than the Chicago campus. The University of Illinois at Chicago required a film unit, so we studied Spike Lee's *Do the Right Thing*, which I replaced with Kerouac's *On The Road* at Ball State. In 2015 the texts resonated deeply with current events. The Indiana state legislature passed a religious-freedom law, widely interpreted as permission to discriminate against and refuse service to gay couples. In addition, the local and national news covered the many incidents of racial violence and police brutality that culminated in the Baltimore protests (Stolberg). These political events frequently added immediacy to the class's discussions of the play, novels, and graphic memoir.

[6]For the poetry unit both courses used *The Making of a Poem: A Norton Anthology of Poetic Forms* edited by Eavan Boland and Mark Strand. In the Chicago course, students used *Critical Terms for Literary Study*, edited by Frank Lentricchia and Thomas McLaughlin, while students in the Ball State course used the less theoretical *Texts and Contexts*, by Steven Lynn.

[7]Students discussed whether or not Beech Creek could be called a segregated neighborhood, which provoked them to question the labeling of Chicago neighborhoods.

[8]In my 2007 course students examined my personal collection of the Firebrand *Dykes* compilations, since *The Essential* Dykes to Watch Out For had not yet been published. The copyright page of the 2008 edition of *The Essential* Dykes to Watch Out For includes information on how to request permission to use reproductions in class. Department or library staff may be able to help instructors secure permission in advance.

[9]I thank Natalee Bird, Stefanie Clark, Ellen Fawcett, Kaitlyn Freeman, Taylor Frymier, Haley Gillilan, Megan Hardin, Raevyn Harper, Amy Hecimovich, Jenn Kunkle, Elizabeth Linder, Krissy McCracken, Samantha Taft, Nolan Swarz, Allison Tunstall, and one anonymous student for permitting me to compile and quote from their group notes.

Imitating Bechdels in Banned Books and Novel Ideas: An Exercise in Rhetorical Unmastery

Eric Detweiler

Course Context

In this essay I discuss an exercise I designed and implemented while teaching Banned Books and Novel Ideas, an undergraduate course offered by the Department of English at the University of Texas at Austin. At the time I taught it, most sections of the course were taught by PhD students. The course served two audiences and purposes: for the general student body, it was one way to fulfill a university-wide writing requirement and, for English majors, it was an introduction to the major. The course was intended to teach both audiences to read, write, and revise formal, historical, and cultural literary criticism.

As its title indicates, Banned Books and Novel Ideas focused on controversial texts. My iteration of the course also emphasized the rhetorical dimensions of book bans and challenges. After a preliminary unit focused on debates around both contemporary textbooks and a 2010 Arizona bill that banned schools from teaching what the bill referred to as "ethnic" studies (State of Arizona, House of Representatives), students read the following: Aristophanes's *Clouds*, a selection from Plato's *Republic*, J. K. Rowling's *Harry Potter and the Sorcerer's Stone*, selections from Gloria Anzaldúa's *Borderlands/La Frontera*, Alison Bechdel's *Fun Home*, Ralph Ellison's *Invisible Man*, and secondary sources detailing controversies around those texts. In concert with *Fun Home*, for instance, students read coverage of ongoing disputes surrounding the book's assignment in undergraduate courses at the College of Charleston and at the University of South Carolina, Upstate—disputes that led the South Carolina legislature to threaten to cut both institutions' funding.

For the course, students wrote and revised six four-hundred-word minipapers and three longer papers: a rhetorical analysis of the controversy surrounding a particular book ban or challenge, an annotated bibliography,[1] and a piece of literary criticism. The minipapers asked students to engage with course texts in less traditionally critical ways, incorporating affective concerns and asking students to reflect on their writing processes, research habits, and relations to literature. In loose terms, these exercises resonate with "postcritical" classroom practices since proposed by Rita Felski (172; see 172–82)—practices that, in their attunement to emotion, affect, and identification, recall longstanding elements of rhetorical education. They were designed to give me a sense of students' approaches to reading, writing, and research; to help students develop meta-awareness of their own academic processes and habits; to make room for students' affective and rhetorical responses to course texts; and to provide starting points for in-class discussions. The six minipaper assignments were as follows:

> Students began by reading Langston Hughes's poem "Theme for English B." I asked students first to describe how they would read the poem if they came across it outside the classroom: What parts might they find memorable, interesting, or emotionally compelling? What parts would they probably ignore? What questions or concerns would the poem raise? In the second half of the paper, students compared their answers to how they would likely read the poem if they were assigned it in an English class.
>
> Students identified the literary text they'd chosen to write about for the course's rhetorical-analysis assignment, explained their choice (including any lingering doubts or misgivings), and described their likely process for researching the text's historical context.
>
> In roughly three hundred words, students summarized a scholarly source relevant to their rhetorical analysis. They then described how they found the source, identified the kinds of literary criticism they thought it performed, and explained how it was or wasn't relevant to their own project.
>
> The fourth minipaper was the imitation exercise I focus on in the remainder of this essay. The entire prompt is included below.
>
> Students read the prologue and first chapter of *Invisible Man*. Noting the different styles of those two sections of the novel, I asked students to identify which they preferred, to compare and contrast their emotional and intellectual responses to the two, and to describe how the style of the prologue shaped their encounter with the first chapter. In the second half of the minipaper, students considered why Ellison might have decided to open the novel in such a manner, focusing particularly on the kinds of responses he wanted to elicit from readers.
>
> For the final minipaper, students reread "Theme for English B" alongside their first minipaper. They then described—based on what they'd learned, read, and written over the course of the semester—how they would or wouldn't read and think about the poem differently from what they wrote in the first minipaper. They concluded by summarizing their main takeaways from the course—things they might return to or make use of in future academic, professional, and civic situations.

Historical Context: Progymnasmata *and Prosopopoeia*

In recent decades, numerous scholars have argued for classical rhetoric's relevance to contemporary writing instruction (see Crowley). Many have concentrated on the *progymnasmata*, a sequence of exercises that was a predominant component of rhetorical education from the classical era through the Renaissance (Fleming; Ray). Specifically, the *progymnasmata* were preliminary ("pro") exercises ("gymnasmata") designed to prepare students for declamation, a fully realized oration that was a sort of capstone assignment in many schools of rhetoric. Young students began with simpler assignments (e.g., explicating a proverb), then moved on to more complicated exercises (e.g., proposing a law) that incorporated skills developed in earlier ones. *Progymnasmata* were structured and sequenced to help students gradually develop a rhetorical dexterity that would make them masterful declaimers, orators, and writers.

One of the later exercises was prosopopoeia, a term that might be more familiar to literature scholars as a figure of speech: giving a voice or a face to a dead, voiceless, or otherwise absent entity (Davis 41–43). As an exercise, prosopopoeia required students to imitate or speak in the voice of everything from inanimate objects to historical figures to abstract concepts.[2] Many historians of rhetoric have noted the curious fact that medieval and Renaissance students, most of whom were boys, often composed and performed prosopopoeiae in the voices of women (Enterline; Woods). Historical and mythical women who had suffered some sort of trauma (e.g., Dido and Thisbe) were especially common subjects. In some ways, these exercises can be read as a surprisingly prevalent form of gender-bending that complicates conservative depictions of premodern education; they also allowed women, despite their frequent exclusion from rhetoric classrooms, a different, if only figural, way into them. It's also possible, however, to read these prosopopoeiae as furthering women's exclusion, appropriating their voices and experiences in ways that fostered misogynist solidarity at the expense of actual women (Woods).

The latter possibility serves as a reminder of Sharon Crowley's warning that classical rhetorical theory, despite its pedagogical affordances, "was devised a long time ago in cultures that were rigidly classbound . . . [and] invented for the use of privileged men" (264). Bearing this warning in mind, in my course I worked to reposition prosopopoeia as an exercise in rhetorical failure rather than rhetorical mastery—one that emphasized the limits the writer encounters in attempting to speak for or as another.

Assignment and Theoretical Rationale

In "Drawing the Archive in Alison Bechdel's *Fun Home*," Ann Cvetkovich argues that, as a genre, graphic narrative "reminds us that we are not gaining access to an unmediated form of vision" (114). Cvetkovich claims that Bechdel's text acknowledges the "unassimilability" of her father's story (124), painstakingly "map[ping] a history that she can't comprehend as a direct witness" (122). That is, though Bechdel notes that "removing one word would be like pulling on a thread that unravels the whole sweater" (qtd. in Chute, "Interview" 1008),

Fun Home is also a necessarily incomplete text—one that can't not encounter the limits of an unassimilable story that even its author doesn't claim to grasp completely.

One of my main goals in assigning the prosopopoeia, then, was for students to encounter *Fun Home* in a way that resonated with Bechdel's simultaneously painstaking and incomplete retelling of her father's story. The prompt was as follows:

> This minipaper asks you to take on the voices of Bruce and Alison Bechdel—to try to engage and imitate *Fun Home*'s language carefully. Your assignment is to imagine the conversation that Alison and her father might have had if they weren't turned away from the bar on page 223.[3] Don't speculate in your voice—write the dialogue that Alison Bechdel speculates "might have been [their] Circe chapter" (223). The book provides evidence of both characters' writing and language habits (Alison's diaries, her father's letter on page 224, etc.), so try to imitate the tone and voice of the character you choose. Keep in mind, however, that Alison the narrator is not identical to Alison the drawn character, that the style in which her father speaks to her is not identical to the style in which he writes, and so on. Your primary task is to try to be faithful to Bechdel's characterization of their relationship.

When class began the day the minipapers were due, I gave students a supplemental task: add three footnotes to your minipaper, pinpointing the specific evidence from *Fun Home* that you used to make three particular rhetorical decisions in your prosopopoeia.

Subsequently, we had an in-class discussion about the difficulties of writing the minipaper—the aporias or gaps students tried to or could not fill, the resistance they felt to appropriating Bechdel's text—but also the feelings of pleasure that attended the assignment. Students had already read Cvetkovich's article, so I emphasized points of overlap between Bechdel's project and the assignment I'd given them, noting the inescapable limits and failures—historical, rhetorical, ethical—of both my assignment prompt and their minipapers.

My goals for the minipaper, both the original assignment and the footnoted iteration, were as follows:

> To build on the archive students had created in their bibliographies (see note 1), thus underscoring the ways in which the course's writing assignments fed into each other and were—like the *progymnasmata*—more than a discontinuous series of isolated exercises.
> To help students differentiate the book's narrative and textual layers (e.g., the differences between Alison Bechdel as author, narrator, and illustrated character).

Perhaps in tension with the first goal, to foreground the "unassimilability" described by Cvetkovich—to call attention to something like rhetorical unmastery, rather than mastery, in students' relation with *Fun Home* and other course texts. To highlight, in other words, the ways in which meticulous, responsible engagement with a text can lead not to comprehension but to interpretive uncertainty.

Two final notes: first, because Banned Books and Novel Ideas is a writing-intensive course, I had students focus on *Fun Home*'s words. In other courses, this assignment could incorporate a graphic component and thus engage the visual rhetoric of *Fun Home* in ways my version did not. As another way of stressing the importance of medium, courses that address the musical version of *Fun Home* could have students remediate into musical numbers scenes from the book that aren't included in the musical in order to foster dialogue about the limitations and affordances of different media.

Second, I structured this exercise as I did—emphasizing unmastery over mastery—in the hope of interrupting the easy appropriation that arguably characterizes medieval students' prosopopoeiae. By appropriation, I mean the possibility of writers taking over the voices they're imitating, assuming they can responsibly and authoritatively speak for another. I do not mean to suggest, however, that my take on prosopopoeia was purely nonappropriative. I am persuaded by scholars who have argued that there is no purely nonappropriative pedagogy (Enders), that any attempt to grasp another's perspective entails translating it into one's own terms and thus slicing off some of that perspective's alterity—that which makes it, to use Cvetkovich's term, unassimilable. Rather than assuming my students and I could circumvent the risk of appropriation, I aimed to foreground the ways in which writing about literature, even when one is writing in more traditionally critical modes, involves some measure of appropriation and thus places a significant responsibility on the writer. In some ways, the most thoughtful response to this assignment might have been that of a student who, after poring over *Fun Home*, claimed that she couldn't write the minipaper—not because she wanted to slack off but because she felt doing so would violate Bechdel's text: the conversation in the bar did not happen, and so this student believed she could not responsibly write a counterhistory in which it did. For her, the most responsible way to characterize Alison was to let what went unrealized and unspoken remain as such. This was a lesson for me at least as much as it was for the student.

NOTES

[1]The bibliography assignment served as important preparation for the minipaper on which this essay focuses. Students were allowed to annotate either *Fun Home* or

Invisible Man. Students who chose *Fun Home* were assigned a roughly twenty-page section of the book and were charged with writing fifteen one-paragraph annotations for their section (e.g., key words or concepts, cultural references, literary allusions). After students submitted the assignment, I combined the annotations into a single document that functioned as a student-generated glossary for *Fun Home*, which served as a reference as students wrote the minipaper this essay describes in more detail.

[2]Classical rhetoricians subdivided this exercise into three categories: *ethopoeia, eidolopoeia,* and prosopopoeia (G. Kennedy 115–16). For the sake of concision, I use the relatively familiar prosopopoeia throughout.

[3]In *Fun Home's* narrative, this happens just after the two go to see the movie *Coal Miner's Daughter* and is followed closely by the visit home from college during which Alison introduces her parents to Joan—a trip that marks the last time she sees her father.

Fun Home on the Stage and in the Classroom

Sue-Ellen Case

Teaching Alison Bechdel's *Fun Home* within the area of theater and performance studies provides an opportunity to explore the transformation of a successful graphic memoir into Lisa Kron and Jeanine Tesori's Tony Award–winning Broadway musical. The shift from a memoir composed of text situated among two-dimensional drawings to dialogue among live actors on the stage challenges the student to engage with just how the particular choices the animator and the director have made affect the significance and meaning of the material. The most obvious change is the representation of Alison at different ages by three live actors, whose gestural appearance radically alters the characterological studies. While the memoir remains as published, staging the piece offers the opportunity to adapt the material to a wide range of production possibilities. In a class designed to translate the graphic novel to the stage, the student may be invited to imagine how other stagings re-create Bechdel's dramatic world.

Along with *Fun Home*'s formal transformation from print to live production, the social and historical reception of the depiction of lesbian and gay characters and their narratives was also altered. Thus, materials that indicate the reception of the play must be assembled from the reviews, the historical and social composition of the audience, and so on. This approach focuses less on a strict analysis of the work itself and more on the changes the work's reception makes to the meaning of the play, from depicting a movement in search of civil rights to one more successful in gaining them.

Like the cells in the graphic memoir that frame the characters and incidents, modules of study may both organize materials and elucidate their signifying elements. The cells on the page of the graphic memoir are directional, yet they also invite the reader to scan, to assemble, and to rearrange their composition in the act of reading. Likewise, modules of study may organize comparisons between the graphic memoir and the musical, while also emphasizing that these relations are merely frames that may be exceeded, scanned, or rearranged, inviting students to imagine directions beyond those determined by the source materials and the instructor. I have posed questions within the frames to suggest where the exploration might expand outward. Directionally, the first module introduces what is arguably the root difference between the page and the stage: the transformation from drawn characters to live actors.

Drawn Characters to Live Actors

In the graphic *Fun Home*, the reader is beguiled and guided by Alison Bechdel's masterful and mature drawings, through which the characters in a dysfunctional family appear. The drawing style is a classic form of realism in comics.

This "classical" realism suggests that the narrative, the conditions, and the composition of characters are historical ones, bound by a set of normative traditions, as is the drawing style. Realism and the bourgeois family drama have enjoyed a long, prosperous history on the page and the stage. Bechdel's consummate artistry makes critical use of the combination. The monochromatic style of the cells is without affect, depicting the characters neither by expressionism in style nor by expression on their faces —what Bechdel refers to as her "cool aesthetic distance" (*Fun Home* 67).

On the one hand, this affect-less world is one of repressed desires and emotions; on the other, the monochromatic approach renders incidents as mapped out rather than expressed, animating a schema or a scenario that locates them within a process of self-discovery, situates them historically, literally figures them out.

The collection of affectless cells on the page might suggest that if the page had a theatrical voice, it would sound like an ancient Greek chorus, standing before the House of Atreus, considering the conundrums and the moral and social implications of the family tragedy. Moreover, the text, though often caught in the traditional comic bubbles exuding from the characters' mouths, also exists outside the cells, like the chorus, critically commenting on the scenes, explicating the ironies of a childhood lived without foreknowledge of coming out and the father's suicide.

The psychological and social histories of closeted repression and coming out are deeply intertwined. Bechdel, after decades of drawing comics about lesbian lives, fully understands how the closet has played a devastating and determining role in the psychological makeup of lesbians and gays. In this story, the closet is represented through the father figure, permeating even the more radical, pleasurable lesbian coming out experiences of Middle Alison. Critical distance is required to make this relationship of father and daughter both historical and psychological.

How, then, to imagine the genre of the musical for this book? Bechdel perceived her memoir in relation to theater when she subtitled it "A Family Tragicomic," punning on the theatrical genres of tragedy and tragicomedy and on comics. Like comics, the genre of the American musical is associated with entertainment and popular culture. Yet the effect of a child actor portraying Small Alison on the stage of the Broadway musical creates an image that is contrary to the memoir's self-criticism. Cavorting and singing exuberantly, the young actor represents the promise of childhood rather than the memoir's tragic ironies, which, as in Greek tragedy, interrupt the narrative with foreboding observations: "and with my father's death following so hard on the heels of this doleful coming-out party . . ." (Bechdel, *Fun Home* 59).

In the form of the American musical, child actors recall Shirley Temple or Annie, not Electra. For, even as the actor in *Fun Home* may offer signals (particularly in the costuming) of gender dysphoria and family conflict, her songs, such as "Come to the Fun Home" (a campy, energetic ad for the funeral home), emerge as light and delightful show tunes that inspire the audience to clap—they thus interrupt the story, not with critical distance but with the sign of successful entertainment.

To compensate for this lack of critical perspective provided in the graphic text, the musical includes Bechdel the author as a character, lurking about the stage watching the scenes, sometimes with pen in hand, sometimes mimicking drawing. But this lurking Alison is a chimera rather than a creator. She watches rather than animates, is simultaneous rather than subsequent. The audience does not know what she knows: the father's suicide, the significance of his continual household renovations, the changes in attitude concerning LGBTQ movements, and so on. Yet onstage these characters are always "there," in the present. Then how could the stage character suggest the perspective of the creator?

Within this module is the invitation for the students to imagine alternative stagings of the musical—specifically, how to stage the critical distance from the events that the memoir conveys. The following are some examples: How would the live stage production differ if the drawings were projected onto a screen behind the performers or on the bodies of the actors? Or what if puppets in the Noh tradition were used instead of actors, with the visible manipulators speaking and singing—an adult manipulating a child puppet, for example, or a woman the father? This would situate the production in the off-Broadway or off-off-Broadway tradition rather than in the Broadway one, leading to changes in the play's production and reception.

In one key scene for the representation of lesbian sexuality, the college-aged Middle Alison has sex with Joan for the first time. The song that follows, "Changing my Major," is perhaps the most popular song in the musical. Whereas, in the memoir, the two are drawn as naked, entwined, in the position of oral sex, in the stage version Middle Alison immediately leaps out of the bed where Joan remains sleeping. The song is witty and lively rather than, say, sultry, naughty, or seductive. Any sense of lesbian sex as passionate or perverse is replaced by the sense that it is charming, nonthreatening, and somehow innocent. Why this choice? How does it differ from the treatment of gay sex in, say, the equally successful Broadway play *Angels in America*? What is the address to the audience and why? Although Bechdel's earlier comic strip, *Dykes to Watch Out For*, never had the sting of Diane DiMassa's *Hothead Paisan: Homicidal Lesbian Terrorist*, Bechdel's work was always firmly situated within the community and its practices. Is this scene?

Bechdel's memoir situates plot and character within a variety of literary allusions that are lacking in the stage production, so altering the unique intellectual, educated, literary, and intelligent flavor of the memoir. Other lesbian plays have managed to retain a literary quality—for example, Bryony Lavery's play *Her Aching Heart* is based on Daphne du Maurier's novel *Rebecca*, imitating and ironizing its florid language and repressed quality. What difference does this choice to excise the literary references make in the politics and aesthetics of the play?

Spatial Difference between Graphic Novel and Stage

The graphic novel provides the reader the choice to directionally follow the cells at a variable pace or to simultaneously scan a set of cells on the page. This device also offers the author-artist the possibility of exceeding the cell frame. So while space may be confined and directional, pace together with space is within the viewer's control. The possibility of simultaneity in viewing matches the collapsed, synchronous time of the story.

Where the memoir is graphic in its compression of space and pace, the stage is mechanical. At the Public Theater production in New York, the action took place on a revolving stage, in order to literally move through the scenes and to offer perspectival change. Where the graphic text depicts the living space, the production at New York's Circle in the Square Theatre used hydraulic lifts, through which set pieces rose and disappeared down stage traps. The stage was bare, but for books, pieces of furniture, and decorative items that were exact replicas from Bechdel's home. The photographs were real family photos (Dziemianowicz). The cast visited her home. How do these gestures enact mimesis? How can autobiography appear onstage? Students could explore some use of drawings as part of the scenic design.

Music versus Animation

While one might imagine a mimetic relation between the memoir and the musical in terms of casting, costuming, and even the set pieces, the incorporation of music is completely foreign to the novel. Exploring a strictly auditory medium—that is, the cast recording—in relation to the strictly visual one, the printed text, requires both a historical and an interpretive perspective. What does it mean for a character to break into song? Specifically, how does it work in this musical? And, in terms of reception, aren't musical theater spectators a special category of fans? How does this relate to Bechdel's address to the reader in the graphic text?

Music without lyrics can nevertheless suggest representational elements and diegetic movement, as in nineteenth-century programmatic music and in movie scores. One might ask whether the music, by Tesori, functions in this manner, and, if not, how does it function?

In my conversation with the eminent musicologist Raymond Knapp, several musical strategies used in *Fun Home* became evident. Knapp pointed out that what is not done is one of the major effects. For example, there is no duet between father and daughter, even when sitting side by side in the car; in fact, with few exceptions, each character sings solo. This lack can represent, Knapp suggested, the lack of contact among the members of the dysfunctional family. It is a compositional choice that would resonate with an audience familiar with musicals. What other functions does the music not adopt? Why? And why is there no duet between Middle Alison and her lesbian lover, Joan? "Changing My Major" is a solo in the tradition of the exuberant declaration of love in the Rodgers and Hammerstein song "A Wonderful Guy." Does Middle Alison share qualities with Mary Martin in *South Pacific*?

Perhaps the choice of exuberance here is designed to contrast with the traditional maudlin, noir depictions of lesbian relations. Lisa Kron, who wrote the lyrics, cocreated the show *Brave Smiles . . . Another Lesbian Tragedy* with the Five Lesbian Brothers. The play satirizes the dark history of lesbian representation so common to most portrayals. Is the joyous celebration in "Changing My Major" intended as an intervention into that tradition?

Reception

The playbill for the Broadway musical includes interviews with successful gay playwrights, such as Harvey Fierstein, Larry Kramer, Tony Kushner, and Terrence McNally. How do these gay celebrities of the stage situate, aesthetically and socially, a lesbian graphic memoir or a lesbian play? Do they create a cavalcade of success into which *Fun Home* is inducted? If so, how is that addressed to the lesbian and gay community and to the broader Broadway audience? Historically, how have audience attitudes changed toward the depiction of a lesbian couple after the right to marriage passed by the Supreme Court? I saw the play in New York that week, amid public LGBTQ celebrations. How does that change the reception of the closet that killed the father? Is it now strictly historical? Has the play "come out"? What does it mean that the critics hail its success? Are there any documents of distress in the reception of the play? If not, what does that mean? Finally, how was the Broadway production funded? How much did it cost to produce?

Much more could be said, much more suggested, in the study of this transformation of *Fun Home* from page to stage, but it is hoped that the questions and issues presented here offer a beginning approach for the classroom.

Narrative and Visual Frames in *Fun Home*

Daniel Mark Fogel

I teach *Fun Home* in a seminar, Graphic Novels and Narrative Theory, offered only to first-semester, first-time undergraduates; the seminar satisfies a general-education requirement for a foundational course in intensive writing and information literacy. Enrollment is capped at seventeen students. Why approach *Fun Home* through narrative theory, when other approaches—feminist or queer theoretical approaches, historicist approaches, genre analysis, thematic and psychological orientations—may be more likely to engage seventeen- and eighteen-year-olds? I have chosen the narrative theory approach to *Fun Home* (along with Bechdel's *Are You My Mother?* and works by Art Spiegelman, Marjane Satrapi, James Sturm, Jason Lutes, and others) in part for its allure for students more oriented toward the sciences than the arts and humanities. Science majors, I have found, respond well to the analytic scaffolding of narrative theory, to the clarity of its concepts and terms, and to the ideas that narrative "is the principal way in which our species organizes its understanding of time" and that the conflict, or agon, at the heart of narrative may provide "a way for a culture to talk to itself about, and possibly resolve, conflicts that threaten to fracture it (or at least make living difficult)" (H. Abbott 3, 55). Narrative theory, I hope, will turn a few of those science majors toward the arts and humanities.

More important, a narrative theory approach can enrich virtually every other approach to *Fun Home*. The growing body of commentary on Bechdel's masterpiece bears this out. Thus, for example, Valerie Rohy's Derridean psychoanalytic reading of the queer destabilization of personal and political history produced by the archive mania manifested in *Fun Home* draws on a fundamental concept of the theory of narrative in comics, the ghostly play of absence in the gutters between comics panels against such acts of presence, of reminiscential and imagined embodiment inscribed in Bechdel's drawings (see McCloud, *Understanding Comics* 60–93). Similarly, Ann Cvetkovich, while focused on intergenerational trauma, postmemory, and the witnessing of sexuality, analyzes Bechdel's "insurgent genre" as providing "a queer perspective that is missing from public discourse about both historical trauma and sexual politics" (112). And Robyn Warhol's "Narrative Approach" to *Fun Home* not only extends the poetics of the genre but also adds depth and complexity to feminist, queer, and other readings. A founder of feminist narrative theory, Warhol faults Scott McCloud for not attending "to gender or sexuality in his universalizing descriptions" of the genre and observes that "[e]xcept for [Hillary] Chute's, the leading models for analyzing comic structure . . . are as gender-blind as classical structuralist narratology" (14).[1] Only as students become familiar with such narratological terms as *diegesis*—not just in its narrow meaning as synonymous with *narrative* or *the telling of a story* but also its indication of the different levels (temporal, spatial, conceptual, inside or outside the storyworld of the primary narrative) on which a narrative may be constructed—are they able to derive meaning and value from discussions like Rohy's, Cvetkovich's, and Warhol's.

I have my students read H. Porter Abbott's *Cambridge Introduction to Narrative* and McCloud's *Making Comics* in tandem with our primary texts. Students regularly respond in writing to study questions designed to help them understand and use the concepts and terms discussed by Abbott and McCloud. Study questions become catalysts for class discussion; most are completed outside class, but occasionally I give the class a few minutes to respond in writing to questions they have not seen before. After sharing highlights of Warhol's essay, for instance, I asked students to respond in the first fifteen minutes of our next class to four study questions and prompts drawing on Warhol, Abbott, and McCloud:

> List as quickly as possible the different kinds of archival materials that extend, deepen, and enrich the diegetic levels (that is, the juxtaposed and interpenetrating levels of the storyworld) in *Fun Home*. Then identify by page and panel (e.g., 30.4) one example of each kind of archival material you have identified.
>
> Comment on how one or more of the terms of McCloud's discussion of body language (*Making Comics* 102–11)—elevation and status, distance and relationship, imbalance and discontent, etc.—might be applied to each of the following panels in *Fun Home*: 19.4, 44.3, 150.3.
>
> In 103.2, how would you characterize the contrast between the language of the voice-over narrative caption above the panel and the language of the labeled odors within the panel? How might the difference be characterized in terms of diegetic levels?
>
> Whose hands are holding the snapshots in 120.3? Whose hand is holding the snapshot in the centerfold of *Fun Home* (100–01)?

Student response to Abbott and McCloud in anonymous questionnaires has been overwhelmingly positive. One commented that Abbott presented aspects of "narrative theory and the different levels of narrative . . . and the author-narrator relationship" that were "important in all the primary texts" and that McCloud "made reading the texts themselves simpler," especially "figuring out what's highlighted or important on certain pages." Another wrote, "I personally loved this text [Abbott] as it gave me concrete operational definitions for so many components of literature that I had simply dismissed." Students also like Jan Christoph Meister's Web site, *The Living Handbook of Narratology* (*LHN*); one student responded, "It was a very valuable resource," and another observed, "This Web site just furthers what Abbott starts. It's very useful as well!"

The questionnaire asks students to score ideas and terms from narrative theory on a five-point scale from least to most valuable for reading each of our primary texts. A few of the twenty items I asked the students to rank referred to the entirety of extended discussions: for example, McCloud on character design, facial expressions, and body language. A discussion of the items that got the highest scores in the *Fun Home* column of the ranking sheet follows.

Autography, Narrative, and Time

Students like the recent coinage *autography* for long-form graphic memoirs and autobiographies because it neatly captures what Gillian Whitlock has termed "the specific conjunctions of visual and verbal text in this genre of autobiography" (966).[2] That long-form graphic autobiography constitutes a distinctive genre is immediately obvious to students, and they are interested in how readers' interpretations are in part shaped by their belief that a work belongs to a particular genre. If autography is a subgenre of autobiography, then autobiography itself has a variety of subgenres, including, among many others, crisis autobiography, bildungsroman, *Künstlerroman*, coming-out story, and trauma narrative. Abbott's discussions of what he calls *masterplots* and of the terms *type* and *genre* prepare students to see that while *Fun Home* may be assigned to various subgenres of autography, that assignment matters: reading *Fun Home* as a *Künstlerroman*, for example, foregrounds Alison's triumphant emergence as an artist, whereas reading Bechdel's "family tragicomic" as a trauma narrative foregrounds the troubling conjunction of Bruce Bechdel's outing and death with his daughter's coming out.

Students understand from McCloud that the comics medium represents time as space; Hillary L. Chute calls the framed panels of comics "boxes of time" (*Graphic Women* 6). Abbott distinguishes "storytime" from "the time of narrative discourse," and relates these terms to the narratological terms *story* and *discourse*, or *fabula* and *sjuzet* (15–19). Putting these ideas together, students are able to distinguish between Alison's *story*, which moves steadily in a single direction (from past to present), and the complex graphic and verbal *discourse* of her autography, which spirals backward and forward, returning again and again to key traumatic events (for example, Bruce's death); which speeds up some episodes in a single panel (for instance, Bruce's insistence that Alison's necklines match [15]) while slowing others through several panels (for example, Alison's handing her father scissors across the open cadaver of a male who died in the prime of life [44]); and which always exhibits the distance in time, perspective, and understanding between the narrating adult and the younger Alison.

Conflict and Closure

Abbott's discussion of conflict and closure provides two interesting frames of reference for students as they interpret *Fun Home*. First, the observation, already cited, "that the representation of conflict in narrative provides a way for a culture to talk to itself about, and possibly resolve, conflicts that threaten to fracture it" (55) invites students to zoom out from the interior theater of Alison's own unfolding discovery of her emotional and sexual truth and the domestic sphere of the Bechdels' family life to the public and political spheres represented by the contrast between the homophobic culture of small-town western Pennsylvania in which Bruce Bechdel is trapped in closeted loneliness and the queer, gregarious cosmopolitanism of New York City and also by allusions to such historical events as the Stonewall riots, Watergate, and the bicentennial celebrations. Second, Abbott's discussion (57) of the narrative codes postulated by Roland Barthes helps students distinguish between closure on the level of expectations and actions (the proairetic code) and on the level of questions and answers (the hermeneutic code): on the proairetic level, we know that Bruce Bechdel died when struck by a Sunbeam bread truck, but on the hermeneutic level we are not completely certain that his death was a suicide. Students can see that while there is substantial closure in Bechdel's autography on the level of expectations and actions, much of the power of the work to haunt the reader resides in the lack of closure on the level of questions and answers, down to the magically ambiguous panels with which the narrative closes.

McCloud: Five Choices, Six Transitions, Character Design, Facial Expressions, Body Language

McCloud's *Understanding Comics* and *Making Comics* are part of a single project, an almost Aristotelian effort to provide a taxonomic description of comics. Although *Understanding Comics* is better on some topics (notably on the function of the gutters in comics), on balance *Making Comics* has seemed a better primer for first-year undergraduates, helping them focus on the panel-by-panel construction of graphic narrative (8–57), on character design (58–127), on the part words play in comics (128–57), and on "world building" (158–211). McCloud helps students read sequential graphic art intelligently and articulately.[3]

He assumes a cartoonist bent on clarity and communication who must make a set of choices for each panel: of moment, frame, image, word, and flow (the guiding of the reader's eye from panel to panel).[4] Every panel in *Fun Home* will reward analysis in terms of these five choices, especially the first four (flow is scarcely an issue in *Fun Home*, though it may be in the two-page spreads in *Are You My Mother?*). The first five of McCloud's six transitions from panel to panel—moment to moment, action to action, subject to subject, scene to scene, and aspect to aspect—also help students attend to the rationale and implications of page design and of sequences of panels within pages and from page to page.[5]

Students are fascinated by Bechdel's process of photographing herself in the garb and poses in which she draws her characters (see, for examples, Chute, *Graphic Women* 201, 203). Knowledge of that process intensifies students' alertness to examples of McCloud's anatomy of what a cartoonist may express through characters' facial expressions and body language. McCloud remarks that well-designed characters need three essential attributes: an inner life, visual distinction, and expressive traits. As Chute emphasizes, in embodying through hand-drawn art both the bodies of human beings and archival materials such as snapshots, literary passages, and legal documents, Bechdel not only interrogates a series of provisional ideas about who her father was and about her own development but also works against the grain of "dominant conceptions of trauma's unrepresentability" (*Graphic Women* 182). McCloud helps students see that the strains of maintaining family secrets and of repressing trauma are drawn in the Bechdel family's predominantly blank facial expressions. Bechdel conveys the inner lives of her characters through textual materials (voice-over narration, dialogue balloons, and such expressive archival artifacts as letters and diaries) and through body language far more than through physiognomy. McCloud's discussions of such facets of body language as "elevation and status" and "distance and relationships" (*Making Comics* 104) help students talk effectively about what is being conveyed in *Fun Home*'s drawings: for instance, in Bruce's "half-bull, half-man monster silhouette" looming above a frightened small Alison (12), in the panel in which Alison poignantly leans toward her father while they enjoy a sunset vista together (150), and in the closing image in which we look down over Alison's shoulder at her half-submerged father as she jumps toward his outstretched arms (232).

Narrative Worlds and Diegetic Levels

Abbott and McCloud present parallel discussions of narrative worlds and diegesis (Abbott) and of world building (McCloud) that prepare students to appreciate the sophisticated narratological commentaries readers like Warhol bring to *Fun Home*. As Warhol observes, "Broadly speaking, prose autobiography inhabits two diegetic locations, the space in which the present self speaks and the space in which the past self experiences the details that constitute the story," whereas autography introduces a "third diegetic level" in its graphic representations of characters, places, and incidents (3). Students find Warhol's analysis particularly trenchant when it draws on McCloud in discussing what Bechdel has called the *Fun Home* centerfold, the two-page drawing of a snapshot of the character Roy reclining seminude, with Alison's (or the reader's) hand running off the left-hand margin of the page.[6] Warhol quotes McCloud's observation that such an image, extending beyond the edge of the printed page, is "known in the print industry as a 'bleed'" and that a bleed "can, well . . . 'bleed' into our world" (7). Not only does that hand implicate the reader (whose real hand is imposed over the drawn hand) but, as Warhol also observes, many of the archival images in Bechdel's autography, such as maps, newspaper headlines, and photos, are "gestures toward real-world referents . . . material objects hailing the implied reader from the reader's world" (6). If there is an intrinsic rationale for approaching *Fun Home* with students who read it in tandem with texts of narrative theory, it is precisely in the way familiarity with narratological terms and concepts prepares them to take in, to appreciate, and to articulate for themselves thrilling insights like Warhol's and Chute's and thus to grasp more fully the meaning and power of *Fun Home* in all its complex emotional and thematic dimensions.

NOTES

[1] I am grateful to Robyn Warhol for having introduced me to *Fun Home* when we cotaught a sophomore honors seminar on narrative theory in 2007.

[2] Whitlock's 2006 essay was the first to apply the term *autographics* to comics autobiography, adapting the neologism from Leigh Gilmore's *Autobiographics: A Feminist Theory of Women's Self-Representation*. See also Whitlock and Poletti. Warhol opens her narratological study of *Fun Home* with a discussion of autography as a genre.

[3] McCloud dedicates *Making Comics* to Will Eisner, who coined the term *sequential art* for comics in his *Comics and Sequential Art*.

[4] McCloud's term *frame* here should not be confused with the panels themselves: by *choice of frame*, McCloud means how the comics artist frames each image as in the lens of a camera with respect to distance from the subject, angle of view, and cropping.

[5] *Fun Home* offers no examples of McCloud's sixth transition, the *non sequitur*, "a series of seemingly nonsensical, unrelated images and/or words" (*Making Comics* 15).

[6] My students have enjoyed debating whose hand is depicted in this image. As a James Marsh Professor-at-Large at the University of Vermont, Bechdel generously visits my class, and while it lies beyond the scope of this essay to discuss student interactions with her, I offer here two observations. The first is that at least half the class is pleased to have their reading of the hand affirmed when Bechdel tells them that she intended the drawn thumb and fingers to be as much the reader's as her own. The second is Bechdel's demonstration of the difficulty, when one is dealing with autography, of adhering to one of the basic principles of narrative theory, that a narrator is never to be confused with the author and that a character is always a narrative device, not to be muddled up with any conceivable flesh-and-blood model. "I know that," Bechdel has told my students, "I know I should just call her 'Alison,' but I just can't help referring to the figure in the book as myself, and I always fall into speaking of her in the first person."

Why Call Them Graphic Novels If They're True? Classifying *Fun Home*'s Mirrors

Michael A. Chaney

Like Art Spiegelman's *Maus*, Alison Bechdel's *Fun Home* may best be classified as an autobiographical graphic novel. Or, to put the matter in pedagogical terms, perhaps the question of classification is best left for students to pursue. With works like *Maus* or Marjane Satrapi's *Persepolis* to provide context, students may investigate the utility of a term like *autobiographical graphic novel* in relation to *Fun Home*. Through writing and discussion they may determine their comfort with or wariness of such taxonomies and genres, labels and definitions, in critical echo of Alison, concept detective par excellence. The term *graphic novel* is contradictory in relation to autobiography, because the latter is predicated on nearly legalistic claims about telling the truth, a concept made all the more problematic when rendered between symbol systems. How do the pictures of *Fun Home* tell truths that words alone cannot convey? Questions of this sort should produce rich classroom discussions of *Fun Home*, because comic art tends to tell the truth in a format that distorts reality, using illustrations that necessarily veer from the look and feel of real life. What sort of truths do graphic narratives tell using comics' inherent facility for distortion?

My students arrive at this conversation by grappling with issues of classification. When the question, what kind of narrative is *Fun Home*? is not simply a point of departure but a critical problem for students to linger over, classroom discussions are primed to explore concepts of self, truth, and reflexivity as well as their complex interplay in Bechdel's narrative. A helpful activity I have used for achieving this puts students into five groups; each group is assigned a different critical or theoretical excerpt that defines a key term. A later version of the activity invites students themselves to research possible excerpts for in-class use; for this activity, they read excerpts I provide and describe the extent to which Bechdel's text matches or differs from them. The five classificatory terms are as follows:

Autobiography. A big term that is rendered manageable for students by Sidonie Smith and Julia Watson's *Reading Autobiography*, covering the theorist Philippe Lejeune's notion of the autobiographical pact, a triumvirate unity of the author, narrator, and actor of autobiography (*Reading Autobiography* 11). As the visual universe of *Fun Home* exceeds Lejeune's categories of authority, students in this group are invited to articulate the intellectual consequences of Lejeune's literal oversight.

Autographics. Taken from Gillian Whitlock's path-finding essay of the same name, this excerpt provokes students to analyze Bechdel's text in terms of its verbal and visual relations and the gendered meanings of its compositions and areas of focalization. Students in this group are thus encouraged to ask, From whose point of view are particular scenes seen and to what effect?

Coming-out narratives. *The Cambridge History of American Literature* (Bercovitch and Patell) links coming-out narratives to gender oppression and to the struggles of individuals versus those of the collective, which students easily apply to the opposing cases of Alison and Bruce (561–62).

Family chronicle. A few lines from the *Routledge Encyclopedia of Narrative Theory* (Herman et al.) has students wondering if *Fun Home* focuses mainly on "the dissection of the family as an institution" or on the "travails of a family as a synecdoche for the development of a class or nation" (158).

Künstlerroman. In *Art, Alienation, and the Humanities*, Charles Reitz summarizes the ideas of the Frankfurt School theorist Herbert Marcuse, who, according to Reitz, saw in this subgenre of autobiography "the harsh duality of the ideal against the real, perceived by modern artists in the alienating quality of their life and activity vis-à-vis the general forms of social existence" (31). Follow-up questions ask students in this group to momentarily distinguish between two forms of becoming, or self-actualizing, that *Fun Home* entangles—that of the artist with that of the sexual adult.

This activity enables students to conceptualize *Fun Home* as a graphic novel in multiple senses: *graphic* in that the narrative prioritizes images and the alternative psychic and symbolic terrains that images open up in relation to words; *novel* in that the narrative has a spine, heft, scope, a sense of completeness to it—but also *novel* in the sense that, despite being the product of a disciplined regime of memory reconstruction, the narrative is a fiction or a construct. That drawn pictures help tell these stories lends them an air of self-reflexive knowingness—texts that seem aware of themselves as constructions of reality rather than as reflections of it, variations on the past rather than verities wrenched from it.

Students can be encouraged to ask these deep questions themselves about the text. One way, for instance, of getting students to consider subtle differences between the pictorial truths of similar texts is have them compare and contrast *Fun Home* as a book object with Bechdel's other major works, *Dykes to Watch Out For* and *Are You My Mother?* There may be as many groups as there are extra copies of the texts, or the comparisons may be conducted as a class. Questions of genre leap to the foreground as the novelesque qualities of the more typical autobiographies stand out against the teeming collection of strips in *Dykes to Watch Out For.* Interestingly, assigning alongside this activity excerpts on queer temporality and queer narrative from theorists such as Jack Halberstam and Lee Edelman leads some students to assert the diary-based

Dykes strips to be more queer in form than *Fun Home*, given their greater openness to subjects, people, and scenes of daily life. Of course, even firm conclusions may furnish the basis for elaboration in subsequent classroom activities geared to emphasize the less obvious radical or open connections *Fun Home* seeks to make within a tradition commercially and critically established by such works as *Persepolis* and *Maus*, Lynda Barry's *One Hundred Demons*, and Craig Thompson's *Blankets*.

Comparisons across the genre or even within Bechdel's own canon eventually point students to Bechdel's drawing style, and the obsessive, even erotic, attention Alison pays to drawing as a practice in her life and text. Because of the overtly drawn nature of every main character, no matter how true or not true the narration may be, the text comes to life by virtue of illustration's fictive lights. And even though my term for the larger genre, *autobiographical graphic novels*, is a mouthful when compared with *autography*, for example, I like the emphasis it places on the instabilities of truth the medium of comics conveys like no other. I also like to introduce students to how autobiographical graphic novels are self-conscious about their formal pictorial insincerities by way of Barry's exemplary opening scene from *One Hundred Demons*.

In two panels, Barry draws herself, cartoony, on what seems to be notebook paper, sitting at a drafting table. In one panel she muses, "Is it autobiography if parts of it are not true?" In the second she transmutes the question: "Is it fiction if parts of it are?" (7). Activities that urge students to attend to these panels aid understanding of the reflexive nature of Barry's graphic novel and its relation to the truth claims of autobiography. Students observe the position of Barry's avatar in the second panel, mirroring the self-portrait of herself, in miniature, that sits on the table before her. The mirror metaphorizes comics' unsteady fixation on unreliability and truth. The prevalence of mirror scenes in graphic memoirs is intriguing for any class reading *Fun Home*: David B.'s *Epileptic* opens with a mirror scene, as does *Persepolis*, where in the first panel Marji identifies herself distinctly from many other girls who seem to be little more than mirror versions of her in the second panel. Even beyond memoir, characters obsessively look into reflective rectangles—so much like the formal comics panel—in a range of comic narratives. Remember the young protagonist trying on his superhero mask in Chris Ware's *Jimmy Corrigan*, and Incognegro, the antilynching crusader of Mat Johnson and Warren Pleece's eponymous narrative? All seem to verify their cartoon existence by looking into mirrors.

Giving students snippets to read from Hillary L. Chute on Barry's use of collage and memory ("Materializing" 290–91) or from Lucien Dällenbach on the mirror in fine art (11) facilitates their understanding of Barry's gesture to inaugurate her autobiography in a space of self-reflexive hybridity—in between genres, as it were. Students may be invited to apply these ideas to significant panels in *Fun Home*. Are there similar mirrors in *Fun Home*, mirrors that make use of the dualities of revelation and fictionalization that underlie comics? Are there any literal mirrors, panels acting like mirrors, or panels seeming to contain mirrors, as with the picture-in-picture mechanics of the *mise en abyme*? What do mirrors do for characters? What do these mirror scenes accomplish for the narrative?

Apart from precipitating catharsis for characters or unity for the plot, some of the mirror scenes in *Fun Home*, as keen students will observe, position reader-viewers to question their assumptions about identity, sexuality, history, family, memory, reading, writing, and textuality—the text's capacity to convey reality. The results of such explorations will finally depend on the students' observation of the mirroring relations established between Alison and Bruce, beginnings and endings, life and literature. What Alison refers to as "the tricky reverse narration that impels our entwined stories" (232) cues readers to one of the most powerful mirroring devices at work in *Fun Home*, one students never fail to notice though it often frustrates their ability to explain. Unlike the tidier examples from Barry or Satrapi, Bechdel's mirroring of panels takes place across the entire narrative, a novel, an autobiography, and a family chronicle (and here we may add a host of other possible classifications—epic, myth, adaptation, family album, biography, and so on). The point is that no span could be imagined as longer within the universe of narrative, no matter the genre, than the opening and the end of the story. The activities outlined above encourage students to see the first and last panels in *Fun Home* as a type of mirror, joining the symbolic birth and death of our entry into and out of the narrative in weird tandem with the characters' journeys into and out of their closets, a course that ends, in the case of Bruce, out of life and into death.

When asked—as reading questions, prompts for in-class writing, or in small-group discussions—to distinguish panels in *Fun Home* containing mirrors from those that perform mirroring functions themselves, students inevitably wrestle with many of the same deep logics of relation and resemblance that perplex Alison. A successful activity with my students walks them through slides dissecting the mirror scenes in Barry along with a few critical passages from Chute on Barry's material entwinement of gender, trauma, and truth. Another slide illustrates the similar mechanics at work in a panel from *Persepolis*, showing Marji before a background whose symbols, the caption tells us, are variously associated with the West and the Middle East. The mirroring dynamic here is clarified with reference to a few key sentences from Whitlock's "Autographics" essay. Armed with these two examples, students may be prompted to identify an analogical mirror panel in *Fun Home*. The only missing element would be another critical excerpt, and this is where we follow up the classification activity: students select critical excerpts related to any significant aspect of *Fun Home* and bring them to class to study alongside the example of panel mirroring.

Despite *Fun Home*'s immanent insistence on a universe entirely drawn by its creator, so much of what is in the text depends on other texts. Once prodded by the text's many verbal allusions, students can easily see the connections between the relationship Alison has with her father and the fatal one Icarus has with his. Students are likely to point out these allusions and others, particularly the heartbreaking symmetry of *Fun Home*'s opening panels and closing panels—in the opening young Alison plays airplane with her father, who hoists her up with his feet in a kind of mirror image of the closing panel, where he is poised to catch her fall at the swimming pool. The visuals coordinate with the written story. But as this is a graphic *novel*, students do well to notice the allusions offered by the pictures, too, such as the mirrored expressions on Alison and Bruce's faces—of mute wonder, half-surprise (having students describe or imitate the expression goes a long way to prod their analysis of it). This similarity of expression tells a different sort of tale about the desire for sameness—one that is not a choice but an inheritance. Students could be pushed to read the visuals against the verbal grain of the narrative further, scouring the Internet for images of faces that seem similar. Kewpie dolls, emojis, even Waldo, from the *Where's Waldo?* phenomenon, may be helpful in piecing together an image repertoire that informs *Fun Home*—whether consciously or not, directly or allusively.

Don't Read This:
Fun Home as Contemporary Visual Culture

Alexis L. Boylan

In my contemporary art history and visual culture courses it is hard to truly shock the students. They are not necessarily especially cosmopolitan, deeply versed in art theory, or endlessly open to new ideas. They are, however, students (BA, BFA, and MFA candidates) who seem to find little at stake in policing the boundaries of what is, or is not, art: such a conversation just does not interest them. They see the art-or-not-art debate as an old fight that has been resolved. A toilet as sculpture? Great. Self-mutilation as performance? Sounds interesting. Random collections of objects tossed together and staged in warehouses? Knock yourself out. Nudity, violence, mixed media—they embrace it all as art, no questions asked. They may not like it, but taste and aesthetics, they readily explain to me, are another matter. Censorship exists, but it concerns systems and culture and the law, not students' definitions of art. For my students, if the creator says it is art or if someone else in the room says it is art, then it is art. Case closed.

Welcoming this spirit of openness and experimentation, I often incorporate novels, films, theater, and music into my contemporary visual arts syllabi. Students seldom balk at this, and so I thought nothing of bringing Alison Bechdel's *Fun Home* into both mid-level undergraduate classes and graduate-level seminars. The conversations about the text were smart and engaged, and the students responded to Bechdel's work with complexity and thoughtfulness. All was fine until I offhandedly asked my undergraduates how they would compare Bechdel with other contemporary artists they considered during the term. The question was not meant to be hard or controversial, just a prompt to connect the work to the broader themes of the course. The discussion went dead. Surprised, I tried the question from a different angle, asking them to consider Bechdel in regard to other visual artists who engage text. Again, crickets. Finally, a student offered that Bechdel isn't a contemporary artist but a novelist, a writer, a graphic novelist. I pressed the student, but the whole class seemed to agree. Everything is art, except *Fun Home*, because *Fun Home* is a novel. It is art but not visual art, which meant that Bechdel was not a contemporary visual artist but an author. All of a sudden these laid-back, freethinking students turned into strict guardians of disciplinary boundaries. I argued all the obvious points, even appealing to the illustrators in the class, but no one budged. Incredulous, I took this conversation to my graduate class, and they agreed with the undergraduates. *Fun Home* is literature, and I was being obtuse in suggesting otherwise. Narrative play and textual art were one thing—bring on Félix González-Torres, Glenn Ligon, and Mary Kelly—but Bechdel's rightful home was in an English department.

The comics scholar Hillary Chute persuasively argues that "comics might be defined as a hybrid word-and-image form in which two narrative tracks, one verbal and one visual, register temporality spatially" ("Comics as Literature?" 452). Yet more often than not the verbal register receives the most attention, both in the classroom and critically, while the imagery of graphic narratives is tended to primarily when it is in antagonism or tension with the words on the page (Chute, *Graphic Women*; Meskin; Miodrag). There is great value in pushing students to see *Fun Home* as primarily a visual text and, more specifically, as a work of contemporary visual art production. In this essay I briefly discuss a few strategies for teaching *Fun Home* as a visual text in conversation with other contemporary visual artists. The resistance my students felt, I believe, mimics a disciplinary divide that they see, and that is encouraged, in the academy; fine arts and creative writing, art history and literature, not to mention theater, music, and design, are often housed in physically separate locations on campus, a separation that is replicated in larger art institutions and in the marketplace. This fissure can be an opportunity to assess what constitutes art and how different forms and materials get categorized and quarantined. *Fun Home* is a conduit for productive debates about what exactly qualifies as contemporary art, about the boundaries of the visual and the verbal, and about how to be more attentive and skeptical about visual work.

So what happens if we think about *Fun Home* as primarily a visual text? I can certainly understand that many readers of the present collection of essays, published by the Modern Language Association, will sigh in frustration at this proposition, as graphic novels have only recently gained value as literature. To have graphic novels reclaimed as visual objects might seem like regression. Likewise, I appreciate that, for those who study literature, it might appear as if our students are drowning in visual culture and imagery. Yet, as an art historian, I would caution that the deluge of images has not necessarily made students more critical viewers or able to discern meaning in imagery. In fact, most media images are so seductive and designed to appear obvious and innocuous that many students are disinclined to look with care, time, or critical distance. By the time they get to college courses, students are far more seasoned at unpacking texts than they are at analyzing visual imagery. As a result students often see the images of graphic novels as simply supporting the text, offering benign and docile visual aids to enhance the words on the page.

A first task then is to help students read the images independent of the text. A good place to start this work, and where I like to begin the conversation about *Fun Home*, is by engaging its first two pages and then its last page. Ask the students to look at the images and not the text—if possible, isolate the images on a *PowerPoint* slide to aid focus on the imagery alone. In the first three panels of the book, Bechdel draws the progression, from three distinct perspectives, that connect her body to her father's. Even without Bechdel's textual narration, the images of a game of airplane, where a child floats in the air supported by an adult's feet, are familiar. It is a game that is both intimate and occasionally uncomfortable for both parties. Yet it allows a parent to accommodate a child's desire to defy corporeality and gravity, to help the child fly. The last panel on the last page replicates this physical act, when Alison (at the same age as on the first page) is again in mid-air, hovering above her father, defying gravity and the sting of the water that she will fall into. It can take students some time to notice this mirroring, but it is productive to point out to them that this repeated imagery is a deliberate choice on Bechdel's part, which connects her body to her father's and highlights familial play with physicality. Continuing to focus on images rather than words, instructors can push students to consider potential shifts in perspective and authority: Does isolating the images make us think differently about Bechdel and her father? What is suggested about their intimacy? Why does Bechdel start and end with her body supported in flight? Do we think differently about how the words and images work, together or against each other, in this moment? Dwelling on these scenes can help students understand the need to read the images and consider visual choices as carefully as they do the written text. Bechdel's visual story is as complex as her verbal one, and it often emphasizes issues she cannot—or will not—write.

Getting students comfortable analyzing Bechdel's complex visual dialogues is critical for the next step, linking *Fun Home* to wider visual cultures and contemporary art conventions and conversations. For this, it is helpful to look at moments when Bechdel literally and figuratively draws the viewer to see the power of imagery to define the self and desire. If *Fun Home* broadly confronts issues of identity and family, it specifically asks how we represent ourselves and signify that self to others. For Bechdel, the answer is found in visuality. Early in the text, Bechdel builds a case for her childhood home as a visceral space reflective of the central antagonisms within her family. She focuses the reader on her father's penchant for Victorian antiques and what she perceives as his overly fussy, overly obsessive attention to decorative objects. This comes to a fine point when Bechdel writes, "I was Spartan to my father's Athenian. Modern to his Victorian. Butch to his nelly. Utilitarian to his aesthete" (15). Crucially, Bechdel here speaks to both taste and sexuality, identifying both as fundamental and intertwined. Not all students readily understand the full meanings of the terms *Athenian* and *nelly*, terms that are themselves markers of class, taste, and education. Pulling back to the images on the page is helpful, highlighting the ways in which Bechdel positions and dresses her younger self in opposition to her father and his form. It can also open up a productive discussion of the ways in which aesthetics stand in for things that cannot be said easily or at all. Here I introduce the concept of camp, Susan Sontag's "Notes on Camp," and Oscar Wilde's use of his body and clothing as a visual canvas as examples for thinking about the long histories of embodiment, sexuality, and aesthetics. This is also a great opportunity to talk about two divergent theories of aesthetics that are essential for contemporary visual culture: Pierre Bourdieu's *Distinction* and Nicolas Bourriaud's *Relational Aesthetics*. In Bechdel's text, aesthetics mark difference, and throughout *Fun Home* the author points to objects, texts, and images as crucial to her self-definition. But do these aesthetic choices really signify anything beyond class yearnings, as Bourdieu might suggest? Are these choices that simply differentiate and make distinctions without offering the possibility of bringing Bechdel and her family together? Are aesthetics always alienating? Or, as Bourriaud might suggest, should we think of aesthetics as a progressive and unifying power? Finally, to make things more complicated, I like to bring in Glenn Ligon's powerful confrontation with race, sexuality, and taste, *Notes on the Margin of the Black Book* ("Glenn Ligon"). The project confronts the power of images to shape or unsettle our self and sexuality in ways that, like Bechdel's, trouble the relation of words and images. Bringing together Ligon, Bechdel, Sontag, Bourdieu, and Borriaud helps students to process the problem of aesthetics in our contemporary moment.

This is but one way to use the contemporary and the visual to interrogate *Fun Home*. I would also encourage spending time with Bechdel's images about writing and overwriting in her diary, which provide wonderful opportunities to speak to erasure and obscuring as powerful tools of expression. Students respond well to a comparison of Bechdel's kind of clarifying and masking with Robert Rauschenberg's erasure in 1953 of a Willem de Kooning drawing ("Robert Rauschenberg"). Just as Bechdel's words are not disappeared, Rauschenberg cannot erase de Kooning's lines. This comparison can inspire a good conversation about mark-making, censorship, and memory. Likewise, comparing how Bechdel reproduced as a drawing the photograph of her former babysitter that her father kept (*Fun Home* 100–01) with the art of Sherrie Levine (specifically Levine's photographs of earlier photographs, such as her After Walker Evans series from the early 1980s) and that of González-Torres provides rich possibilities to talk about reproduction, postmodernism, and even Roland Barthes and the power of photography and images. Likewise, Alison's experience seeing the calendar with a naked woman on the cover (112–13) offers an excellent opportunity to introduce Mickalene Thomas's paintings and Grayson Perry's tapestries to generate a conversation about imagery, desire, and gender.

My teaching of *Fun Home* emphasizes choices that Bechdel makes as a contemporary artist. Placing her work in conversation with other contemporary visual artists does not limit the work to narrow disciplinary codes but broadens *Fun Home*'s complexity. *Fun Home* is, after all, not tangential to visual culture but deeply embedded in contemporary visual dialogues, highlighting the power, potential, and limitations of the visual. It is good to look—really look—sometimes.

Photo Graft:
Revision, Reclamation, and the Graphic Photo

David Bahr

> Certainly drawing this about my family, it felt like I
> was—and all the pictures of my dad, with close-ups of his
> face—it was really like touching him.
>
> —Alison Bechdel

> From a phenomenological viewpoint, in the Photograph,
> the power of authentication exceeds the power of
> representation.
>
> —Roland Barthes

In 2013 I taught the first comics course at my community college. I called it
Rebels, Rousers, and the Graphic Narrative and included *Maus* by Art Spiegelman, *Persepolis* by Marjane Satrapi, and *Fun Home*, Alison Bechdel's memoir
about growing up queer with a closeted gay father whose early death may or
may not have been a suicide. I conceived of the seminar two years earlier at a
private liberal arts college, where *Fun Home* was popular with students. This
time, however, my students—mostly from urban areas, some struggling with
writing skills—were less keen on *Fun Home*, largely because of the literary allusions and vocabulary.[1] To work through this resistance, I focused on the family
photograph as a site of memory and revision.

My interest in the family photograph is charged. A former foster child, I became a ward of the state at eighteen months old. My mother, Sadie, single and
battling mental illness, reclaimed me within six years but still could not raise
me, and, by age ten, I was returned to the care of the state. Five years later, Sadie died of cancer. Aside from a couple of cousins I barely knew, my mother was
the sole blood relative in my life. I possess one photo of her, which I took while
I was at a boarding school for troubled youth. I have studied the image for hours
in search of clues of who she was and who I have become. It has prevented me
from forgetting the twist of her closed-lipped smile, the sad cast of her gaze, her
tattered clothes. For my doctoral dissertation on autobiography and the psychological breakdown, I wrote a chapter on comics, at the end of which I attempted
an illustration of my mother. The attention required to draw the photo invited
a troubling yet illuminating intimacy.[2] Consequently, Bechdel's use of the illustrated photograph—as a means of revision and reclamation—speaks to me. And
I bring that personal connection into my teaching of *Fun Home*.

Each of the seven chapters of *Fun Home* begins with an illustration of a personal photograph. Elsewhere in the memoir, there are over half a dozen drawings
of photos, not including two passport pictures, several snapshots of literary icons

and their families, and one photonegative strip. Many students were disinclined to engage with the memoir, which they found wordy and unrelatable. In response, I devoted an entire class on Bechdel's use of the illustrated photograph, or, *photo-graphics*, as I call it. I asked students to bring in an old family snapshot. Intrigued, a few wondered why. Many had not yet recognized the formal and thematic significance of the photograph in *Fun Home*. I wanted them to think about the illustrated photograph as a narrative tool and heuristic device.

I began the lesson by asking students to freewrite about what they perceived to be the purpose of illustrated photographs in Bechdel's memoir, notably those serving as visual epigraphs at the beginning of each chapter. We had already discussed *Fun Home* as a recursive narrative—one that obsessively returns to and retraces historical events (like the father's possible suicide)—and several students identified these opening images as temporal place markers. The illustrated photos situate the reader within a specific moment in the Bechdel family history that Alison revisits. I then invited the class to explore the strategies and effects of the drawn photograph. This line of inquiry encouraged students to think further about comics as a mode of mediating the world. How is a photograph—retraced and reimagined—transformed by the human hand? How is the mediation of an already mediated artifact a means of reclaiming, reimagining, and revising? How might the drawing of a photograph simultaneously demystify and obscure its subject? And, finally, how might discussion prompted by these questions add to our understanding of Bechdel's memoir, perhaps encouraging identification with her process?

In *Graphic Women*, Hillary Chute addresses some of these questions in relation to Bechdel's composition of *Fun Home*, particularly in regard to the mediation of an already mediated artifact as a means of reclaiming, reimagining, and revising (176–217). Chute notes how Bechdel re-created family photographs by photographing herself posing as the subject of those photos, adding an additional layer of mediation between the family photo and the illustrated snapshot. According to Chute, *Fun Home*'s narration is rooted in acts of looking at archives: "in *Fun Home* the regeneration of archives is about asserting the power of comics as a form to include and also to fruitfully *repurpose* archives, not about solving any epistemological crisis" (200). I would add that while comics' use of archives might not solve an epistemological crises, such repurposing of archives could in fact raise questions that produce an epistemological crisis. This crisis may be fruitful and cause the author-cartoonist to view archives differently, experiencing them anew. As Chute notes, Bechdel's drawn photos tell readers little about her past, which remains "ambiguous" and "blurry" (200). But as an excavator of my own disintegrating history, my interest is in how illustrating personal archives can be a means of discovery for the illustrator, and, in turn, for readers of *Fun Home*.

Drawing my mother, I sketched an adjacent self-portrait, our ears interlocked (fig. 1). This effect unexpectedly highlighted a psychic bond.[3] As I closely examined the photo to re-create her distinct eyes, mouth, chin, and forehead, such

Figure 1. Self-portrait of the author with his mother.

attention resurrected our shared emotional lability through the unraveling lines of my mouth, her furrowed brow and worried orbs for eyes. In my class, I shared the illustration of my mother as well as the photo on which it was based. Unlike Bechdel's precise photographic reproductions, my drawing is not meant to be a faithful replica but a product of memory and archival inspiration. Likewise, I encouraged my students, who possessed a wide range of drafting talent, to sketch an image based on, or inspired by, a family photograph. First, I asked students to freewrite a paragraph or two about the snapshots they brought to class, jotting down whatever came to mind. Most students focused on positive and idealized aspects. One woman, Sherlin Minaya, noted how "happy" a great-aunt looked and that she seemed to have forgotten "all her problems." Another student, Grace Mathre, observed how, in a picture of her grandparents, "even in photographs my grandpa was reserved, yet [in this photo] his love [for his wife] is still captured." I then asked them to draw the photo. I went around the room, offering encouragement, especially to those who seemed insecure about their drawing skills. I reminded students of the expressive power of comics, referring to the underground comix artists of the late 1960s and early 1970s, which we'd studied at the beginning of the semester. After about twenty minutes of drafting, I asked students to write a page about their drawn image, reimagining the story behind, and the people within, their photographs.

The experience of one student, Kelvin Santos, best encapsulates the process of discovery experienced by many in the class. Beneath his sketch of a Polaroid of a man and woman, he identified the woman as his mother in Santo Domingo, Dominican Republic—she often went there to see her mother (fig. 2). "I'm going on memory here," he cautioned. The couple is "dressed up," so he guessed that "they were having fun," and added, "I think this is the only time I don't see my mother stressed out in a picture."

Figure 2. Kelvin Santos, drawing after a photograph of his mother and a man.

As he continued to reflect on the photograph, questions emerged. "My mother looks young in this picture and writing about it is beginning to trigger some of my old memories about where this might be. . . . My mom never left my side without her taking me with her unless it was important or she had some lover on the side. So this could probably be one of her boyfriends from her past that I didn't know about." As Kelvin wrote further, his memory and imagination caught fire. "I remember the guy taking care of me when I went to the Dominican Republic. He used to take me on his motorcycle around the beach . . . when I was bored at my grandmother's house." Still, he doubted himself. "It's hard to tell if he actually was my mother's boyfriend or if he is my uncle. I've never heard from him again but he is in some pictures of my father's side [of] the family." This epistemological crisis caused him to reflect on the process. "This is pretty interesting how I have no full memory of this guy . . . and I'm beginning to wonder if he was important in my life." He concluded: "The more I think and look at the picture, the more I begin to wonder who the hell was this guy and why is he so important that I found this picture I didn't even know we had in a photo book we keep."

As it did for Kelvin, the exercise problematized initial idealizations of family photos for a number of students, raising questions about a picture's date, location, and narrative context. Interestingly, most responses centered around loss. Often the photographic subjects were dead, estranged, or never personally known. Alicia Hoe wrote, "Doing the photo assignment, specifically of a family member that I don't have any memory of—my grandfather—really brought me closer to the subject. It made me wish I was closer to him. . . . I wonder if [Bechdel] drawing photos of her father helped her feel a sense of closeness with him on paper, much like I did with my grandfather." While *Fun Home* remained not relatable for some students, the exercise caused many students to express a greater appreciation of Bechdel's technique. Grace wrote, "Bechdel's process of going back and forth between what she knows firsthand and secondhand makes sense now. She uses the flashbacks to help set the tone, as well as fill in the missing info. Using photos helps us understand the space a person was in. The picture is a way of getting a glimpse of who someone was that we may have never met." Grace added how she "loved drawing" her grandfather because she "focused on details [she'd] never looked at before: his nose, his eyes, his hands, etc. It was quite cathartic, actually."

Although all my students did not share my passion for, and identification with, Bechdel's comic, the photographic exercise proved to be pedagogically useful in helping them think about the critical work that *Fun Home* is doing. Bechdel has stated about the work's genesis: "I do think I sensed on some level that if language was unreliable, and appearances were deceiving, then maybe somehow by *triangulating* between them, you could manage to get a little closer to the truth" (Chute, *Graphic Women* 191). My goal in conceiving the course was to deepen students' understanding and appreciation for what graphic narratives can do, and in this sense the exercise was effective. I was moved by students' reflections and saw Bechdel's story as belonging to a larger communal narrative of loss, especially as it pertains to individual and collective memories. "Our memory is never fully 'ours,' nor are the pictures ever unmediated representations of our past," Jo Spence and Patricia Holland have stated about family photographs. "Looking at them we both construct a fantastic past and set out on a detective trail to find other versions of a 'real' one" (13–14). My student Richard Lee, unfamiliar with the work of Spence and Holland, came to a similar conclusion after participating in the class exercise: "most 'posed' photos don't depict the truth, but rather something we're trying to be. The 'candid' or 'off-guard' photos are more likely to depict the truth at a particular moment. However, with time, the 'truth' *changes* because our memory is bad and quite possibly because we change, as [do] our interpretation/interpretive skills."

NOTES

This essay was made possible by a Borough of Manhattan Community College faculty development grant.
[1] I wrote about this experience in my essay "Outside the Box."
[2] See Bahr, "Labile Lines."
[3] See Bahr, "The Things We Carry" and "No Matter What Happens."

Is It Okay to Laugh?
Bechdel and the Triumph of Gallows Humor

Audrey Bilger

A few pages before the conclusion of Alison Bechdel's *Fun Home*, an eight-frame sequence depicts Alison's memory of being asked by someone in a record store how her summer is going, shortly after her father's death. First, she says, "Okay. I'm working in the library," then, laughing, she adds, "Oh, and my father died!" Her interlocutor, believing she must be joking because of the laughter, replies, "Right. Good one." At this point, Alison, declares, "No, I'm serious! He did!" To prove her veracity, she physically pulls her lips down into a forced frown, and repeats, "My father died," but she cannot keep a straight face and in the next frame begins to laugh uncontrollably, declaring, "He got—ha, ha, ha—hit by a truck!" In a text-only frame, the narrative commentary explains, "The idea that my vital, passionate father was decomposing in a grave was ridiculous." An image of Alison doubled over in laughter, her acquaintance looking on, perplexed, concludes the scene (227). Even though *Fun Home* is not a comedy, the book repeatedly invokes and deploys humor. The title is an inside family joke ("fun home" being short for funeral home), and the subtitle, "A Family Tragicomic," refers simultaneously to comics as a genre and to the memoir's intertwining of the comic and the tragic.[1] Bechdel dedicates the book to the surviving members of her nuclear family, highlighting the bright side: "We did have a lot of fun, in spite of everything."

When I decided to teach *Fun Home* in a first-year writing seminar entitled The Power of Laughter, I knew that students would resist the idea of seeing anything laughable about the book and that they would probably wonder why it was on the syllabus at all. Having taught courses on humor, comedy, and satire for over two decades, however, I have found that once students learn to think theoretically about the relation between comedy and tragedy, they come to understand that the comic spirit functions not just as a diversion but as a temporary respite from the certain knowledge that death is the end of human life and as a strategy for survival in the face of ambiguity. I placed *Fun Home* toward the end of the course so that by the time we reached it students would have already read other works of literature that show how tragedy and defeat hover in the margins of even the lightest and brightest comedies. For example, in the resolution of Shakespeare's *Much Ado About Nothing*, Hero, after being forced to fake her own death, achieves the classic comic happy ending of marriage, but the restoration of her reputation and honor takes place in a manner so arbitrary and coincidental (Dogberry and the night watch happen to overhear the plot against her and eventually reveal what they know) that it's just as easy to see how the play could have concluded as a tragedy. Similarly, Jane Austen's *Pride and Prejudice* takes a grim turn in the last third of the novel, and Elizabeth Bennet just barely makes it to the altar with Darcy, benefiting from the insulting visit from Lady Catherine de Bourgh, an incident that again almost accidentally leads to the comic finale (Lady Catherine tells Darcy that Elizabeth would not refuse to marry him). Comedy is a hard-won victory, a removal of obstacles to happiness, and we like to celebrate with the winners.

In *Fun Home*, Bechdel invites us to consider the proximity of tragedy to comedy in human life, as she struggles to make sense of her family, her identity, and her father's untimely death. When Alison returns home for her father's funeral and sees her brother, we are told—and shown—that they "greeted each other with ghastly, uncontrollable grins" (46). An explanation for this incongruous response appears in a block of text above a frame with a closeup image of Alison's and her brother's grinning faces: "It could be argued that death is inherently absurd, and that grinning is not necessarily an inappropriate response. I mean absurd in the sense of ridiculous, unreasonable. One second a person is there, the next they're not." In a box inserted between the two faces, another statement continues in a darker vein: "Though perhaps Camus' definition of the absurd—that the universe is irrational and human life meaningless—applies here as well" (47). Absurd, ridiculous, unreasonable, irrational—death leads us to question the meaning of life. Alison's and her brother's grins are an incongruous response to the gravity of the moment. Their frozen expressions are both intimate and detached in ways that resonate throughout the book.

Although comic theorists tend to agree that there is no universal sense of humor—so much of what makes people laugh is inflected by culture, place, and time—one unifying element across most types of comedy is incongruity. Alison's grin and laughter at the ridiculousness of her father being dead are not idiosyncratic expressions of inexplicable mirth but actually illuminate something fundamental about the way humor operates. Freud's theory of humor as a coping mechanism for dealing with harsh realities provides a useful lens to help students make sense of *Fun Home*. In the 1927 essay "Humour," Freud expresses the view that humor provides people with a measure of control over distressing circumstances. To illustrate this point, he shares what he calls "the crudest example," an anecdote about "a criminal who was being led out to the gallows on a Monday," who says, "'Well, the week's beginning nicely.'" Here the man about to die is afforded a "certain sense of satisfaction" from his own humorous observation. Freud imagines himself as a "non-participating listener" to the criminal's remark, able to "feel, like him, perhaps, the yield of humorous pleasure" (161). This example fits the term *gallows humor,* a mode of dark humor that allows the subject to triumph over reality and that provides vicarious pleasure to those who hear or observe that victory. Central to Freud's theory is the notion of the "humorous attitude" as an active stance that can be shared by a reader or hearer: "To sum up, then, we can say that the humorous attitude— whatever it may consist in—can be directed either towards the subject's own self or towards other people; it is to be assumed that it brings a yield of pleasure to the person who adopts it, and a similar yield of pleasure falls to the share of the non-participating onlooker" (161). Those who adopt the humorous stance reap great benefits, according to Freud: "Humour is not resigned; it is rebellious. It signifies not only the triumph of the ego but also of the pleasure principle, which is able here to assert itself against the unkindness of the real circumstances" (163). Freud views humor as "the victorious assertion of the ego's invulnerability" (162) and posits the superego as an atypically benevolent figure when it comes to humor, associated with a parent, especially a father, who "tries, by means of humour, to console the ego and protect it from suffering" (166).

Students in my seminar responded well to the idea of humor as an act of rebellion and to the idea that humor yields pleasure for writers and readers alike. Students participated in an online discussion forum, where they posted twice for each session, once before and again after the class, reflecting on what they had learned. In their earliest posts on *Fun Home,* they grappled with the difference between this book and our other literary selections and sought to articulate the relation between text and image, which I emphasized as an added dimension for interpretation. In one student discussion post, Aviva Bhansali said that she had discovered that in *Fun Home,* "words and images perfectly complement each other to generate dark humor." Christophe Rimann remarked on the way that "Bechdel repeatedly chooses imagery that is at odds with what is written" and suggested that she "questions the trustworthiness of the visual."

In examining humorous incongruities, students also gained an appreciation of the twin stories of Alison's coming out and the discovery of her father's secret affairs with young men. That Alison learns about her father's sexuality shortly after coming out to her parents in a letter is highly ironic, something that Bechdel accentuates in the commentary: "I'd been upstaged, demoted from protagonist in my own drama to comic relief in my parents' tragedy" (58). Philippa (Pippa) Straus was struck by this moment and analyzed it in one of her posts:

> Here, Bechdel reveals that she felt as though her father's sexuality rendered her own sexual orientation secondary, a footnote on her parents'

"tragedy" rather than a distinguishing individual characteristic. She seems almost to have wanted [her sexual identity] to separate and render her distinct from her parents, and seems upset that it played again into a narrative about her father rather than herself. . . . Despite the fact that she seems to somewhat resent this part of her identity being co-opted by her father, she nevertheless almost yearns for that connection which she did not have with him when he was alive, almost hoping that her coming out is tied to his death, in what she calls "that last tenuous bond."

Other students registered the father's closeted life as a product of his era, contrasting it with Alison's greater opportunities for sexual freedom and the positive trajectory of her life.

In their final posts on *Fun Home*, students applauded Bechdel's ability to present her unusual family in a relatable fashion. They expressed their identification with Alison's coming-of-age and recognized aspects of their own stories in her simultaneous desire for independence and fierce attachment to her family. They viewed the last frame of the book, with its statements about the "tricky reverse narration" and the image of Alison leaping into her father's raised arms, as defiant concluding gestures belonging more to comedy than tragedy (232). Khadija Hassanali, referring to Freud, noted that the book is "filled with incongruities that, although [they] may not be completely resolved in the end, come very close to a resolution, allowing the audience to experience some humor or relief." Mingliang Zhang wrote, "By adopting a lighthearted attitude, convincing herself that her father has almost an eternal presence in her life, Bechdel diminishes the suffering from her loss. In a way, Bechdel's father does live metaphorically [in the book]." Adriana Lopez echoed, "I would definitely agree that Bechdel brings her father back to life at the end of her book."

By including *Fun Home* in a class focused on laughter and humor, I wanted students to see how Bechdel puts gallows humor to serious use. I also wanted to complicate their understanding of comedy in a more general sense. One student, Jie Tang, perfectly expressed in her last post on the memoir what I was hoping to convey in the class: "I love Bechdel's ending. It is a perfect reflection [of the book's] beginning and gives me the sense that her father has never truly died, but extends his life in Bechdel's memory. In this sense, though she mainly discusses the negative part of her family and childhood, the ending can still be considered as a comedy. . . . [T]he comic can be tragicomic." In fact, humor and comedy can be all the more satisfying when blended with the tragic. The victory is bigger, and the laughter lasts.

NOTE

[1] Bechdel titles her follow-up family memoir *Are You My Mother? A Comic Drama*, its subtitle a playful reversal of *Fun Home*'s that once again has a double meaning and invites the reader to conflate comics and comedy.

"Ring of Keys":
Butch Lesbianism, Queer Theory, and
the Lessons of *Fun Home*

Dana Heller

I begin this essay with a classroom discussion question: how does the culture dictate the terms of lesbian visibility and vision to the exclusion of what actually appears before our eyes? For many of my students, mainstream popular culture's dalliances with girl-on-girl attraction, such as Katy Perry's 2008 bubblegum hit, "I Kissed a Girl," overwrite Alison Bechdel's *Fun Home*, creating a contradictory palimpsest of media myths and the text itself. A case in point: when ten-year-old Alison unfurls a calendar pinup that her father warns her not to look at because "it's dirty," students tend to misread the visual encounter as a pleasurable first brush with same-sex desire. In fact, when young Alison disobeys her father and confronts the image of a naked woman she feels only distress and humiliation. In Bechdel's words, "I felt as if I'd been stripped naked myself, inexplicably ashamed, like Adam and Eve" (112). How could Alison's traumatic disidentification with the pinup be interpreted as pleasurable?

Another disturbing visual encounter occurs in *Fun Home* a few pages later (fig. 1). Young Alison is having lunch with her father in a Philadelphia diner, when she suddenly beholds "a most unsettling sight," something she's never before seen (117). A butch lesbian truck driver with cropped hair, dungarees, flannel shirt, and a large ring of keys hanging from her belt loop swaggers into the diner. In that instant, Alison is awestruck, her world opening to possibilities that she has never before imagined. "I didn't know there were women who wore

Figure 1. Alison Bechdel, *Fun Home*, p. 118.

men's clothes and had men's haircuts," Bechdel writes. "But like a traveler in a foreign country who runs into someone from home—someone they've never spoken to, but know by sight—I recognized her with a surge of joy" (118). Many of my students have misread this joy as sexual desire or as Alison's awakening to lesbian sexuality. On the contrary, to me it seems quite clear that Alison is not sexually attracted to the masculine woman; rather, she apprehends the enticing possibility of becoming one herself.

Taken together, Alison's viewing of the calendar pinup and the butch are about not the initial stirrings of sexual arousal but the beginning of "gender trouble," an unsettling of the apparently oppositional and natural categories of masculine and feminine (Butler).

To put it another way, Alison's different emotional reactions to two different viewing encounters of two different female bodies are linked by a visual rhetoric of disidentification and identification, a disruptive practice with roots in queer theory that exposes the failure of normative gender and opens up prospects for reclaiming that which feminist literary history and the cultural imagination have rendered largely invisible and unthinkable: the butch dyke. These textual moments also encapsulate a major theme of *Fun Home*, as well as a problem I've confronted in teaching it. Thematically, *Fun Home* is a book about disidentification and the queer body. It's about the predicament of misrecognizing oneself in a father who appears inexplicably strange and the joy of recognizing oneself in a stranger who appears inexplicably familiar. The problem is getting my students to disidentify, or simply suspend, their own assumptions about gender and queerness and to open themselves to the possibility of identifying with the butch.

I teach *Fun Home* as a book about the triumphs and perils of queer disidentification, which enables deviations from normative practices of seeing and doing femininity. As a graphic memoir with aesthetic origins in queer comics, *Fun Home* enables us to see femininity and masculinity differently and therefore encourages a thorough interrogation of the means by which gender is rendered socially visible. For this reason, *Fun Home* is a narrative that could only be conveyed through the logic of comics, which Scott McCloud calls "the invisible art" in the subtitle of *Understanding Comics*. According to McCloud, in their unique formal fusion of words and images, comics breach "the wall of ignorance that prevents so many human beings from seeing each other clearly . . . " (198). *Fun Home* demonstrates that graphic texts can elucidate gender differences in ways previously unexplored. The challenge is getting my students to pay attention to the visual cues and to recognize the work as less a memoir about sex and death than a joyful record of butch survival against the odds.

Fun Home is the final text I assign in an upper-level undergraduate course, Women Writers, which is populated with English majors, the majority of whom will become secondary public-school teachers. Our reading list begins with Mary Shelley's *Frankenstein* and proceeds through Kate Chopin's *The Awakening*, Zora Neale Hurston's *Their Eyes Were Watching God*, Toni Morrison's *Sula*, Maxine Hong Kingston's *The Woman Warrior*, and Marjane Satrapi's *Persepolis*, with stops at Virginia Woolf's *A Room of One's Own* and Adrienne Rich's *When We Dead Awaken*. By the time we reach *Fun Home*, my students have been immersed in monstrous mayhem, casual infidelity, sexual betrayal, suicide, homicide, madness, alienation, loss, and bloody revolution. Asking them to see *Fun Home* as an uplifting finale to the class may be a tall order. But my hope is that they will leave the course understanding the social and material conditions that enabled women to enter the literary marketplace as professional writers, the strategies through which women writers have sought to establish literary authority and community, the cultural anxieties that have long framed women's public voices as suspect and scandalous, the formal echoes that allow us to imagine lines of artistic influence and aesthetic commonality in women's literature, and the differences among women writers that ultimately make a category that contains them too heterogeneous to imagine in general terms.

Fun Home marks the end of the course, yet at the same time it returns us full circle to the semester's opening conversations about Shelley's *Frankenstein*. Like Shelley's abandoned creature, young Alison is positioned as the latest in a series of "hideous progeny," a baby dyke (abandoned by her father's suicide) who similarly seeks to understand the questions, "Who was I? What was I? Whence did I come? What was my destination?" (Shelley 112). Like the monster, Alison immerses herself in a program of educative reading, seeking to discover in the archives of great literature a legitimization of her family's essential humanity, the meaning of her father's life and death, the mythical dimensions of her relationship to him, and—as she matures—the political contours of her lesbianism, which she initially embraces as "a revelation not of the flesh, but of the mind" (74). Most important, *Fun Home* returns us to a discussion about the monster as "aberrant signifier," a "disturbingly prolific producer" of multiple signifying problems—aesthetic, linguistic, physiological, sexual, national, and gendered—all of which arise from that which we (as readers) cannot properly see: the monster's hideously unnatural body (McLane 961). A visual and biological anomaly, the monster serves as a critique of human beings as a category of species and as a threat to the presumed natural order in its defiance of taxonomy. To what kingdom, genus, or family could such an unspeakable thing belong?

Although she lacks visible sutures, the anomalous butch body in *Fun Home* similarly inspires a "most unsettling" array of taxonomic problems, the first of which becomes immediately apparent in Bruce's reaction to his daughter. Bruce recognizes something in Alison's fascination with the butch, which signals his daughter's disidentification with him, or, more precisely, with the conventional feminine aesthetic that he relentlessly pushes upon her despite her staunch opposition to all things girly. Bruce asks, "Is that what you want to look like?" (118). Caught in the act of identifying, and with no words to explain or rationalize her emotions, Alison has little choice but to say "no." In a subsequent panel, we see her being led by the hand away from the diner; young Alison stares back at an empty expanse of street, and the adult Alison recalls, "the vision of the truck-driving bull dyke sustained me through the years . . . as perhaps it haunted my father" (119).

Yet another unsettling sight from Alison's childhood is recalled immediately before the diner scene. On a camping trip Alison and her brothers happen upon an enormous snake in the spring near their campsite. They run back to alert Bill, an "outdoors type" (110) who is the latest of Bruce's young male companions. Bill grabs his pistol, which shocks Alison, but when the children lead him back to the spring, the snake has disappeared. The experience subsequently produces a peculiar state of melancholy in Alison, as she senses that she has somehow failed at "some unspoken initiation rite" (115). She is haunted by the figure of the serpent, "a vexingly ambiguous archetype," which, she admits, is "obviously a phallus, yet" also an "ancient and universal symbol of the feminine principle" (116). What's unsettling about snakes, the adult Alison ruminates, is "this undifferentiation, this nonduality," which, ironically, is also the point. The serpent takes on an additional sinister dimension in view of Alison's speculation that her father's death might not have been a suicide at all but the result of a snake on the side of the road causing him to jump back in the path of an oncoming truck.

The tissue that connects these three memories is Alison's engagement with gender misrecognition and disidentification. Affectively and intellectually, her encounters with the calendar pinup, the shadowy serpent, and the butch lesbian form a rhetorical set piece, a proliferation of associations beyond duality or difference, ultimately linking the truck-driving butch to the truck that kills Bruce and to the snake that may have caused the accident. At the same time, the generative nonduality of the snake signifies the sustaining androgyny of the butch. In sum, all roads lead to the butch, which then point to Alison as a potential agent in her father's death. Indeed, the appearance of the butch in *Fun Home* marks the beginning of Alison's truth and the unraveling of Bruce's lie. That truth—simultaneously shameful, terrifying, and joyful—positions the butch body as a rupture in the fabric of gender intelligibility, a critique of the illusory foundations of gender, an unmasking of the lies and artificial embellishments that Bruce has built his identity around as a husband and a father. *Fun Home* renders starkly the discursive and material consequences of gender disidentification and identification. It's a matter of life and death.

Still, the butch—butchness—is not an easy topic to broach in class. For the vast majority of students, butch women are curiosities to be politely ignored or laughed at. Usually, the first time I utter the word *butch* the entire class falls conspicuously and awkwardly silent. I have come to anticipate this reaction. By acknowledging the butch—by simply saying the word out loud—I knowingly unsettle the class. And in an age of trigger warnings, the authority that I claim in unsettling the class is neither simple nor sanctioned by my own privilege, not even by my lesbianism. Indeed, every time I teach *Fun Home*, my ability to open the floor to discussions of butch identity is something that we, as a class, must collectively negotiate. Once, a student chuckled nervously (but not maliciously) when I echoed the term *bull dyke*, and a cadre of students seated nearby turned angrily on him, silencing him on the spot. For many years, this has been my predicament in talking about the butch, a body that long defied taxonomic classification. While the culture has already made it difficult to talk about butch women, my students' policing of one another's responses, even if well intentioned, makes conversation virtually impossible to spark.

This changed when I discovered a *YouTube* video of Sydney Lucas, the eleven-year-old actress who plays Small Alison in the musical adaptation of *Fun Home*, singing "Ring of Keys," a powerful anthem about Alison's transformational encounter with the butch lesbian (*"Fun Home* Performance"). I posted it on the course *Blackboard* page with an optional assignment for students to create a blog about a "Ring of Keys" moment in their own life. The following week, we watched the video together, and the class opened up. In part, I attribute this to the originality of Jeanine Tesori and Lisa Kron's composition. But the real credit goes to Lucas, whose poignant rendition moved my students on a visceral level. Finally, they could talk about the butch because they could see her (and themselves) in Lucas's performance of innocent, inarticulate awe.

> Someone just came in the door,
> like no one I ever saw before
> I feel . . . I feel . . .
> . . . .
> It's probably conceited to say
> But I think we're alike in a certain way
> I . . . um

The flustered, halting pauses that punctuate the lyric speak to the dilemma of the "aberrant signifier" and also reflect Tesori and Kron's challenge in composing "Ring of Keys," the first song in American musical theater history about a young girl's awakening to butch consciousness. Tesori and Kron had to put aside ingrained cultural assumptions about butch women as ugly or comical and discover a "new language" for the telling of a different kind of truth. Their efforts were rewarded when they became the first female composing team to win a Tony Award for Best Musical. Accepting the award, Tesori shared her own "Ring of Keys" epiphany about the importance of making butch women visible. "For girls, you have to see it to be it," she thoughtfully explains. "['Ring of Keys'] is not a song of love. It's a song of identification" (Clement).

My students' blogs describing their own "Ring of Keys" moment produced no great discoveries about human nature and variation. The assignment did, however, position them as stakeholders in the discursive world that *Fun Home* invites readers to identify with or misrecognize. Some did not write of their own experiences at all but chose to elaborate on the ring of keys in Bechdel's text, seeing it as a coded signifier of female power, a metaphor portending Alison's escape from a life of shame and secrecy, her unlocking of the closet that quite possibly killed her father. Others told stories that were personal accounts of family crisis and romantic partnering. Their moments were as ordinary as eating lunch in a diner, and that may be exactly the point. In the future, I will try to clarify my expectations for the assignment, but for now I am hopeful that "Ring of Keys" will unlock a conversation, enabling us to talk meaningfully about what has been disavowed or monstrously displaced throughout the history of women's literature: the eight-hundred-pound bull dyke in the room.

Her Father's Closet:
Bruce Bechdel in *Fun Home*

Monica B. Pearl

I have taught Alison Bechdel's *Fun Home* in several courses, including a course on American self-representation, a course on canonical twentieth-century American texts, and master's-level courses on gender and sexuality. *Fun Home* is an excellent text for teaching close textual analysis because there are so many levels on which to read it and read into it. *Fun Home* is deceptive. It looks like—well, a comic strip. And it looks also like a storyboard, the rough structure of a film on the page before the film gets made, which is what initially made me feel that, as someone who has written about literature as well as film, I was ideally situated to comment on *Fun Home*. But I was wrong—graphic novels are not like film and prose together: as most scholars and aficionados of the form know, it is its own genre, not a combination of other genres. This did not stop me writing on *Fun Home*, but it slowed me down considerably and taught me a lot in the process. Mainly it taught me how to look: how to look differently, how to think about the ways that words and images might connect and clash to tell a story, rather than accompany each other, one foregrounding while the other comments upon. So, although I have taught *Fun Home*, and taught it while I was writing on it, my most pronounced understanding of how to think about *Fun Home* heuristically comes from thinking about what it taught me (Pearl, "Graphic Language").

Fun Home is devoted to Bechdel's father—to uncovering and mapping out his secrets—and also to restoring him, making him into a "good enough father."[1] *Fun Home* suggests the torment and irresolution that comes from not knowing or understanding one's father. That Alison's father died in her early adulthood (an untimely death that she is convinced is a suicide) makes this irresolution even more poignant, for it suggests an unsolved mystery: "It's true that he didn't kill himself until I was nearly twenty," she writes, "but his absence resonated retroactively, echoing back through all the time I knew him" (23). However, *Fun Home* is compelling for the ways that it charts a common mystification about a father's unknowability: "Maybe it was the converse of the way amputees feel pain in a missing limb. He really was there all those years, a flesh-and-blood presence steaming off the wallpaper, digging up the dogwoods, polishing the finials . . . smelling of sawdust and sweat and designer cologne. But I ached as if he were already gone" (23).

In his short essay on the family romance, Freud confirms an Oedipal truth, that "[i]ndeed, the whole progress of society rests upon the opposition be-tween successive generations" ("Family Romances" 221). Generational opposi-tion is often understood as rebellion—one must cast off one's parents' modes of thinking, doing, and being to formulate a separate, autonomous personality and character—but opposition might work in more nuanced, deeper, even antitheti-cal ways.

The Oedipal complex is the child's psychological development that involves fantasy desire for one parent and the wish to kill the other parent, who is the child's rival for the coveted parent's love; when these fantasy urges are thwarted, it is the resolution of that profound disappointment that makes the individual able to choose an appropriate object of desire as an adult. Growing up does not necessitate killing the father: in the more anodyne version of the family ro-mance, the father is restored, resutured. Freud concludes "Family Romances" with the idea that the more a child finds avatars of more convincingly heroic par-ents, the more the child restores her original, dazzled admiration for the parent.

For a child to separate from a parent by establishing differences, rather than killing off the parent, those differences must be clearly recognized or created. In order to know how one is different from one's father, one has to know him—secrets and all. A closeted father thwarts the effort to enact the normal dis-course of the family romance. *Fun Home* is Bechdel's story of the attempt of her graphic childhood persona, Alison, to know her father in order, I suggest, to separate from him and restore him. This proves difficult, for every discovery or way of knowing her father, and indeed every effort at growing up or knowing herself, shows their similarity rather than their difference. The book illustrates this struggle.

Freud tells us that the "liberation of an individual, as he grows up, from the authority of his parents is one of the most necessary though one of the most painful results brought about by the course of his development" ("Family Ro-mances" 221). Like Alison, who "in [her] earliest memories" sees her "dad [as] a lowering, malevolent presence" (*Fun Home* 197) and later admits that although "[m]y father had slipped somewhat in my estimation . . . I was still sympathetic toward him" (174), Freud's account of the family romance is one in which a child must recognize a diminishment in the parent's original grandeur.

The memoir paints Bruce Bechdel as inscrutable and unavailable in myriad ways—unavailable to be known or loved by Alison or by anyone else in her fam-ily. The answer to his inscrutability turns out to be his secret homosexuality, from which all his behavior and preoccupations can be made legible. But *Fun Home* seems to be about knowing something and not knowing something at the same time: a story or set of truths that Alison is concealing from herself but also trying to tell herself—and us. The recursive nature of the narrative, the way that it is told not chronologically but back and forth, revisiting different mo-ments in Alison's past, renders the story always already known but also always mysterious, more details and aspects continually unfolding and being revealed. Like Alison's attempt to know her father and understand what might have led to his untimely death, *Fun Home* conceals and displays what it knows as the narrative unfolds.

Fun Home is an excellent text for thinking about the ways that the form of a work can recapitulate and put a reader in the mind or the sensibility of the story that is being conveyed. For example, its recursiveness is a nice illustration of how memory itself works: that is, one does not remember in a straightforward, progressive narrative; one remembers in a kind of back and forth, one thought leading to another, not necessarily adjacent chronologically. Its recursiveness also makes it an especially useful text for thinking about queerness and the closet. The notion of the closet—that domestic storage space in which secrets are hidden—is continually enacted in the book: the family is living with secrets that are hard to discern. The only image of an actual closet in the book comes right after young Alison dares to kiss her father's knuckles. With an image of a closet at the end of the corridor, Bechdel narrates:

> The embarrassment on my part was a tiny scale model of my father's more fully developed self-loathing. His shame inhabited our house as pervasively and invisibly as the aromatic musk of aging mahogany. In fact, the meticulous period interiors were expressly designed to conceal it. Mirrors, distracting bronzes, multiple doorways. Visitors often got lost upstairs. (20)

Bruce's great preoccupation is restoring the Gothic Revival house in which Alison grows up. This grand house, we come to understand, is the closet in which Bruce lives. His house is his sublimation for a desire that cannot be expressed or enacted. The closet is constructed and sustained by silence.[2] But the opposite of silence is not (only) speech but expression. Even sublimated communication can be a kind of announcement; indeed it often leads to perfectly legible coded communication for anyone who knows how to look or listen properly.

The truth of Bruce's desires does not unfold slowly; the recursiveness of Bechdel's memoir means that readers know everything at once. There is no narrative closet and subsequent prosodic disclosure. Indeed, insofar as Bruce's secret was hardly a secret—available to scrutiny and knowledge by those in the know—the narrative, the prose and the images, reproduces Bruce's closets. Bruce's other closet is his great love of literature and reading. He hides behind books. (There is no shy, bookish child—or adult—who does not understand how this works.)

The closet that Alison perceives her father to have been living in all his adult life is a closet that hides and contains not just his homosexuality but his (and his wife's) more artistic and bohemian leanings, the life they began in Europe and had to relinquish when Bruce's own father died. Our fathers thwart us.

Alison finds more similarities between her and her father than differences. Although she insists that they "were inversions of one another" (98), suggesting that they express each other's unacceptable gender dispositions, that is not the only mirrored dynamic she sets up between them. Alison wonders, for example, if under similar circumstances she would have lived a different life from that of her father: "Would I have had the guts to be one of those Eisenhower-era butches? Or would I have married and sought succor from my high school students?" (108). If Alison imagined, when coming out to her parents, that her transgressive sexuality might distinguish herself from her father, she is quickly disappointed. His own predilections are revealed over the telephone by her mother soon after she comes out to them (211).

Even her love of books—not the books he wants her to read but her own lesbian-feminist books—ends up mirroring the ways her father hides behind books. Books are her closet as well. She recognizes she is a lesbian through books: "a revelation not of the flesh, but of the mind" (74). "My researches," she admits, "were stimulating but solitary" (76). Books lead to sex for Alison—"[i]t became clear I was going to have to leave this academic plane and enter the human fray" (76)—as they do for her father: "whatever else might have been going on" when Bruce distributed books to his protégés, "books were being read" (61).

What allows her to distinguish herself from him finally is her artistic ambition. She describes her parents' indulging in their own frustrated artistic talents as their way of sustaining themselves when emotional interconnection fails: her father's reading and preoccupation with the house and her mother's immersion in acting and piano playing. "It's childish, perhaps," she writes, "to grudge them the sustenance of their creative solitude. But it was all that sustained them, and thus all-consuming" (133–34). Her story of their marriage exposes their failed artistic ambitions from the beginning. They leave Europe to return to Beech Creek, and it is on the occasion of the first family visit to Europe that Alison vows never to leave the Europe that stands for the artist's life. She will not lug a suitcase back (which she is shown doing obstinately) but stay there, where she can wear swim shorts and hiking boots ("See?" young Alison pleads with her mother, "girls wear them too"): "Perhaps this is when I cemented the unspoken compact with them that I would never get married, that I would carry on to live the artist's life that they had each abdicated" (73).

Alison escapes a conventional life but her father can't; death is his only escape. She imagines speaking this truth at his funeral: "There's no mystery! He killed himself because he was a manic-depressive, closeted fag and he couldn't face living in this small-minded small town one more second," adding, "I'd kill myself too if I had to live here" (125). In this moment Alison states her intention to live a life different from her father's. In this story a daughter tries to distinguish herself from her father so that she can separate from him. In unearthing her father's secrets, however, Alison finds that she and her father are more alike than different.

But this recognition is in keeping with Freud's conclusion to the narrative of the family romance, in which the child's wish is to see the parent restored to his original magnitude: "in fact the child is not getting rid of his father but exalting him" ("Family Romances" 224). Alison suggests of her father's death that "the end of his lie coincided with the beginning of my truth" (117), confirming her need to dislodge him from his closet but also to reinter him in her book. One resolution of the Oedipal complex is claiming our parents' narratives, telling their stories.

An obvious point about this book that makes it instructive for teaching is the historical change, within a generation, with regard to open, public expressions of queer sexualities. While Alison's father lived a closeted life, Alison came out and lives openly as a lesbian. But a perhaps more subtle point is that the family romance, the Oedipal separation, is painful for everyone—even for those who are not artists or lesbians, whose parents are not gay or artistically inclined. We may not have to force open a closet from our childhood home or bury a parent to grow up, but, like the myth and literature that Alison uses to understand her father and her relationship to him, *Fun Home* lets us see—visually and narratively and prosaically—how hard it is to forge our own sexualities and lives.

NOTES

[1] The psychoanalyst D. W. Winnicott's concept of "the good enough mother" describes the virtues of the ordinarily devoted mother, not only relieving the parent (and the child) of unrealistic, superheroic parenting expectations but also suggesting that these ordinary efforts are sufficient for a child to thrive. By borrowing and misquoting this phrase I am suggesting that Bechdel does something in *Fun Home* that she does more literally in her subsequent memoir, *Are You My Mother?*, where she actually invokes Winnicott, and the parent under interrogation is her mother.

[2] See Sedgwick.

Witnessing Queer Identities:
Teaching *Fun Home* and
Contemporary Memoirs

Jennifer Lemberg

When a young Alison Bechdel calls home from college to tell her father, Bruce, that she will be reading James Joyce's *A Portrait of the Artist as a Young Man*, he responds with a stern directive: "You damn well better identify with every page" (*Fun Home* 201). Bruce's command communicates one of the central themes of *Fun Home*, which is concerned throughout with the modes of identification between Alison and her father before his death at a young age, likely by suicide. By demanding that she "identify with every page," Alison's father addresses her as a talented reader of one of his favorite books.[1] More important, he charges her with recognizing his unfulfilled dreams of artistic and sexual expression, with bearing witness to his life story. *Fun Home* is partly a response to this directive, as it chronicles Bechdel's experience of growing up with a queer, closeted father in the 1960s and 1970s. The book is in many ways a singular achievement, with its humor, obsessive re-creation of archival material, and interest in what Julia Watson calls the "the erotic and the necrotic" (35). Yet it also belongs to a body of literature dedicated to exploring queer identities, and teaching *Fun Home* in an undergraduate classroom invites us to seek out companion texts in order to highlight its importance to the genre.

Much of the critical literature on *Fun Home* stresses Bechdel's depiction of her younger self as a witness to her father's traumatic past. In her analysis of how graphic narratives create "an expanded *idiom of witness*," for example (*Graphic Women* 3), Hillary Chute discovers connections between *Fun Home*, Art Spiegelman's *Maus*, and Marjane Satrapi's *Persepolis*, pointing especially to similarities between *Fun Home* and *Maus* as accounts that "concentrate deeply on identification and concomitant *disidentification* with fathers" (176). Ann Cvetkovich also views the three books as examples of "second-generation witnessing," "each . . . haunted by questions about the effects of growing up in the vicinity of powerful combinations of violence and secrecy"; *Fun Home* is distinguished by the "queer witnessing" it presents (113, 126). By dealing openly with Bruce's "illicit" desire and its place within the family, Cvetkovich writes, Bechdel makes queer identity visible and legitimizes his experience as traumatic (113).

These readings draw attention to the book's representation of multigenerational queer identities, or what Valerie Rohy has termed a "queer genealogy" (341). For Bechdel, what Chute describes as the "*re*-visioning" of the past (*Graphic Women* 199) serves as a trope for the attempt to understand the movement of nonnormative identities across gender and generational lines within her family.[2] Alison's decision to come out to her parents, her mother's subsequent revelation of Bruce's affairs with underage boys, and Bruce's death shortly thereafter inspire Bechdel's exploration of the ways in which her lesbian identity is rooted in her family history. Bechdel rereads her family life within the frame created by her belated insight, revisiting her childhood memories as well as archival materials in order to create a new understanding of her father's story.

Teaching *Fun Home* alongside other memoirs that testify to complex gender identities and desires within the context of the family can move students toward a deeper appreciation of Alison's role as witness. By reading narratives that foreground the challenges to representing these subjects, students are encouraged to reflect on the ability of queer memoirists to develop new forms of vision. We may lead students to consider the importance of what Marianne Hirsch calls the "familial look," or "the ways in which the individual subject is constituted in the space of the family through looking" to the project of documenting queer identity (9). If the intimate "familial look" refigures a more public "familial gaze" that "situates human subjects in the ideology, the mythology, of the family as institution" (11),[3] we can examine other narratives that document coming to see in new ways in order to consider how they reshape ideas about family and identity.[4]

With this in mind, instructors may choose to assign Minnie Bruce Pratt's *S/he* (1995) and Maggie Nelson's *The Argonauts* (2015), which bracket *Fun Home* (2006) within a period of twenty years. Distinct from Bechdel's volume in their purely narrative, rather than graphic, form, *S/he* and *The Argonauts* nevertheless reflect a similar interest in the family within the context of nonnormative sexual desire. Each text explores the experience of living with a transgender spouse and foregrounds the author's effort to describe her partner's gender expression and its meanings for her lesbian identity. Where Bechdel is troubled by the generational distance that makes it impossible to fully comprehend her father's experience as a gay man ("like a version of Nachträglichkeit," Cvetkovich notes [114]),[5] Pratt and Nelson acknowledge the obstacles to understanding their spouses' experience even as they navigate the spaces mapped by shared desire and family bonds.

All three works show the memoirist taking on the role of witness to a loved one's gender expression, refining her vision in order to better accomplish her goal. Tracing each author's shift in perspective helps illuminate the gaps between ideology and lived experience as well as the interplay of ideas about gender, family, and identity. In *Fun Home* Bechdel makes revisions to her early descriptions of her relationship to her father, which emphasize their opposing personalities, temperaments, and tastes.[6] As Alison grows older, her perception undergoes a shift, in a movement "from simple dichotomies to complex interrelations, from differences *between* to differences *within*" (Rohy 344). In *S/he* and *The Argonauts* Pratt and Nelson undertake similar explorations, as each considers the meanings of her partner's transgender identity for the picture of the family unit they have created as well as the limits to and possibilities for identifying with the person to whom they are most intimately connected.

Describing her memoir as a book written "to give theory flesh and breath" (22), Pratt charts her journey as a lesbian, a poet, a mother, and, eventually, as the wife of the author and activist Leslie Feinberg.[7] Recalling her childhood in Alabama, Pratt explores how her own and others' gender expression was shaped around heteronormative restrictions. She is aware of writing at a time when gender theory is striving to "make clear that every aspect of a person's gender expression and sex will not be consistently either masculine or feminine, man or woman" (21), and records her personal knowledge of this idea. Important to the book are her reflections on how coming out as a lesbian and the life she shares with Feinberg are experiences that enlarge her understanding of sex and gender as well as the concepts of home, family, and motherhood.

Initially finding Feinberg so completely outside expected gender categories that she "had no language to talk about her or us together" (14), as the book progresses Pratt demonstrates the ways in which her vision expands to be more inclusive. On meeting a transgender friend of Feinberg's, for example, Pratt employs spatial terms to imagine the three of them living "on the edge of town, a place out of my view when I was growing up" and likens that space to one inhabited by "the women-men of the sideshow at the circus" (89). However, she writes, she now knows that "the people there have lovers, marriages, children, poor-paying jobs. . . . You live there, and now I live there too, with those who know they are both *man* and *woman*" (89–90); in other words, they have been made visible, made real to her through her broadening awareness. Pratt is eager to cross the distance between her earlier experience and the location at which she arrives, in response to a "desire that has heated up slowly over the years" (104) but also to a growing sense of solidarity with queer movement.

S/he chronicles an increasingly urgent need for language that can bear witness to this change, as Pratt insists, "*if we dare claim our lives as our own, we must read all of the poems we write with our bodies*" (134). By reading the text with an emphasis on how that act of claiming requires new ways of seeing the self, the family, and established gender categories, students are asked to consider a form of familial looking able to recognize and give name to shared experience and individual histories. Cvetkovich reminds us that "to become a 'witness' (either literally or more indirectly) to anyone's sexuality is a difficult documentary task, given its frequent privacy or intimacy, and this general secrecy can be further heightened when that sexuality is constructed as immoral or criminal or perverse" (114). Reading Pratt's account of her deepening intimacy with Feinberg, we see that her experience demands an increasingly complex understanding of gender and desire. Her memoir helps us grasp Bechdel's move, more than a decade later, toward acknowledging differences "within" rather than "between" (to recall Rohy) not only as the personal responsibility of the writer but also as an active intervention into readers' understanding of queer life stories.

The Argonauts takes on questions similar to those posed by *S/he* but with a sensibility corresponding to its more recent publication. Like Bechdel and

Pratt, Nelson is concerned with whether she truly knows her subject and with the project of writing her way past conventional forms of gender expression. She recounts her experience of falling in love with the transgender artist Harry Dodge, describing in detail their romance and the period during which she is pregnant with their first child and Dodge undergoes top surgery while continuing to take testosterone shots. Although they are already part-time parents to Dodge's son, the shifts that Nelson and Dodge experience—alluded to in the titular reference to Roland Barthes's discussion of how the *Argo*, like love, keeps its name even as its constituent "parts may be replaced over time" (*Argonauts* 5)—bring them closer while creating new differences.[8]

Students reading *The Argonauts* will find that it resonates with both *Fun Home* and *S/he*, as Nelson struggles to describe her new partner (early on, she has a friend perform an online search in hopes of finding clues to Dodge's preferred pronoun) and questions the ability of language to bear witness to experience. Nelson negotiates issues of proximity and distance, saying, "I want the you no one else can see, the you so close the third person never need apply" yet asserting the need for her writing to remain solely her own (7). Here, as in *S/he*, belatedness is replaced by another kind of distance, with Dodge's transgender identity sometimes presented as being beyond Nelson's understanding, an idea she recognizes as invoking traditional femme/butch dynamics but one that she also goes on to complicate. Before Dodge's surgery, Nelson recalls his saying that "*I will never feel as free as you do. I will never feel as at home in the world, I will never feel as at home in my own skin*" (31). Afterward, when the surgery has brought about a "measure of peace" that is highly liberating for him as an artist, she observes, provocatively, "as I labor grimly on these sentences . . . I'm no longer sure which of us is more at home in the world, which of us more free" (52). Dodge's changes are meaningful, and Nelson recognizes them as such even as she draws a tentative connection between the effects of being unsettled in these different ways.

There is poignancy in following a study of *Fun Home* with *The Argonauts*, as it seems to offer up a version of the queer parent's story for which Bechdel may be searching. Like Bechdel, Nelson insists on the need to engage in the act of seeing the family as it is constituted by queer identity, but she does so in the present rather than belatedly. *The Argonauts* repeatedly draws our attention to the images that are part of this process, as Nelson considers the meanings of a mug emblazoned with a family photograph that prompts a friend to tease, "*I've never seen anything so heteronormative in all my life*" (13) and admires a photographer whose work "reminds us that any bodily experience can be made new and strange . . . that no one set of practices or relations has the monopoly on the so-called radical, or the so-called normative" (72–73). Attending to Nelson's interest in the visual can return us to the ways in which Bechdel intertwines word and image in addressing questions of gender and desire and to our own participation in acts of familial looking.

Significant differences exist among these suggested companion texts and *Fun Home*, of course. *S/he* and *The Argonauts* foreground spousal relationships and transgender identities and feature recognized artists and activists. Yet the intersections with *Fun Home* offer rich possibilities for the classroom. All three works engage deeply with theoretical questions and situate personal stories within the longer history of queer life in America; all deal openly and explicitly with sex and desire. We may recall Pratt's challenge: "*if we dare claim our lives as our own, we must read all of the poems we write with our bodies.*" Reading these books together can help locate *Fun Home* within the genre of queer memoir and make space in the classroom to explore the ways in which we read, and write, and see.

NOTES

[1] For a detailed discussion of the importance of Joyce's text to *Fun Home*, see Chute, *Graphic Women* (203–08, 211–14).

[2] Chute conceives of "*re*-visioning" as "a form of touch" in the way it brings the author and artist into contact with the past and with the page (*Graphic Women* 199).

[3] Hirsch here refers specifically to the role of the family photograph in this process. Much of the criticism on *Fun Home* explores the complexity of how Bechdel incorporates her own family photographs into the book, including Hélène Tison's recent discussion of the ways in which "drawing and redrawing" the photographs serve to repair broken connections between Alison and Bruce (361).

[4] For Cvetkovich, *Fun Home* "provides a welcome alternative to public discourses about LGBTQ politics that are increasingly homonormative and dedicated to family values" (111). The concept of family values is discussed in Minnie Bruce Pratt's *S/he* and Maggie Nelson's *The Argonauts* and could usefully be addressed in the classroom.

[5] Gabriele Schwab defines *Nachträglichkeit*, a term borrowed from Freud, as "writing belatedly or in deferred action from within trauma" (64) or "belatedness" (202n67).

[6] My discussion throughout is indebted to Valerie Rohy's analysis of how Bechdel establishes and then goes on to "complicate" the differences between Alison and Bruce (344).

[7] Feinberg, the author of *Stone Butch Blues* and several other books, passed away in 2014 (Weber).

[8] In her review of *The Argonauts*, Jennifer Szalai offers insight into the resonance of the book's title with the physical changes Dodge and Nelson experience.

Rural Space as Queer Space:
A Queer-Ecology Reading of *Fun Home*

Debra J. Rosenthal and Lydia Munnell

Many students reading Alison Bechdel's *Fun Home* for the first time express surprise that a queer narrative can take place in a rural setting. They imagine that the civilized, accepting communities in which queer-identifying folks can safely come out and escape small, backward-thinking hometowns are found in urban areas. However, literary, historical, and phenomenological evidence shows that this model does not always match the lived experiences of queer-identifying people in rural areas. Numerous queer folks choose to live and form communities in rural settings. In fact, the rural, with its mountaintop removal mining, repurposed architecture, and, at times, anachronistic culture, can reveal itself to be already queer. When we teach *Fun Home* to undergraduates in our Feminist Literary Criticism and our Introduction to Queer Studies courses, we explore queer space and the ways that the author's youth in rural Pennsylvania can challenge students' assumptions about the queerness of city and country. We recommend that teachers consider an environmental reading of the memoir that focuses on the queering of rural space so students can understand the "strong relationship between the oppression of queers and the domination of nature" (Mortimer-Sandilands and Erickson 29).

Construing rural areas as either precious or backward has led to what Bud Jerke calls "queer metronormativity," the belief that "queer culture and identity can only be situated in an urban geography" (268). In problematizing queer metronormativity and framing Bechdel's Beech Creek, Pennsylvania, as essentially queer, it is helpful to use Jack Halberstam's understanding of queer space in opposition to white, male, postmodern geographies that privilege the global over the local and the cosmopolitan over the rural. Halberstam argues that "[u]ntil recently, small towns were considered hostile to queers, and urban areas were cast as the queer's natural environment. . . . [T]he division also occludes the lives of nonurban queers" (15). We recommend exploring with students Emily Kazyak's point that formulaic stories about queer folks often involve a rural-to-urban migration story—one that may or may not accurately describe their experience. Kazyak argues, "At the heart of the narrative is the 'stock character' of the 'oppressed rural gay': those who must flee to the city to come out, find a queer community, and become liberated" (562). Clearly, this urban/rural binary, in which the urban is privileged and the rural devalued, runs deep in American culture, paralleling the Great Migration of African Americans from rural Southern oppression to opportunities in Northern cities. It runs so deep that it affects our views of hate crimes in rural areas, the fairness of our legal system, and even the narratives of queer-identifying folks in rural areas. These ideas can then be paired with students' personal reflections in order to create a background for the metronormativity that Bechdel's Beech Creek subverts.

We also explore the ways Bechdel shows the urban environment to not necessarily normalize queer identity. Moving quickly to the text provides our class with interpretive evidence and talking points. For example, the urban site that promises liberation turns out to be humiliating: Alison gets "eighty-sixed," or refused admission, at a New York City bar when out with a group of lesbian friends (*Fun Home* 106). Alison had "come to New York after college, expecting a bohemian refuge," but instead she finds that "[Greenwich] Village in the early eighties was a cold, mercenary place" (107). These instances challenge the concept of queer metronormativity and help students see the way *Fun Home* reorients space and sexuality.

In our Introduction to Queer Studies class, we also complicate Bechdel's understanding of place, environment, and sexuality by studying the way the rural town of Beech Creek was, for young Alison, a place of repression and death as well as one of acceptance and beauty. The map illustrations demonstrate that Bruce Bechdel's entire life and family are situated on the same two-mile stretch of land in the Susquehanna River watershed region. *Fun Home*'s deep interest in mapping reveals Alison's efforts to understand place and her sexuality amid such tightly bound connections to a rural locale. Young Alison literalizes Adrienne Rich's invitation to begin with "the geography closest in—the body" ("Notes" 212) by explicitly linking her body to the land: for example, Bechdel's illustration of her father's obituary highlights the words "Beech Creek" at least seven times as if to emphasize his (and by extension, her) rural placedness. She muses that her father's fate might have been different "if only he'd been able to escape the gravitational tug of Beech Creek" (125). In another example, Bruce Bechdel writes in a letter to Alison, "It's ironic that I'm paying to send you North to study texts I'm teaching to high school twits. Faulkner IS Beech Creek. The Bundrens ARE Bechdels" (200). While Bruce sees his family mirrored in Faulkner's deeply rooted characters, Alison claims that the "narrow compass" of her father's life "suggests a provincialism on my father's part that is both misleading and accurate" (30).

Fun Home's depictions of Alison's engagement with the environment reveal that what appears as natural is socially constructed and can hide ecological degradation: there might not be anything natural about human-polluted nature. For instance, young Alison describes her childhood place with inspired nostalgia, punctured by an awareness of human-made biohazards. She reflects on "Bald Eagle Mountain's hazy blue flank" and the way the sun "set behind the strip-mine-pocked plateau." She realizes that the "pyrotechnic splendor" of beautiful sunrises indicates that the atmosphere is contaminated "due to particulates from the pre–Clean Air Act paper mill ten miles away." As a girl she wades in Beech Creek's waters and understands that "with similar perversity, the sparkling creek that coursed down from the plateau and through our town was crystal clear precisely because it was polluted. Mine runoff had left the water too acidic to support life . . . " (128). Beech Creek's translucency is thus anything but natural: the crystal-clear water is caused by the strip mine's acidic industrial runoff, which obscures its pollution and so normalizes acceptance of a toxic environment marked by "perversity." Thus, the supposedly natural environment of colorful skies and transparent water proves to be a nonnormative deviation: the rural environment may already be queer.

A queer-ecology reading of *Fun Home* exposes young Alison's awareness of the parity between "ecological degradation and sexual inequality" (Sbicca 33) and usefully opens up the scene of the Bechdel children's visit to a strip mine. Alison's interpretation of their visit overlays environmental exploitation onto sexual oppression and thus presents as "anthropocentric heteronormativity" (Griffiths 294) the exploitation both of the ecosystem and of the naked white woman on a pinup calendar hanging in the strip miners' office. The mining equipment looms huge and threatening, dominating the background and damaging the landscape as it removes the top of a mountain to extract coal for the creation of electricity. The environmentalist Bill Conlogue argues that "to write about the region is to record trauma both human and environmental. . . . Although coal mining here has all but ended, strip mines still scar mountainsides, . . . and streams run stained with acid" (18). At first, Alison and her brothers do not question the damage and violence wrought by mining but instead are "excited about seeing the monstrous shovels that tore off whole mountaintops" (112). As they drive to the strip mines, young Alison picks up a roll of paper lying in her father's car, but Bruce admonishes her not to open it because it is "dirty." She misunderstands his meaning and muses that the white paper "looked clean enough to me" (111). When she unrolls it and sees a naked woman being used to advertise a local company, she expresses her newfound understanding of the connection between compulsory heterosexuality and dirt with a simple "Oh" (112). Feeling exposed by the calendar image, she says, "I felt as if I'd been stripped naked myself" (112), in an echo of the miners' stripping of the mountaintop. Her identification with the white pinup woman may open up the question to students about the ways that race infuses the woman-as-land trope. She feels "inexplicably ashamed, like Adam and Eve" (112) by the nudity (this reference to the Garden of Eden will resonate with Alison's later thoughts about a snake and a "postlapsarian melancholy" [115]). When Alison sees a similar nude calendar hanging in the strip miners' office, she feels "astonished" by what seems to be a "bizarre coincidence" (113) that both her father and the miners have calendars that exploit white women's presumed erotic availability.

Compulsory heterosexuality is evident when Bruce holds up a loaf of Stroehman's Sunbeam bread so that Alison's face appears directly between the naked pinup girl and the too-wholesome Sunbeam girl on the bread package (manufactured by the company whose truck will later kill Bruce). The juxtaposition cannily positions young Alison between two types of female identity: a highly eroticized white woman available for male consumption and a virginal, traditional, innocent, white-bread (literally), maiden girl (112). Caught between these opposing choices of heteronormative female sexuality, Alison suddenly feels it is "imperative" (113) that the strip miner not know she is a girl. She finds a queer way out of this virgin/whore binary: she asks her brother to call her Albert (113). As the heavy machinery repurposes the mountain into a commodity, Alison performs a different type of repurposing. Throughout the visit to the strip mine, the heteronormative, masculinized space of the miners exposes Alison's deviation from expected sexual and gender norms. She cannot identify with the highly eroticized female body on the calendar that reflects and ensures straight male dominance. As Greta Gaard argues, "By attempting to 'naturalize' sexuality, the dominant discourse of Western culture constructs queer sexualities as 'unnatural' and hence subordinate" (121). Alison's desire to reassign her gender and to repurpose her identity as Albert, when juxtaposed with the mine's goal of repurposing the environment, reflects the queerness of strip mining, an exclusively rural activity. Although Alison's brother ignores her request for a new name, she connects her experience to a "Proustian transposition" that melds "Proust's real Alfred and the fictional Albertine" (113).

In the woodland scene that follows the strip mining sequence, the Bechdel children practice shooting a gun, and they become frightened by a large snake. Young Alison feels a "postlapsarian melancholy" as she reflects that she "failed some unspoken initiation rite" (115) associated with the trope of "rurality being grounded in macho-masculine gender expression" (Sbicca 48). Bechdel continues the memoir's theme of the incommensurability between word and meaning as she wonders why she did not record the full woodland adventure in her diary: "No mention of the pin-up girl, the strip mine, or Bill's .22. Just the snake—and even that with an extreme economy of style." The accompanying illustration shows the children in the woods with a text box of young Alison's diary that reads simply: "Saw a snake. Had lunch" (143). Later she wonders if her father was struck mid-road by a truck because he had come upon a large snake, a "vexingly ambiguous archetype" (116). By failing to have a successful adventure out in nature or to kill the phallic snake, Bechdel revises the typical coming-of-age story. Her struggle to recast her gender assignment within her rural context is mirrored in her inability to write about such a recasting; both constitute a search for identity where sexuality and rural placedness share an ineffable link.

In these scenes, Bechdel challenges the natural-unnatural dichotomy to reveal how the environment and sexuality can be mutually queered.[1] As Gaard points out, queer sexuality has historically been considered against nature, which suggests that nature would be valued and prized in a heteronormative society. However, Western culture actually devalues nature and queers and instead grants primacy to culture and heterosexuality. Gaard theorizes this contradiction: "from a queer perspective, we learn that the dominant culture charges queers with transgressing the natural order, which in turn implies that nature is valued and must be obeyed" (120). But an ecofeminist perspective shows "that Western culture has constructed nature as a force that must be dominated if culture is to prevail"; thus "the 'nature' that queers are urged to comply with is none other than the dominant paradigm of heterosexuality . . . itself a cultural construction . . ." (121). Against a backdrop of strip mines, highways, polluted air, and toxic creeks—products of the cultural mandate of heterosexuality—Bechdel's depiction of her rural natural world can be reframed as akin to her queer identification.

Bechdel's queering of herself and her environment within the context of the heteronormative makes *Fun Home* so accessible. Because many students identify with the specifics of young Alison's middle-class, rural-suburban, gender-traditional upbringing, they are easily led to the more complex and subversive implications of this upbringing. Bechdel's understanding of place in *Fun Home* is far more nuanced than the typical urban/rural binary; she artfully works the queer and the straight so that they cannot be unraveled. The memoir challenges assumptions about metronormativity through its decidedly queer depictions of rural life and and the unnaturalness of mountaintop strip mining. Reading *Fun Home* with a queer-ecology focus can give students an increased understanding of place, of the complications inherent in the queer rural-to-urban migration narrative, of the link between sexual and environmental exploitation, and of the ways metronormativity is problematized in Bechdel's queer depictions of rural life.

NOTES

For their insightful comments that helped us clarify our arguments, we are grateful to Yvonne Bruce and Cathy Hannabach.

[1] Goldsmith extends the natural-unnatural dichotomy to architecture by discussing the liminal positioning of porches and the way they straddle inside and outside, nature and culture.

Teaching Traumatic Narrative in the English Classroom: Psychoanalysis in *Fun Home* and *Are You My Mother?*

Erica D. Galioto

"I wanted to write about the problem of the self and the relationship with the other," Alison Bechdel reveals about her purpose for writing *Are You My Mother?* (Bechdel and Chute 203). Both *Fun Home* and *Are You My Mother?* reflect Bechdel's attempts to better understand her parents as her primary others as well as the construction of her "self" in relation to each. Whereas *Fun Home* primarily describes Bechdel's analysis of her father's suicide alongside her own coming out as a lesbian, *Are You My Mother?* centrally focuses on her relationship with her mother during the time when she is composing *Fun Home*. Both memoirs showcase Bechdel's trauma, or "an experience that is not fully assimilated as it occurs" (Caruth 5), and the author's multiple attempts to integrate loss into her consciousness. As she represents these painful events in an effort to work through her relationships with her parents, Bechdel illustrates that trauma often operates on two different registers. On one level, she endures overwhelming experiences of personal pain such as her father's suicide, exposure of his hidden homosexuality, gradual acceptance of her own lesbianism, and lonely emotional distance from each of her family members, but on the other level, she undergoes isolating alienation from both her parents as she psychically separates from each to become her own autonomous self. Bechdel's unexpected significant losses and her ultimate psychic separations from her parents are both traumatic because they result in unassimilated lack that must be worked through to be accepted. Exposing both traumatic registers, Bechdel's memoirs foreground psychoanalytic lack as generative rather than reductive and offer space for discussion about how working through trauma necessitates an open lack at its center and how autonomous subjectivity relies on the opening of a traumatic lack caused by psychic separation from one's parental other or others.

In Reading and Writing about Trauma in the English Classroom, I introduce students to the field of trauma studies through the overlap of psychoanalysis, pedagogy, and literature.[1] As shown in the selected essay prompts and student writing below, my instruction of *Fun Home* highlights how Bechdel's representation of the psychosocial dynamics embedded within "the problem of the self and the relationship with the other" significantly moves from an encounter with painful internal lack to productive movement outside the self.

Fun Home *as a Traumatic Narrative*

To launch our study of *Fun Home*, I begin with Bechdel's use of the graphic memoir genre in relation to our ongoing analysis of trauma and its various narrative representations. Bechdel deliberately situates her work in the realm of narratives of trauma that are expressed in comics—by subtitling *Fun Home* a "tragicomic" and *Are You My Mother?* a "comic drama." In so doing, her memoirs engage the evocative disjunction between image and text that befits descriptions of both comics and trauma in their fragmented, incomplete reconstruction of emotional events. Early class discussions analyze Bechdel's drawings in terms of her desire to relive her childhood as a working-through mechanism to both understand the past and distance herself from it. In this way, Bechdel's employment of the graphic memoir genre supports two of Marian MacCurdy's points in "From Trauma to Writing: A Theoretical Model for Practical Use": first, "that traumatic memories are likely to be tied to sensory, iconic representations, not strictly linguistic, intellectual concepts about those memories" (163); and second, "re-experiencing sensory details encoded during extreme life moments is at the core of trauma recovery" (165).

In both *Fun Home* and *Are You My Mother?* Bechdel painstakingly relives traumatic experiences, recreates these images graphically, signifies them through narrative, and connects them to the evolution of her developing self. Following Freud's trajectory of remembering, repeating, and working-through, she first recalls the memories associated with her images, then repeats them as she re-creates the scenes that become her panels, and finally works through them as she confronts their centrality to her subjectivity, though she ultimately separates from and moves beyond them. To represent the two levels of her traumatic experiences in her graphic memoirs, Bechdel employs memories, dreams, free associations, family archives, and even therapy to work through what Freud describes as "experiences which occurred in very early childhood and were not understood at the time but which were *subsequently* understood and interpreted" ("Remembering" 149). Both the agents and the representatives of her working-through, Bechdel's uniquely graphic narratives of trauma join MacCurdy's sensory encoding with Freud's healing reproduction. One student, Stephanie Ehrets, aptly echoes the centrality of the graphic form to Bechdel's sensory healing process:

> In her article, Marion MacCurdy uses research to validate her theory of trauma recovery through writing. She states, "Research into trauma recovery indicates that healing is more likely to occur when survivors can describe not just the event of their trauma but the images their memories have encoded" (166). Similar results are present in *Fun Home*, as Bechdel is able to confront her memories by illustrating them. Like MacCurdy's students, Bechdel is able to make sense of her trauma as she re-creates it

through images. She is able to accept her trauma, which is shown through her eventual identification with her father, her embraced sexuality, and her acceptance of her father's suicide.

To expand beyond the graphic representation of Bechdel's memories, I then push students to consider the relation between presence and absence in *Fun Home* and in trauma more generally. Collectively, we complete a Venn diagram graphic organizer that places "Form: How *Fun Home* Is Written" on the left side, "Content: What Is Written about in *Fun Home*" on the right side, and "Trauma: The Complex Relation between Knowing and Not Knowing" in the overlapping center (Caruth 3). This exercise shows how the graphic memoir form allows Bechdel to maintain the slippage between absence and presence that conveys "the complexity of loss itself" (*Fun Home* 120) and permits her to state that "the book is all about this sorting out what happened in that strange little knot of sexual coming of age and death and trauma" (Bechdel and Chute 210). As Bechdel explains, loss paradoxically grants generation, and it is this production that is significant for the intersection between *Fun Home* and trauma studies. As illustrated in the Venn diagram, *Fun Home* and *Are You My Mother?* represent content that is both present and absent, hidden and revealed, and known and unknown through a graphic memoir form that is framed by white space and conveys a narrative structure that is recursive, fragmented, and dissonant. Trauma's own muddled definition is similarly paradoxical and confusing; yet rather than avoiding or sanitizing projects that seek to represent the unspeakable, invisible, and inaudible, Bechdel presents trauma's messiness as well as its potentiality to readers who witness her telling and listen "to a voice that [they] cannot fully know but to which [they] nonetheless bear witness" (Caruth 9).

Following Hillary L. Chute's cogent analysis of these same issues, I intend for students to understand that "*Fun Home* does not stitch up the gap at its center—Bruce Bechdel's death—so much as give a substance to loss; in its form, it actually *caresses* the loss" (*Graphic Women* 199). In *Fun Home*, the absences persist as potential, not to be filled in or ignored but to provide space for movement and interpretation. Extending his analysis to reader-witnesses of Bechdel's narratives of trauma, my student Bryan Smith writes,

> The lack of connection between the witness and the victim doesn't end with the limited emotions of the graphics in *Fun Home* and *Are You My Mother?* The gap between the reader and Bechdel can be seen in the emptiness of the pages, which helps readers see the lack in Bechdel even clearer. . . . The uniqueness of graphic memoirs (and other visual media) is that the lack, gap, emptiness can be depicted, despite the fact that it shouldn't be possible to do so. Just as the silence in oral communication helps witnesses bridge the gap, the white space and emotionless depictions are able to do the same. And just like words, graphics are able to communicate even with a lack of something.

By representing trauma through lack, Bechdel emphasizes an important dimension of the theory itself: loss may never be recuperated, but it may inspire future movement. Absence and loss persist; they are neither unrepresentable nor closed up, but they endure as a complex presence that opens a generative space of potentiality. As Smith emphasizes, Bechdel's ability to represent her lack without filling it in allows her to confront loss and expand beyond it, while her readers, or witnesses, experience a similar confrontation with lack and its potential for movement. The gap is not "stitch[ed] up" for either the testifier or the witness but remains as a catalyst for future movement. Whereas remembering or repeating would stymie Bechdel's progression, working-through necessitates her confrontation with lack's empty and enigmatic center at the same time that she allows its absence to awaken forward movement in her relationships, artistic productions, and language use.

Bechdel's Family Dynamic and the Experience of Loss

On the final pages of *Are You My Mother?* Bechdel draws a game she used to play with her mother called "the crippled child," where she would pretend to be physically disabled and her mother would help her until she could move without assistance. Over the illustration of a nearly autonomous child Alison, she writes: "There was a certain thing I did not get from my mother. There is a lack, a gap, a void. But in its place, she has given me something else. Something, I would argue, that is far more valuable. She has given me the way out" (288–89). I encourage students to recognize in this multilayered ending not only the psychoanalytic explanation of her unique artistic birth but also that the negotiation of her parental lack is a universal experience. Subjectivity is uniformly traumatic, in the sense that we all must deal with, as Freud puts it, "excitations from outside which are powerful enough to break through the protective shield" of the ego, but the development of the self is also generative, in that we need to endure the lack created through those excitations to propel forward to adult autonomy (*Beyond* 607).

As Bechdel asserts in *Are You My Mother?* through her direct use of psychoanalysis, psychic separation from parental others is a prerequisite for independent subjectivity, though it also creates the central "problem of the self and the relationship with the other." My student Allison Goodman describes Bechdel's process of separation from her parents and how Bechdel must embody them physically and destroy them psychically to inculcate the necessary lack for her independent subjectivity:

> We see Bechdel struggle, going back and forth between what something meant then and what it means now that she is older, wiser, and looking from various perspectives. She can analyze events differently as an adult than was possible as a child in the moment. This is achieved by posing as

each person in the book and viewing situations in the perspective of that person. In order for this to be effective, Bechdel must [be] open to the experience of healing and remain objective for the duration of the posing. In *Fun Home* and in *Are You My Mother?* Bechdel does not shy away from confrontation but gravitates toward her trauma and uses embodiment to work through and heal from said traumas.

As Goodman explains colloquially and I can emphasize more psychoanalytically, what happens in *Fun Home* with her father and continues in *Are You My Mother?* with her mother is that Bechdel separates from both her parents to achieve the autonomous subjectivity gained at the conclusion of "the crippled child" game, when she stands on her own feet after having been helped by her mother. In *Fun Home* Bechdel must become her father to separate from him, and in *Are You My Mother?* Bechdel must destroy her mother to separate from her.

In both separations, she must endure the confrontation with loss that is commensurate with any experience of trauma. She must realize, as she does in a recounted dream, that "[n]ow there was nothing between me . . . and nothing" (*Are You My Mother?* 272). The separation from each parent that prompts this confrontation with nothing also initiates the forward, productive movement that is first affiliated with pain and loss. Once again aligning her creative process to simultaneous destruction and expansion, Bechdel nervously admits, "I am literally in my basement recreating my childhood. [laughter] But I feel like this is my way to the outside world. And that when I'm writing about my family, my family is like a little country . . . and I'm trying to like overthrow it [laughter]" (Bechdel and Chute 207). Despite her mitigating laughter, Bechdel's psychic separation is indeed the coup she describes, and it is riddled with deception, death, isolation, and pain, but it also grants her necessary sovereignty. In her poignant words, "the lack" is also "the way out" and "that is far more valuable." Through her graphic narratives of trauma, she transforms her pain into art that is at once self-healing and catalytic for her witnesses. By remembering, repeating, and working-through her own losses and offering them for her audience's consumption, Bechdel always already proves that trauma is productive; lack inspires generation.

NOTE

[1] For broad introductions to trauma studies that are approachable for undergraduates, see Kaplan; Sontag, *Regarding the Pain of Others.*

Teaching *Fun Home* as a Disability Memoir

Cynthia Barounis

While few would dispute *Fun Home*'s relevance to queer studies and modernist studies, the memoir's relation to disability studies remains more ambiguous. Yet Bechdel's recollections of her childhood experience with obsessive-compulsive disorder open the possibility that the text is not only a queer bildungsroman but also a disability memoir. Because the pairing of *Fun Home* with disability studies is neither straightforward nor intuitive, it poses some interesting challenges in the disability studies classroom. Yet such a framing has the potential to generate a rich and provocative classroom discussion regarding the boundaries of disability identity and the politics of disability representation. Some of the approaches that I outline here are included in my article "Alison Bechdel and Crip-Feminist Autobiography," which can supplement this essay.

Disability studies focuses on how norms of able-bodiedness (and, more recently, able-mindedness) attach cultural stigma to disabled bodies and create barriers to access. Against a limiting medical model that frames the disabled body as a site of organic deficiency or brokenness in need of repair, the social model proposes instead that disability is a category that is created and sustained through a built environment designed for a narrow range of bodies and abilities. The social model is based on the assumption that disabled people do not need cures or medical interventions but rather a world that is constructed for a diversity of bodies and abilities. While activists and scholars in the social sciences have taken on disability-based injustices by advocating for inclusive education, accessible buildings, and public support for independent living, humanities scholars focus primarily on challenging the dominant image of disabled lives as tragic, inspirational, monstrous, or not worth living. More recently, disability scholars have adopted queer studies approaches that highlight the performativity and epistemological instability of disabled identity. Newer trends have also challenged the field's traditional focus on physical disability and mobility impairments, opening up important new inquiries into psychiatric disability, cognitive impairment, and neurodiversity. A class discussion that takes up *Fun Home* from the perspective of disability studies might be organized around three key questions: How is the social construction of Alison's childhood obsessive-compulsive disorder similar to or different from the social construction of her lesbian identity? To what extent does *Fun Home* participate in or subvert the cure narrative? And, finally, how do Bechdel's narrative strategies compare with other disability memoirs, particularly those that address mental disability?

I have taught selections of *Fun Home* in the context of an upper-level undergraduate course in women, gender, and sexuality studies, titled Feminist and Queer Disability Studies. The lesson on *Fun Home* occurred midway through the semester and concluded a brief unit on feminism and psychiatric disability.

Before introducing *Fun Home*, I wanted students to have a working understanding of the standard vocabularies, tools, and critiques of disability studies. Specifically, they had been trained to recognize ableism as a system of oppression and to understand disability as a site of political community and activism. We had also briefly covered the genealogy of hysteria as a gendered disorder and followed recent conversations about psychiatric disability as a distinct (and often marginalized) site of experience within the broader category of disability activism.

The sections of *Fun Home* most useful to a disability studies approach include chapter 3, which charts the emergence of Alison's lesbian self-identification, and chapter 5, which details the emergence of Alison's obsessive-compulsive disorder. These can be assigned individually or taught together in the context of the full memoir. I was aware that some students might resist reading Alison's temporary adoption of obsessive-compulsive behaviors as a disability. Rather than presenting *Fun Home* as a straightforward example of disability memoir, I explained that it would be the task of the class to evaluate whether or not the text could legitimately be assigned to the genre of disability memoir. By inviting debate on the topic, my aim was to validate students' important concerns while also making room for counter-readings that acknowledge *Fun Home*'s potential contribution to disability studies as a field and to disability memoir as a genre.

Though many students accept the labels applied to sexuality as social constructions, they may resist the idea that disability is a social construction. Pairing chapters 3 and 5 provides the opportunity to closely compare and contrast these two seemingly different identity categories. Chapter 3 depicts the process though which Alison gradually embraces a lesbian identity and comes out to her parents, culminating in the revelation of her father's own closeted sexual history with men. Chapter 5 revisits a period of several months of Bechdel's childhood during which she experienced a set of symptoms that she comes to recognize as manifestations of obsessive-compulsive disorder. To begin a comparative reading of these chapters, one might ask students to consider the role of the library in creating both identifications. In chapter 3, Bechdel describes her father's library as a "fantasy" that was "fully operational," "so authentic in its details, that it stops being pretense . . . and becomes for all practical purposes, real" (61, 60; ellipsis in original). While Bruce Bechdel uses books to fashion himself as heterosexual, Alison's parallel "revelation" (74) of her lesbian identification begins with the dictionary and progresses through a lesbian literary archive before joining the "human fray" (76) in a "novel fusion of word and deed" (80). These passages will give students the opportunity to reflect on the differences between acts and identities and to consider the way language does not simply name preexisting categories of sexuality but produces the very contexts for their emergence.

Once my class had established this understanding, I turned to chapter 5's staging of another "epistemological crisis" (141) that raises similar questions regarding the material effects of diagnostic labeling. Following a detailed description of her "actual obsessive-compulsive disorder" that "began when [she] was ten" (135), Bechdel observes that her mother's concern over her behaviors most likely derived from reading Dr. Spock's *Baby and Child Care* (138). Acknowledging that she herself had "spent many an hour browsing in that edifying volume," Bechdel recalls that "the section on compulsions came closest to describing my symptoms. So close, in fact, that I wonder if perhaps that's where I picked them up" (138). Reading these passages alongside one another should generate a provocative dialogue on similarities and differences between the way queer and disabled identities are fashioned. Students may point out, for example, that both identifications are presented as the effects of the very discourses and vocabularies meant to describe them. However, neither identity is presented as merely constructed; both are materially grounded by a set of embodied practices that Alison experiences as an authentic expression of selfhood.

Of course, while Bechdel may claim obsessive-compulsive disorder as a diagnosis, she does not explicitly claim a disabled identity. Such comparison may also, therefore, open a conversation about certain key differences between Bechdel's lesbian identity and her obsessive-compulsive subjectivity. While a rich canon of autobiographical literature helps Alison "elaborate on" the dictionary's limiting, clinical definition of *lesbian* (74), ultimately enabling her to situate herself in a queer community and to fashion a feminist politics, her experience with the literature of obsessive-compulsive disorder remains within the realm of the clinical. Individualized through the vocabulary of medicine, Alison's self-diagnosis appears neither to connect her to the disability community nor to lead her to develop a recognizable critique of ableism. Thus, unlike her lesbian identity, Alison's obsessive-compulsive disorder could be read as a personal obstacle to be transcended rather than a site of identity and experience. One student, for example, suggested that it is problematic to situate *Fun Home* within the genre of disability memoir because of the way Alison's struggle to overcome her obsessive-compulsive disorder aligns with the medical rather than the social model of disability.

Observations like this provide an opportunity to reflect on the extent to which *Fun Home* is complicit with or subverts the traditional cure narrative—a cultural trope that assumes that disability is a problem to be eliminated rather than a rich category of experience and identification. Because the chapter ends with Alison's recovery from her obsessive-compulsive behaviors through individual discipline and personal commitment, it would be easy to read the chapter's narrative arc through the framework of overcoming. Keeping these concerns in mind, I encouraged the class to entertain counter-readings that explore some of the ways that the memoir validates obsessive-compulsive behaviors, both in Bechdel's narrative style and her painstakingly precise drawing techniques. This discussion might be usefully supplemented with Bechdel's own account of her creative process. In a brief video, for example, Bechdel describes the way her commitment to detail and accuracy has resulted in the persistence of certain "obsessive" practices that she found necessary to complete the manuscript of *Fun Home* ("OCD"). In the light of these counter-readings, students can consider the extent to which the narrative affirms obsessive-compulsive disorder as a site of artistic creativity.

Finally, I found it especially useful to pair these chapters with Margaret Price's article "'Her Pronouns Wax and Wane': Psychosocial Disability, Autobiography, and Counter-Diagnosis," which provides a framework for comparing *Fun Home* to other disability memoirs. Elucidating a shared commitment to "counterdiagnosis," Price identifies the way various memoirs of psychiatric disability have adopted narrative strategies that overturn "key assumptions of autobiographical discourse, including rationality, coherence, truth and independence" (17). Because Price's arguments are complex, I focused discussion around the concepts of rationality, coherence, truth-telling, and independence. Students used *Fun Home*'s approach to each of these concepts as a litmus test for determining the extent to which the memoir is engaged in "counterdiagnosis." Students observed, for example, that Bechdel's commitment to realism and factual accuracy corresponds to an autobiographical impulse to tell the truth and that Bechdel's logical puzzling out of her family's past places the memoir in the realm of the rational. They also noted the extent to which *Fun Home* unravels those rationalist commitments by performing their impossibility. After all, pushed to their extremes, Bechdel's commitments to truth and rationality collapse into the diagnosable symptoms of obsessive-compulsive disorder. Thus, while *Fun Home* appears to uphold Price's "key assumptions of autobiographical discourse," a strong case can also be made that the memoir regularly undermines them.[1]

A discussion of independence is particularly fruitful here. Keeping in mind the commitment in disability studies to interdependence and care, I led the class through a close reading of the sequence in which Alison's mother writes Alison's diary entries for her when obsessive-compulsive symptoms make it impossible for Alison to write them: "For the next two months, she took dictation from me, until my 'penmanship' improved. And slowly, I did improve. On my wall calendar, I set myself deadlines by which to abandon specific compulsions, one at a time," which produced "a definite sense of relief, even if it only barely outstripped my lingering anxiety" (149–50). In this scene, Alison's desire to overcome her obsessive-compulsive disorder independently through the rigorous application of deadlines exists in tension with her reliance on her mother's gestures of collaboration and accommodation. Here, *Fun Home* aligns with disability studies by revealing complete autonomy and independence to be fantasies.

NOTE

[1] Charissa King-O'Brien's short documentary film *The Paper Mirror*, which records Bechdel's artistic collaboration with the prominent disabled artist Riva Lehrer, provides an additional tool for exploring Bechdel's connection to the disabled community and disability aesthetics.

Teaching *Fun Home* Online: Complicating Bechdel's Memoir through Slippage and Queer Temporalities

Ellen Gil-Gómez

Alison Bechdel has explained her view of the destabilizing nature of the comic form, and her attraction to it because of its combinations of image and text and the continual "slippage" between representation and meaning. She argues that comics texts uniquely highlight the gaps between representation and meaning in lived truths as well as those truths based in prose and image. She describes this interplay as a "disjuncture between appearance and reality," a "slippage between words and the picture, between the expected and unexpected . . . [between what an author] was saying and what you were seeing" (Bechdel, "Reading" 00:12:36, 00:12:55). I see *Fun Home* as a multilayered masterpiece that both enacts and demonstrates slippage. In my course Reading Comics and the Graphic Novel, despite students' growing ease with analyzing graphic structure, design, and narrative as the course progressed, most students, if unaided, tenaciously clung to a notion of the text as simply "queer" or "gay," describing it as the coming-out story of a "confused" tomboy who "becomes" gay because of her father's "problem." To my surprise, when the course reached *Fun Home*, students' earlier progress would suddenly come to a screeching halt when we reached this text. However, Bechdel's form allowed me to facilitate a more challenging approach to *Fun Home* that responded to students' resistance and encouraged reading beyond stereotypes. I introduce Bechdel's narrative strategies, and more specifically her concept of slippage, as similar to, but distinct from, Scott McCloud's analytical approaches in *Understanding Comics*. I also find that teaching the text online aids my success in developing students' analytical abilities, despite their resistance, as they consider the relations between image and word.

I created Reading Comics and the Graphic Novel, a junior-level English class, to introduce analytical reading strategies for graphic texts. It attracts English majors, liberal studies (pre-education) majors, and general-education, comic book enthusiasts. I provide the analytical tools discussed in Will Eisner's *Comics and Sequential Art* and in McCloud's *Understanding Comics* and a history of mainly American, though also Japanese and European, comic forms for historical and cultural context. Required texts are in chronological order of publication, beginning with Art Spiegelman's *Maus*; we read *Fun Home* the penultimate week. Students encounter a variety of genres throughout the course: autobiography and memoir, children's and young-adult fiction, periodical fiction, online comics, and graphic novels. Students also practice analyses of textual images, lines, and fonts as well as of visual narrative structure and time. Thus, they encounter class texts in the context of both their literary history, genre, and thematic or subject matter as well as their individualized use of image elements and design. This encourages students to compare and contrast a text within its own contexts as well as with other texts.

Given the visual nature of online teaching, I find comic and graphic narratives are a natural fit. They provide an excellent opportunity for students to consider how to analyze imagery alongside text in order to more fully understand how they interrelate. I concur with the view that teaching online gives students more opportunity for "deep" learning, a concept from educational psychology, usually attributed to F. Marton and R. Säljö, which describes "deep-level processing" as opposed to "surface-level processing." Deep learning requires students to "stand back and conceptualise, seek out interconnections between concepts and data while reflecting on their learning," and, more pointedly, it "involves the bringing together of thesis, antithesis and synthesis. What is important is that the synthesis shows not simply progression but a reconceptualization of the inquiry" (Rosie 109, 110). The online format allows students to consider and reconsider course materials and their scaffolding throughout the term in order to expand their comprehension. Quite simply, students can review earlier discussions, analyses, lectures, and contextual and research materials at any time and at any pace. This deep-learning approach is particularly helpful for studying comic narratives, as most students are wholly unfamiliar with reading and analyzing them and understanding their histories. The online format allows the teacher to require students to watch introductory *PowerPoint* presentations or *YouTube* or other videos before discussing or analyzing the specifics of the text. Because there is no need to manage time, in contrast to the traditional classroom, instructors can require students to review several lectures or presentations to inform the discussion that follows. Thus, teachers can take advantage of ever-growing online materials to help students engage in deep learning.

In my class students watch the hour-long *YouTube* lecture "Reading and Discussion by Graphic Artist Alison Bechdel," in which Bechdel discusses her desire to foreground "slippage"—the gaps of meaning between image and text—in her comics. I highlight this term in my discussion questions so that students can compare Bechdel's understanding of the relation of word and image with McCloud's tools from *Understanding Comics*, which they've studied earlier. Bechdel's lecture also includes the history of her comic strip series, *Dykes to Watch Out For*, and detailed personal background from her childhood and her career as an artist and writer. I ask students to consider the generic differences between *Dykes* and *Fun Home* in order to consider how form might determine function. Autobiographical details from the lecture supplement the memoir's account of how the moment of her father's death affected Bechdel's life and the memoir's portrayal of her autobiographical character, Alison. The lecture also includes examples of slippage in *Fun Home* and relates some of what she wanted to accomplish with them. In addition, students watch Bechdel's five-minute *YouTube* video that demonstrates her photorealism technique of replicating family photos and using digital stills of herself as artistic studies for all the characters in the memoir ("Alison Bechdel: Creating *Fun Home*"). The video reveals her process in detail and again demonstrates some relations between image and text and between the real and the imagined.

In addition to these videos, I require that students view their peers' presentations on *Dykes to Watch Out For*, the history of photorealism in art, and the history of gay and lesbian comic characters. After they have reflected on the broader contexts that these materials bring to *Fun Home*, I have the students go back through the memoir and note the path of photorealistic moments in the narrative, reviewing how, even though these moments are apparently direct transcriptions from reality, Bechdel creates slippage by locating these panels within specific narrative time frames. For example, the text opens with chapter 1's photorealist image of Bechdel's father as a younger married man: bare chest exposed, hands on hips, turned to the reader in what might be seen as a self-conscious fashion pose. The portrait is located directly in front of the family house's front door. The chapter title, "Old Father, Old Artificer," contextualizes the father instantly. In order to show how narrative time functions in the text, I ask students to read this image on its own before reading the text and then again afterward. Most of them initially see the father as a rather sad and "old" man, and they're unsure if the word *artificer* is a positive or negative comment by the author. They tend to approach the memoir trying to find the answer to that question. After they read the first chapter, they see things anew in its opening image: the importance of the position of the man in front of the house; the construct of "artificer" as a reflection of the father's identity as gay, as revealing of his secret; Bechdel's creation of reality at the start of the text. They can more easily see numerous examples of slippage between the points of view of Bechdel the author and of Alison the character. Through this exercise they become aware of the importance of how images tell a story versus how the text does and of the importance of the memoir's narrative structure.

After they've read the full text, students answer one discussion-board question so that they can speak to one another about these concepts and illustrate their knowledge with support from the course texts. They might compare and contrast the use of photorealism in *Maus* and *Fun Home*—how the photographs function in the two texts—and the impact of Bechdel's dual histories provided by her text and her drawings of photos. Because the class has already studied the history of the detective comic, they can read Bechdel's text in answer to the prompt of how the book can be read as one: Who is the investigator? What is the crime? When they read the character Alison as the investigator, they see the crime as the dysfunctional relationship between her parents and the lies, silences, and spoken and unspoken expectations of the parents as the evidence. Alternatively, if they read the author as the investigator, they tend to identify the crime as the father's closeted homosexuality, against which Bechdel came out as a lesbian: the evidence then is found in the house, her father's obsessions, the photographs, and his death. If they read the text and its components within these different paradigms, they can see the importance of both genre and narrative structure in comic texts.

The final assignment is a private journal entry (an informal writing assignment on *Blackboard* that only the student author and instructor can read) that contains the student's general map of the memoir—image and text showing what the student believes to be the skeleton of the work—and a two-page study of how photorealism, embedded in narrative time, creates slippage, which they write by analyzing Bechdel's style, word bubbles, lines, panel shape, orientation, point of view, and so on. For one example of this approach, I ask the students to use the photorealistic chapter-heading images to create their own version of the story: the father in front of the house; the father's grave; a portrait of both parents with a wide gap between them; a photo that appears to be a woman but, the chapter reveals, is actually Bechdel's father dressed in a woman's bathing suit; a landscape shot of an early evening sky; the mother in front of a dressing-room makeup mirror; and Alison as a girl jumping off a diving board toward her father. How do these images create a narrative? How do they shape the reader's understanding of what's true or real and what belongs to slippage? How does that narrative compare with Bechdel's own discussion of her quest for the real in reading comics or her goal in the memoir of understanding her father's story? Students consider the literal and symbolic importance of these photorealistic moments. Some see them chronologically as indicative of the creation of the father's false life, which leads inevitably to his death. Others see the negative effects of the father's artifice on the entire family. Other students read them as Alison's quest to find meaning within the photographs themselves, thus accounting for their circular placement at the beginning and ending of the book. The course's online context gives students both deep content and time to reflect thoughtfully on these issues with one another and individually. I have found these contexts and techniques encourage deeply evocative analyses by students.

Through these exercises my students also notice Bechdel's creation of what Jack Halberstam calls a "queer temporality": "'queer time' and 'queer space' [that] develop, at least in part, in opposition to the institutions of family, heterosexuality, and reproduction. They also develop according to other logics of location, movement, and identification" (1). Thus, when students consider Bechdel's text as a memoir—individual or familial—I ask them to consider how or if it is queer in the way that Halberstam describes. If students compare the use of memory and documents in *Maus* and *Fun Home*, they see how Bechel demonstrates queer time, whether or not I use the term in class. Either way, I have found the concept of queer temporality to benefit students' reading and understanding of *Fun Home* both within and outside their own understanding of family identity and construction.

To my surprise, most students end up writing their final research paper on *Fun Home*. It is unprecedented in my classes that are not focused on LGBTQ literature to have students choose a queer text for their final assignment. I believe that the combination of deep learning, contextual analyses, and respect for Bechdel's concept of slippage encourages this affinity, even though most of my students are initially resistant to understanding *Fun Home* as more than an example of gay identity derived from psychological trauma or as a straightforward coming-out narrative. The online format's capacity for facilitating deep learning seems to encourage students to move away from opposition to the text and instead to strongly identify with the memoir's complex family stories.

Representing Queer Identity:
A Blogging Exercise

Christine L. Quinan

In our current era, where images are omnipresent and inescapable, Alison Bech-del's graphic memoir *Fun Home: A Family Tragicomic* poignantly speaks to the importance of visual representations in shaping our worlds. A hallmark of the present moment is the ubiquity of social media, with networking sites like *Facebook*, *Tumblr*, *Twitter*, and *Instagram* affecting how we connect, document, and remember. Given this craving for the visual and the digital, particularly for younger generations, it is worth asking how we might draw upon technology to allow for exchanges of knowledge and increased opportunities for students of diverse backgrounds, abilities, and personalities to engage with academic material. Indeed, because social media structures how information is communicated and learned, our institutions, including universities, will benefit from finding effective ways to make pedagogical use of these tools (Davidson 64). Blogging as a reading-response exercise for students reading *Fun Home* works particularly well to harness the combined potential of social media and the graphic memoir's visuality and thematics; it also allows students to connect to difficult topics, particularly around sexuality and gender.

To achieve the pedagogical objective of fostering critical questioning and dialogue in a compassionate and supportive environment, online networking tools allow for the expansion of learning outside the four walls of the classroom by supporting community building and creative engagement; they also stimulate bidirectional and *double-loop learning*, a learning model that encourages reflection on assumptions, beliefs, and goals (Argyris and Schön). Margee Hume summarizes some of the key benefits of blogging: "Many recent authors suggest using weblogs for knowledge sharing and learning in information spaces. They suggest blogging is successful for text-based collaboration. These authors posit that blogging relaxes norms allowing introvert participants to share their ideas on equal terms with extroverts" (53). An especially important feature of blogging is that it encourages quieter students who may not feel comfortable speaking in large groups to offer input and feedback that the entire class can read. It also allows students to explore new ideas, exchange knowledge, and actively participate in discussion both inside and outside the classroom, offering a space where students can productively agree or disagree and can become actively and collaboratively involved in their own learning.

It is crucial, however, to not overlook privacy concerns as well as the potential for online harassment. These issues have become ever more salient not only because of the sensitive nature of blog postings related to sexuality and gender but also because of the increase in trolling and online bullying and harassment. To address these concerns, I require that course blogs be set to private so that they are only accessible to course participants. This precaution cannot guarantee safety, but having a closed group creates intimacy among members and a greater sense of security in discussing sensitive topics.

While I have taught *Fun Home* in various gender studies courses—undergraduate writing courses, queer literature and film survey courses, even a course called What Is a Classic?—I focus here on a blogging assignment in an undergraduate writing course entitled Representing Queer Identity: Post-Stonewall LGBT Literature and Film. In this composition course blogging offers students a venue in which to practice their writing skills. However, I see this approach and assignment as offering productive possibilities in a number of undergraduate courses, across disciplines and institutions. I always teach the entire text of *Fun Home*, which is normally covered during four sessions (approximately six hours). A central component of the course is investigating how varied genres are differently able to recount gay, lesbian, and queer identity, and *Fun Home* uniquely narrates sexuality and desire in a highly accessible format. Its prompting of larger questions about inclusion and exclusion, with respect to both literary canonization and social marginalization, is often a central point of discussion. Students overwhelmingly appreciate the memoir, often naming it as their favorite—and most effective—course text.

For this assignment students create their own blog using a free hosting site, such as *Blogger*, *Wordpress*, or *Tumblr*, and post weekly entries of about 250 words related to class content. Students are also expected to follow other classmates' blogs, thereby facilitating dialogue both in and outside class. Blog posts can follow several formats: a brief summary and analysis of the main ideas or common themes of the assigned texts; a response to comments, questions, or debates brought up during class discussions; or commentary on a classmate's blog entry. The blogs are evaluated on a check-plus, check, check-minus scale. At the end of the semester, students present a written and oral portfolio that requires them to revisit their blogs to revise previous reading responses and arguments formulated about class material and discussions.

While the students blogged throughout the semester, I found that our unit on *Fun Home* lent itself particularly well to blogging for several reasons. First, because the reader plays an active role in making meaning in graphic texts like *Fun Home*, students were able to bring their analysis to another level by including visual representations of the memoir. Graphic novels generate new and alternative meanings through a juxtaposition of word and image; they experiment with form and content in their constantly changing arrangements of words and visuals, creating different forms of signification than other types of literature (Quinan 156). They also play spatially with different temporalities in a single panel or page, layering the past on the present. Reading a graphic novel is not a passive process; the reader is drawn into the iterative construction of the visual and written elements. Hillary L. Chute elaborates: "a reader of comics not only fills in the gaps between panels but also works with the often disjunctive back-and-forth of *reading* and *looking* for meaning" ("Comics as Literature?" 452).

In this respect, students often posted about the emotions (including discomfort) that the images evoked in them, almost mirroring the meta-reflection on word, image, and memory that Bechdel herself engages in.

Blogging also proved to be successful in dealing with challenging themes related to gender and sexuality. Perhaps because of its graphic nature, *Fun Home* seems to give students permission to engage in their blog entries with topics like coming out and the fluidity of sexuality, topics with which students may be grappling on a personal level. As students quickly notice, Bechdel's constantly changing frames on the page—and subversion of traditional narrative techniques—force readers to question the boxing in of identity. The text points to the unspeakability of nonnormative genders and sexualities, but as a visual text it also illustrates queer identities and desires, which blogging and social media platforms also effectively do. Inevitably, students blog about the importance of the images (adding images from the novel to their posts) and emphasize how Bechdel's drawings gave them a sense of stepping into a world of queer possibilities—and impossibilities—which turned out to be important for both queer and nonqueer students. Because, as a memoir, *Fun Home* is a study in getting personal, the text encourages similar responses from readers, inviting reflection on identity, family, and sexuality. In this sense, reading and commenting on one another's blog posts brings students inside the text in a different way, while having the added benefit of allowing them to develop skills in providing and receiving feedback.

Chute writes of the rich tradition that female graphic novelists like Bechdel are currently establishing through a focus on themes like childhood and sexuality that are often unvoiced. She writes that these writer-artists exemplify "how graphic narrative can envision an everyday reality of women's lives, which, while rooted in the personal, is invested and threaded with collectivity, beyond prescriptive models of alterity or sexual difference." She elaborates on the significance of this work: "In every case, from the large-scale to the local, graphic narrative presents a traumatic side of history, but all these authors refuse to show it through the lens of unspeakability or invisibility, instead registering its difficulty through inventive (and various) textual practice" ("Comics as Literature?" 459). While graphic novels are poised to make significant political and creative contributions that reformulate identity, visibility, and voice, so too is social media, particularly when harnessed as a learning tool.

This experiment has only touched the surface of the deep potential that social media holds for learning outcomes. Blogging has led to exchanges of knowledge and has increased opportunities for quieter students and differently abled students to engage with the course material. *Fun Home* exemplifies a complex interplay between genre and form. The intricate relation between words and images in both graphic novels like *Fun Home* and the exercise of blogging allow us to uncover the continual negotiation between these two systems and to see social, cultural, and personal relationships in a different way.

Teaching *Fun Home* to Instill Reading Resilience in First-Year Literature Students

Judith Seaboyer and Jessica Gildersleeve

Recent studies show the value of what has come to be known as flipping the classroom as a way to foster student engagement through preclass preparation. In a flipped classroom, traditional teaching methods are reversed: students are exposed to new material before they come to class, so class time may be used to engage with that material at a sophisticated, critical level. This chapter draws on a recent Australian study of student reading habits and provides evidence that using a flipped model to instill reading resilience in undergraduate literature courses can encourage students to prioritize reading in the same way as they prioritize other assessment tasks. The work we report here is the trial and rollout of a two-year, cross-institutional, Australian government–funded research project called Reading Resilience: Developing a Skills-Based Approach to Reading in Higher Education.

The catalyst for the Reading Resilience project—which aims to address "confident and articulate advanced reading skills" that students need in the literature classroom ("What Is Reading Resilience?")—was contemporary pedagogical research (e.g., Arum and Roksa; Scholes) that confirmed the investigators' classroom experiences across five Australian universities, all of which showed that most undergraduate students cherry-pick from a required reading list the minimum number of texts needed to achieve a passing grade in written assessment, typically the research essay. This failure to read with the care and attention necessary to the humanities is exacerbated by changing technology. Synopses, often unsophisticated and wrong-headed, and readings of difficult texts are just a click away on sites like *eNotes* and *Shmoop*. As the library and information technologist Ziming Liu reports, "students now spend more time on browsing and scanning, keyword spotting, one-time reading, non-linear reading . . . and less time on in-depth reading, concentrated reading, and sustained attention" (705). Maria Konnikova summed up that "the more reading moved online the less students seemed to understand," and that "skimming has become the new reading." We argue that as long as such pragmatic approaches to reading, or not reading, are allowed to pass for what should be the transformative process that is an education in the humanities, we are the ones failing: we fail our students because they do not develop deep-reading skills, what J. Hillis Miller terms "slow reading" (122), that will enable them to go beyond surface skimming and enjoy, rather than simply survive, a tertiary education. This is at the heart of our philosophy as teachers of literature. In the 2011 case study for the Reading Resilience project, slow reading was emphasized from the outset: students in a first-year literary studies course at the University of Queensland, called Reading and Writing Contemporary Literature, began the course by discussing the chapter "How to Read Literature" from Miller's *On Reading* (115–31).

Broadly speaking, our research has shown it is possible to encourage preclass engagement and to foster not only more but also better reading across the Australian thirteen-week semester (Poletti et al.; Douglas et al.). A reading-resilient classroom is flipped: the day before the first class on any text, students must have completed the set reading and uploaded to the online study environment (e.g., *Blackboard* or *Moodle*) a critical, closely argued, 250-word response to one of a number of prompts that are part of a tailored, two-page reading guide. To ensure students move toward critical engagement and away from purely reflective observation, we insist that they produce a coherent discussion, including an explicit argument stated within the first fifty words, and that their discussion is expressed in coherent discursive prose that adheres to the conventions of the argumentative academic essay—no bullet points or other shortcuts. This tight word limit means that students must write clearly and concisely; Helen Sword's *The Writer's Diet* and Gerald Graff and Cathy Birkenstein's *They Say / I Say* have proved invaluable in helping students develop this skill, which in turn results in better writing in longer essays, in both the current course and beyond it, as well as greater clarity in classroom discussions.

This essay discusses the benefits of reading-resilience practices for engagement with texts students find difficult, particularly Alison Bechdel's *Fun Home*. The techniques we tested worked especially well with Bechdel's structurally and thematically challenging memoir. Our experience convinced us that reluctant students can become resilient readers of texts they might otherwise find too difficult, and they learn to value reading as a practice that uses particular skills and to recognize that reading is work, just as writing an essay is work. We remind them that in most courses in the humanities, they will spend more time reading than on marked assessment. Knowing that students are immersed in a grade-centered culture, we explain that, while reading literature is pleasurable, it takes time, patient attention, and persistence, and therefore the time-consuming work that is good reading will be assessed with marks toward the final grade. In other words, they will see an immediate return on investment.

Our experience has been that even those who struggle with the reading responses have begun the critical thinking that can then bear fruit in classroom discussion. Lectures and tutorials blossom into learning communities in contrast with sessions in which the teacher and the few who have completed the reading must outline the text for the rest of the students and rely on, for example, the in-class, close reading of an extract, which may be the only part of the text some students ever read (Poletti et al. 2).

For the University of Queensland rollout of the Reading Resilience project, we taught a module on *Fun Home* across two weeks to a class of 170 students, most of them first-year literary studies majors and others from a range of disciplines who were taking the course as an elective. *Fun Home* was one of six texts studied.[1] Together, the fortnightly responses were worth a substantial thirty percent of the final grade.

The reading guide for *Fun Home* consists of a brief introduction to the text, an invitation for a compulsory but ungraded affective response, and a series of writing prompts.[2] The introduction positions Bechdel's text as a graphic memoir within the subgenre of life writing. It cites two recommended secondary readings. Ariela Freedman alerts students to Bechdel's overt intertextuality. Bechdel, Freedman argues,

> positions her memoir at the intersection of image, narrative, autobiography and history [as she] makes an additional play for high literary status by larding her book with the influence of canonical modernist literature, not only through frequent and explicit citation and reference but also by subtler formal, thematic and textual gestures. In telling her story, Bechdel explicitly places the graphic narrative in irreverent, iconoclastic dialogue with literary modernism.   (126)

Freedman's argument signals the need to engage with scholarly responses to a text and models a way of doing so. In addition, by positioning *Fun Home* on a symbolic bookshelf with James Joyce, F. Scott Fitzgerald, and Marcel Proust, it immediately warns against passing over this book as simply a comic and therefore not literary. Finally, it encourages students to consider what place Bechdel's intertextual references have in her narrative. This approach might form the basis for a student's affective or critical response (or both).

The introduction concludes with practical advice on how to read a graphic narrative, a literary mode with which students might be unfamiliar: "Examine each frame in the opening page. Reading this graphic memoir will require you to negotiate the relationship between text and image within each frame, and the relationship between frames." We cite the second recommended critical reading, by Hillary Chute and Marianne DeKoven, so that students begin thinking about how image and text intersect: "The images are not illustrative of the text," Chute and DeKoven point out, "but comprise a separate narrative thread that moves forward in time in a different way than the prose text, which also moves the reader forward in time" (769). This idea helps students see "the dynamic interaction between text and image that [not only] makes comics a particularly evocative form of life writing" but also requires readers to "slow down enough to make the connections between image and text and from panel to panel" (770). *Fun Home*, then, allows our students to see more clearly the importance of Miller's "[s]low reading, critical reading [that is] suspicious at every turn, interrogating every detail of the work, trying to figure out by just what means the magic is wrought" (122). We conclude by confirming the writerly nature of *Fun Home*, and of graphic narratives in general, and their insistence on the reader's active engagement in meaning making. All this builds students' confidence in their own critical skills prior to classroom discussion of the text.

The reading guide's introduction trains students in the ways we approach literary texts. The critical response is central, but our iteration invites students to begin the process by thinking about the text in terms of affect, which encourages them to distinguish between this particular response and the analysis that underpins the discipline of literature. Typical responses noted students' surprise at the literary value of a graphic novel, difficulty engaging with both text and image, and resistance to the confronting nature of the content (in particular, Bruce's homosexuality and his relationships with his male students and images that explicitly depicted lesbian sexuality). By acknowledging and then setting aside affective response as a barrier to understanding, students found that they could move on and engage the text critically. Alison's father's overt attraction to his male students became a topic for open discussion rather than one that was too easily closed down by hostile or prejudged responses. Students teased out what it was they found disturbing: the student's age, his gender, or the violation of the teacher-student relationship? Some were surprised to discover that they would have felt even more disturbed had the student whose photograph becomes the centerfold of Bechdel's text been a seventeen-year-old female rather than a male, which led to a discussion of how deeply gender stereotyping shapes our responses.

Students then prepared and uploaded the reading response, which, together with ten minutes allowed for the affective response, formed the basis of tutorial discussion. They chose one from a series of prompts:

Think about how Bechdel's graphic memoir works on the page compared with, say, *Atonement* [another course text]. Take a page you find particularly interesting and be prepared to analyze its structure in terms of the relation of the linguistic and the visual, of one frame to another, of the function of the gutter, etc.

Where would you place *Fun Home* on the readerly-writerly continuum, and why?

How does the opening page of *Fun Home* operate as what Miller refers to as an "open Sesame" (24)?

Discuss the wordplay in the full title of Bechdel's text: *Fun Home: A Family Tragicomic*. What literary weight does each word carry, and how does each, separately and together, contribute to the meaning of the text?

If you look up the myth of Icarus on *Wikipedia*, you will see how often it has been appropriated in modern art, including literature. One famous example is W. H. Auden's lyric poem "Musée des Beaux Arts." Discuss why Bechdel might have chosen this particular myth as an intertext. Can you think of other contemporary texts that take up classical myth in similar or different ways?

Linked to the guide is the marking rubric that allows students to check how well they have fulfilled the requirements before they submit.

We have already indicated that rewarding reading through the preclass production of short responses improves student engagement and the quality of longer research essays. In addition, we have found that techniques of reading resilience are particularly useful for texts that deal with confessional or traumatic content. In particular, the invitation to students to produce a brief affective response prior to completing the assessed activity enables self-reflection and modes of response that promote interaction with the literary other. To encourage this kind of ethical engagement, the course drew students' attention to Roland Barthes's work on *lisible* ("readerly") and *scriptible* ("writerly") texts (*Pleasure*). Developing Adrielle Mitchell's argument that "*Fun Home* is an intensely writerly . . . text in its rich layering of non-contiguous series [and] the reader is required to gather the strings offered on many different pages in order to be hoisted and transported by the balloons of [Bechdel's] tale" (2), the lecture identified *Fun Home* (and literary texts more generally) as "writerly," and underscored for students the need to work to make meaning. Combined with the critical reflection and affective response already produced before the lecture, this position encouraged students to take responsibility for their interpretations and claim ownership of their arguments, thereby increasing confidence and originality in assessment tasks. Perhaps more important, this emphasis on the reader's role equipped students to deal more readily with texts that may be confronting in theme or technique. For example, we developed a seminar activity that asked students to analyze *Fun Home*'s centerfold, in which Bruce's sleeping student is unquestionably the object of his teacher's gaze. Consideration of the way in which the reader's hands holding the book overlap the illustrated hands holding the photograph allowed students to see this as an epiphany for the character, the narrator, and the reader. In this recognition students came to view trauma as a condition of the narrative rather than something limited to their own experience.

Fun Home can be a difficult text for first-year literary studies students. Practicing reading resilience techniques that reward reading and preparation improves student engagement and writing skills. By emphasizing slow reading, reading resilience is also a form of ethical inquiry in the discipline and figures for students a type of responsible engagement with texts like *Fun Home* and the cultural work they perform.

NOTES

[1]The other texts were Simon Armitage's *Selected Poems* (2001), J. M. Coetzee's *Disgrace* (1999), Louise Doughty's *Whatever You Love* (2010), Jennifer Egan's *A Visit from the Goon Squad* (2010), and Ian McEwan's *Atonement* (2001).

[2]A version of the *Fun Home* reading guide is available in the "Reading Resilience Toolkit" (R. Kennedy et al. 32).

Fun Home as Young Adult Literature and the Ethics of Mentoring Teacher Candidates

Donna L. Pasternak

Classifying graphic narratives as young adult literature is common among teacher candidates as they approach selecting and teaching literature for middle and high school students.[1] In "Why Comics Are and Are Not Picture Books: Introduction," Charles Hatfield and Craig Svonkin note that picture books—stories that empower readers to participate in cultural literacy—are often conflated with comics—stories that are "fugitive reading" that work against literacy norms (431). The debate as to what is and what is not young adult literature occurs frequently in classes I teach for teacher candidates. One year, Alison Bechdel's *Fun Home* was at the center of this debate, providing a complex literary model for my students to think deeply about what literature they will teach and how they will teach it.

Teaching Young Adult Literature to Teacher Candidates

Reading Interests of Adolescents is partly a young adult literature survey and partly a pedagogy course in reading workshop following Nancie Atwell's design from *In the Middle: New Understandings about Writing, Reading, and Learning*, engaging readers in minilessons about literary study, book talks, teacher and peer conferencing, and small- and large-group activities while they read various texts (87–299). Differing from most traditional university-level literary study, this class asks teacher candidates to participate in whole- and small-group inquiry and collaborative learning.[2] Class meetings are spent reading silently and documenting primary texts, making critical observations about texts, and designing the formats and guidelines to teach literature through reading workshop.[3] Students also engage in an online discussion forum between class meetings to share their reading journals with one another.

The philosophy that underscores the teaching of this class is the notion that if teacher educators tell teacher candidates what to think, we will merely cultivate submissive teachers and not smart, activist educators.[4] Therefore, on the first day of Reading Interests of Adolescents, students engage in a know–want to know–learned (KWL) strategy about constructivism, critical inquiry, reading workshop, and young adult literature. From this activity, we build the inquiry questions we will explore for the rest of the semester. The students then go to the library or online and find a book that they feel is young adult literature and a scholarly definition of young adult literature. Students bring to class texts that range from Orson Scott Card's *Ender's Game* to Mark Twain's *Adventures of Huckleberry Finn*. Unbeknown to them, these selections become the class reading list, a list that underscores critical conversations about the culture wars, breadth, remedial reading, literary texts, student- or teacher-centered learning, and how young adult literature may differ from texts read in their other literature classes. After a few weeks with this list, someone generally asks how to add new texts to it. To do so, students must substantiate the new text as quality young adult literature by using the scholarship learned in their inquiry work.

Fun Home *as* Young Adult Literature

After engaging in the KWL exercise, Derek DeVinney brought *Fun Home* to class because it was a story told through graphic narrative. Student online discussions centered on the misconceptions that James B. Carter details in "Going Graphic": that graphic narratives were "low culture" and too easy for high school students (68). Others thought graphic novels were exciting because they were subversive. Derek posted why he added *Fun Home* to the list:

> [It] takes the reader through the protagonist's life, starting as a young adolescent, and leading into adulthood. It deals with real-world anxieties ranging from broad spheres like societal, to smaller spheres, like the domestic as well as individual. . . . [Where the] definition [of young adult literature] speaks to the value of young adult literature being able to connect students by using central issues in the reader's lives, I am able to think of instances where *Fun Home* is valuable. Homosexuality, suicide, dysfunctional families, and OCD are only a few of these real instances dealt with in the novel that young adults may be suffering through and find reassurance through reading this text.

Despite defining *Fun Home* as young adult literature, Derek did not think he would teach it because "[t]he content can be pretty provocative, but that is not the main reason. Basically, I just feel it is a really advanced work." Erin Day, a student in another class, echoed Derek's concerns:

> This book is very intertextual, creating symmetries between the story Bechdel is telling and the narratives and authors her father loves most (Henry James, Oscar Wilde, F. Scott Fitzgerald) and also the later manifestation of the bibliophagic tendencies her father nurtured in her as she comes to her own "erotic truth" through independent studies of lesbian feminist literature in college. For these reasons, I would definitely suggest this book for older readers, perhaps seventeen and above. There were times that I didn't feel like I fully got everything Bechdel was doing because I wasn't familiar enough with *The Odyssey* or *The Importance of Being Earnest*, so I think this book might be a little advanced both in structure and in the kinds of texts referenced for younger readers. Additionally, the vocabulary of this text is so advanced that I have a whole page

of words I was not familiar with before I read this book, so that leads me to situate the book at the level of older readers, as well.

Both Erin's and Derek's unease with *Fun Home*'s content prompted other students to want to teach it, because they thought it would help students coming to terms with their sexual identity. Nick Bodette wondered "how widespread and commonplace homosexual topics are taught in schools. I agree that at least an understanding should be established in kids to stop abusive and emotionally detrimental name-calling, but I wonder how it would go over with some parents, or religiously inclined people." Ultimately, Derek decided that

> given sufficient resources and student interest, . . . this book would be best taught in some sort of graphic novel elective class where the curriculum would revolve around exploring genres and themes within the specific literary format. This would be a great book to show both the style of a graphic memoir and the theme of sexuality. . . . [I]t took me a while to get through *Fun Home*, and although I agree that the graphic novel style can be more accessible for young students, I would not say so with this specific title.

Because of *Fun Home*'s advanced language, sexual content, intertextuality, and graphic illustrations of the human body, content also found in word-based young adult literature, *Fun Home* challenged notions of what could be taught in secondary schools, what is appropriate content for young adults, what is literary text, and what is young adult literature—conversations the course was designed to generate. By engaging in discussions about sophisticated literary works like *Fun Home*, Derek, Erin, and Nick explored the shifting tastes of culture and analyzed the factors that complicated their decision making about what is appropriate literature for their future students. By engaging in the complex decision-making process about the appropriateness of a text like *Fun Home*, they came to understand how and to whom it could be taught, a process that will support their future curriculum design.

Mentoring Teacher Candidates

When Derek brought *Fun Home* into our class, he challenged our notions about literature and the teaching of it. By engaging teacher candidates with literary choices that connect to their own lives and interests and by supporting an environment in which they can conduct intertextual, critical conversations about literary works they plan to teach, studying a text like *Fun Home* as young adult literature in reading workshop provides teacher candidates a model of literary study that fosters a democratic, informal, active learning community that teacher candidates should want to replicate. Studying Bechdel's *Fun Home* encouraged critical conversations that helped us define young adult literature and consider the memoir's appropriateness for young readers.

NOTES

When I was awarded an overseas student-teaching placement in 1976, my teacher education program assigned Bruce Bechdel as my cooperating (mentor) teacher in the United States while I waited to leave for South America. In the six weeks I spent with him, I took on all his classes: Poetry, Humanities, Courtship and Marriage, Science Fiction, and Coming of Age, the last the class Alison Bechdel identifies in *Fun Home* as the Rites of Passage class (198). She was one of my students for those few weeks. Not having heard from Bruce since late 1978, I did not know he had died in 1980. Only when one of the teacher candidates described in this essay brought *Fun Home* to a class I was teaching did I discover that it was about the Bruce and Alison Bechdel I knew from my own student teaching. This knowledge added a layer of complexity to studying this book that would not otherwise have been present in another young adult literature class. Bruce Bechdel's influence on how I teach my young adult literature class is apparent on a number of levels. He taught me to give students the opportunity to choose books they could relate to by providing his own students with lists of texts he created for independent or small-group study (although he did not teach literature through reading workshop but through whole-class reads involving lecture and other seat work), to support students to share poetry and lyrics of their choosing that aligned intertextually with the themes discussed in class, to structure discussion so that students connect books to their own lives as they analyze the texts with respect to social class and religion, and to vary the genres and difficulty of texts by his including the works of Judy Blume and Paul Zindel alongside those of Jane Austen and Shakespeare—unusual in the 1970s, when young adult literature was just being recognized as a genre.

¹For discussion, see Carter; Reid.

²For a variety of inquiry and collaborative learning activities that underscore why reading-workshop literary study is empowering to students, see Fecho; Freire; Golub; Jennings and Smith; Mitchell and Christenbury; Pasternak, "Combat Ready"; and Soter et al.

³For a sampling of materials that discuss critical literary study for college students, high school students, and teacher candidates, see Applebee; Appleman; Gaughan; Giroux; Graff; Pasternak, "Poetry and Pop Culture"; and Soter et al.

⁴See the following works that discuss the politics of teaching and teacher empowerment: Giroux; hooks; Noddings; and Pasternak and Scott.

Afterword

Alison Bechdel

It's been very strange seeing my memoir *Fun Home* adopted by so many college English courses, if only because one strand of the book is about my own ambivalence toward English classes when I was in college. Where once I struggled to understand the Jungian symbolism in *The Sun Also Rises*, a new generation of students is decoding the events of my personal, real-life, 1970s adolescence, through critical strategies that in the 1970s had not even been invented yet. Of course, I'm very lucky that my book has struck a chord with English professors and students—and as the child of two high school English teachers I am also very gratified by the whole phenomenon. Yet it remains a bit odd to have the intimate material of my life analyzed in this way by scholars.

But I suppose I asked for it. As I was writing *Fun Home*, the analytical training I had learned so reluctantly in my youth began to prove useful for making sense of my own history. I started to envision the book's structure as a Daedalian labyrinth, which I illustrated for the book proposal (see frontispiece). In a way, my wanderings through this labyrinth constitute not so much a story as a kind of literary analysis of my life, in particular my relationship with my father. In fact, the labyrinth, with the puzzling quest at its center, its perils, cul-de-sacs, and divagating threads of inquiry, seems as good a model as any for the critical enterprise that a book about approaches to *Fun Home* is also engaged in. I haven't yet read the essays in this book, but I'm curious to see what the writers have to say—almost as curious as I am to see whether they've each found their way back out.

NOTES ON CONTRIBUTORS

David Bahr is associate professor of English at Borough of Manhattan Community College, City University of New York. His work has appeared in *The New York Times*, *GQ*, *Poets and Writers*, *Publishers Weekly*, the *Village Voice*, *Prairie Schooner*, *The Advocate*, *Reconstruction: Studies in Contemporary Culture*, *Lifewriting Annual*, *Boys to Men: Gay Men Write about Growing Up*, *Affective Disorder and the Writing Life: The Melancholic Muse*, *American Creative Nonfiction*, and *Class, Please Open Your Comics: Essays on Teaching with Graphic Narratives*. His essay was made possible by a Borough of Manhattan Community College Faculty Development Grant.

Cynthia Barounis is a lecturer in the Department of Women, Gender, and Sexuality Studies at Washington University in St. Louis. Her articles on queer theory, disability studies, and American literature and culture have appeared in the *Journal of Modern Literature*, *Women's Studies Quarterly*, and the *Journal of Visual Culture*, among others. Her book, *Vulnerable Constitutions: Queerness, Disability, and the Remaking of American Manhood*, is forthcoming from Temple University Press.

Alison Bechdel is a critically acclaimed graphic artist and the author of *Fun Home: A Family Tragicomic* and *Are You My Mother? A Comic Drama*. Her work has appeared in numerous publications, and her award-winning comic strip is collected in *The Essential Dykes to Watch Out For*. She is the recipient of both the Guggenheim and MacArthur fellowships.

Audrey Bilger is vice president for academic affairs and dean of Pomona College. She is the author of *Laughing Feminism: Subversive Comedy in Frances Burney, Maria Edgeworth, and Jane Austen* and the editor of the Broadview edition of Jane Collier's 1753 *Essay on the Art of Ingeniously Tormenting*. With Michele Kort, she edited the anthology *Here Come the Brides! Reflections on Lesbian Love and Marriage*, a 2013 Lambda Literary Awards finalist. Her work has appeared in *Ms.* magazine, the *San Francisco Chronicle*, the *Los Angeles Times*, and the *Paris Review*.

Alexis L. Boylan is associate professor at the University of Connecticut, with a joint appointment in the Art and Art History Department and the women's, gender, and sexuality program, and associate director of the Humanities Institute. She is the editor of *Thomas Kinkade: The Artist in the Mall* (2011) and the author of *Ashcan Art, Whiteness, and the Unspectacular Man* (2017). She is currently working on an exhibition about the painter Ellen Emmet Rand, and her next book focuses on the murals and sculpture created for the American Museum of Natural History in New York City.

Sarah Buchmeier is a PhD candidate at the University of Illinois, Chicago. Her research interests include nineteenth-century American literature, literary aesthetics and the postsecular, and history and theory of the novel.

Sue-Ellen Case is distinguished professor and director of the PhD program in theater and performance studies at the University of California, Los Angeles. She has published numerous books, anthologies, and articles in the fields of feminist and lesbian performance.

Michael A. Chaney is professor of English at Dartmouth College. He is the author of *Reading Lessons in Seeing: Mirrors, Masks, and Mazes in the Autobiographical Graphic Novel* (2017) and *Fugitive Vision: Slave Image and Black Identity in Antebellum Narrative* (2008) and the editor of *Graphic Subjects: Critical Essays on Autobiography and Graphic Novels* (2010) and *Where Is All My Relation? The Poetics of Dave the Potter* (2018).

Eric Detweiler is assistant professor of rhetoric and composition at Middle Tennessee State University. His research puts the ethically oriented work of modern rhetorical theorists in conversation with historical and contemporary pedagogical practices. He also studies digital rhetoric and its resonances with sound studies. His work has appeared in the journals *Philosophy and Rhetoric, Enculturation, Rhetoric Society Quarterly*, and *Kairos*, and he produces and hosts a rhetorical theory podcast called *Rhetoricity*.

Julie R. Enszer is a scholar and a poet. Her book manuscript, "A Fine Bind," is a history of lesbian-feminist presses from 1969 until 2009. Her scholarly work has appeared or is forthcoming in *Southern Cultures, Journal of Lesbian Studies, American Periodicals, WSQ*, and *Frontiers*. She is the author of four poetry collections, *Avowed* (2016), *Lilith's Demons* (2015), *Sisterhood* (2013), and *Handmade Love* (2010). She is the editor of *Sinister Wisdom*, a multicultural lesbian literary and art journal, and a regular book reviewer for the *Lambda Book Report* and *Calyx*.

Daniel Mark Fogel is professor of English and former president at the University of Vermont. He was the founding editor of the *Henry James Review* and the long-time executive director of the Henry James Society. He has published books and articles on James, Virginia Woolf, James Joyce, A. R. Ammons, Wallace Stevens, and Samuel Taylor Coleridge, among others. He is currently writing a book titled "Everybody's Henry James: A Guide for Social and Solitary Readers."

Ariela Freedman is associate professor at Concordia University, Montreal. She is the author of *Death, Men, and Modernism* (2003) and has published articles on modernism, James Joyce, the First World War, and contemporary literature and graphic novels in journals and collections including *Modernism/Modernity, James Joyce Quarterly, Journal of Modern Literature, Literature Compass, Joyce Studies Annual, Partial Answers*, and *Texas Studies in Literature and Language*. Her work on Charlotte Salomon has appeared in *Criticism* and *Graphic Details: Jewish Women's Confessional Comics in Essays and Interviews* (2014).

Erica D. Galioto is associate professor of English at Shippensburg University, where she teaches courses in American literature, psychoanalysis, and English education. Her research focuses on a concept she calls real-world therapy: everyday experiences in fiction and life that occasion therapeutic effects outside a clinical setting. Her article "Split Skin: Adolescent Cutters and the Other," in *Skin, Culture, and Psychoanalysis*, adds a psychoanalytic dimension to the growing body of work that recognizes cutting as a form of self-therapy.

Judith Kegan Gardiner is professor emerita of English and of gender and women's studies at the University of Illinois, Chicago. Her publications include two monographs, three edited collections of critical essays, and over one hundred essays and chapters, including two essays on Bechdel's work. Other recent publications discuss feminist theories, masculinity studies, contemporary women writers, popular culture, and pedagogy. She is a member of the editorial collective of the interdisciplinary journal *Feminist Studies*.

Jessica Gildersleeve is associate professor of English literature at the University of Southern Queensland. She is the author and editor of a number of works on affect, ethics, and literature, including *Christos Tsiolkas: The Utopian Vision, Don't Look Now*, and, with Richard Gehrmann, *Memory and the Wars on Terror: Australian and British Perspectives*.

Ellen Gil-Gómez is professor of English at California State University, San Bernardino, where she teaches Chicano/a cultural studies and literature, comparative American literatures, comic narratives, graphic novels, and feminist and LGBTQ theories. Her book is *Performing La Mestiza* (2001), and she has published numerous articles and chapters in Chicano/Latino studies and women of color studies. Her most recent publications focus on lesbian activism, contemporary comics, disability studies, and online pedagogies.

Dana Heller is dean of the College of Arts and Sciences at Eastern Michigan University. She holds an MFA from Columbia University and a PhD from the Graduate Center, City University of New York. She writes about popular culture, television, and queer arts. Her most recent books are *Loving* The L Word: *The Complete Series in Focus* (2013) and *Hairspray* (2011).

Soo La Kim is assistant dean for graduate programs at the School of Professional Studies at Northwestern University. She has a doctorate in English from the University of California, Irvine, and is a specialist in nineteenth-century British literature. Her dissertation on the performative dimensions of the novel of manners has proven invaluable in her work in college administration and faculty development. She is a founding partner of Learners at the Center, an educational consulting group.

Jennifer Lemberg teaches interdisciplinary research seminars at New York University's Gallatin School of Individualized Study and is associate director of the Olga Lengyel Institute for Holocaust Studies and Human Rights, a professional development organization for middle school, high school, and college faculty members. She has published essays on American Indian literature, Jewish American Holocaust fiction, and television studies. Her article "Closing the Gap in Alison Bechdel's *Fun Home*" appeared in *Women's Studies Quarterly*.

D. Quentin Miller is professor of English at Suffolk University, where he teaches contemporary American literature and African American literature. His most recent books are *"A Criminal Power": James Baldwin and the Law* (2012), *The Routledge Introduction to African American Literature* (2016), *Understanding John Edgar Wideman* (2018), *American Literature in Transition, 1980–1990* (2018), and *James Baldwin in Context* (2019).

Lydia Munnell earned an MFA in fiction from Bowling Green State University, where she worked as fiction editor for *Mid-American Review*. Her short stories have appeared in *The Adirondack Review* and *Appalachian Heritage*, and her journalism and reviews have appeared in *Cleveland Scene Magazine* and the *Detroit Metro Times*. Originally from rural Pennsylvania, she lives in Cleveland, where she teaches, writes, and serves as creative director of the literary reading series Brews and Prose.

Donna L. Pasternak is professor of English education at the University of Wisconsin, Milwaukee. Her teaching and research interests include the teaching of literature and writing, the integration of technology into the English language arts, adolescent literature, and critical inquiry and teacher development. She has published on these topics in *The English Journal, Professional Development in Education, Profession, Arts and Humanities in Higher Education, Review of Education*, among others. Her coathored book, *Secondary English Teacher Education in the United States* (2018), studies how secondary English teachers are educated in the United States.

Monica B. Pearl is lecturer in twentieth-century American literature at the University of Manchester. Among her publications are "Graphic Language: Redrawing the Family (Romance) in Alison Bechdel's *Fun Home*"; *AIDS Literature and Gay Identity: The Literature of Loss*; essays on the writing of W. G. Sebald, on AA Bronson's photograph "Felix, June 5, 1944," on Eve Sedgwick's "White Glasses," and on the play and film *Angels in America*; and two essays on opera.

Christine L. Quinan is assistant professor of gender studies at Utrecht University. Christine works at the intersection of queer theory and postcolonial studies and has published work in several journals and edited volumes, including *Interventions: International Journal of Postcolonial Studies, Women: A Cultural Review*, and *Women's Studies: An Interdisciplinary Journal*.

Valerie Rohy is professor of English at the University of Vermont. She is the author of *Impossible Women: Lesbian Figures and American Literature* (2000), *Anachronism and Its Others: Sexuality, Race, Temporality* (2009), and *Lost Causes: Narrative, Etiology, and Queer Theory* (2015).

Debra J. Rosenthal is professor and chair of the English Department at John Carroll University. She is the author of *Performatively Speaking: Speech and Action in Antebellum American Literature* and of *Race Mixture in Nineteenth-Century U.S. and Latin American Fictions*; the editor, with David S. Reynolds, of *The Serpent in the Cup: Temperance in American Literature*; the editor of *A Routledge Literary Sourcebook on Harriet Beecher Stowe's Uncle Tom's Cabin*; and the editor, with Monika Kaup, of *Mixing Race, Mixing Culture: Inter-American Literary Dialogues*.

JoAnne Ruvoli was assistant professor in the Department of English at Ball State University. Previously, she was a Mellon postdoctoral fellow and visiting assistant professor at the University of California, Los Angeles. Ruvoli earned a PhD in English at the University of Illinois, Chicago, where she specialized in multiethnic American literature. She published articles on literature, cinema, comics, and Italian American cultural history. She died in 2018.

Judith Seaboyer teaches nineteenth-century and contemporary literatures at the University of Queensland. Her research areas are the turn to pastoral in contemporary fiction and the pedagogy of reading well. Her pedagogy publications include work on reading resilience and an essay in *Approaches to Teaching Woolf's* Mrs. Dalloway. She has held fellowships in teaching and learning from the Australian Government Office of Learning and Teaching and the University of Queensland.

Rasmus R. Simonsen is lecturer in communication design and media at the Copenhagen School of Design and Technology. He is the coeditor of the collection of essays

Critical Perspectives on Veganism and the author of a book chapter on Cormac McCarthy's *The Road*. He has published articles in *Leviathan: A Journal of Melville Studies*, *Children's Literature*, *Journal for Critical Animal Studies*, and *American Studies in Scandinavia*. He also writes about design and fashion theory.

Susan Van Dyne is professor emerita of women and gender at Smith College. Her research examines how archives provide windows into the creative process and richly textured social histories. Her publications based upon archives include *Revising Life: Sylvia Plath's Ariel Poems* (1993) and a microhistory of female friendships, "'Abracadabra': Intimate Inventions among Early College Women in the U.S." (2016). Her essay "Inside the Archive of *Fun Home*" is forthcoming in *The Comics of Alison Bechdel: From the Outside In*, edited by Janine Utell. The Alison Bechdel papers are held by the Sophia Smith Collection, Smith College.

Julia Watson is professor emerita of comparative studies, a former associate dean, and a core faculty member of Project Narrative at the Ohio State University. She and Sidonie Smith have coauthored the recent *Life Writing in the Long Run: A Smith and Watson Autobiography Studies Reader* and *Reading Autobiography: A Guide for Interpreting Life Narratives*, coedited five collections, and recently published articles on testimony, on online life narrative, and on women's graphic memoirs. Watson has published three other essays on *Fun Home* as well as recent essays on visual diaries, voice in Patti Smith's *Just Kids*, and scholarly publishing online.

SURVEY PARTICIPANTS

Melanie Adley, *University of Pennsylvania*
John Alberti, *Northern Kentucky University*
Kathryn Allen, *University of North Carolina, Pembroke*
Steven Ambrose, *Michigan State University*
John Dennis Anderson, *Emerson College*
S. R. Anderson, *Lamar University*
Leah Anderst, *Queensborough Community College, City University of New York*
David Bahr, *Borough of Manhattan Community College, City University of New York*
Josef Benson, *University of Wisconsin, Parkside*
Robin Bernstein, *Harvard University*
Alexis L. Boylan, *University of Connecticut*
Edward Brunner, *Southern Illinois University, Carbondale*
Shanna Carlson, *University of Chicago*
Patricia K. Connolly, *State University of New York, Adirondack*
Karlyn Crowley, *St. Norbert College*
J. Cuevas, *Syracuse University*
Renata Lucena Dalmaso, *University of Federal de Santa Catarina, Brazil*
Julie Daniels, *Century College*
Lisa Day, *Eastern Kentucky University*
Stephanie DeGooyer, *Willamette University*
Eric Detweiler, *Middle Tennessee State University*
Stacey Donohue, *Central Oregon Community College*
Erin Douglas, *Miami University, Hamilton*
D. J. Dycus, *Point University*
Sari Edelstein, *University of Massachusetts, Boston*
Jill Ehnenn, *Appalachian State University*
Julie R. Enszer, *University of Mississippi*
B. J. Epstein, *University of East Anglia*
Logan Esdale, *Chapman University*
Ellen Feig, *Bergen Community College*
Shannon Finck, *George State University*
Daniel Mark Fogel, *University of Vermont*
Hannah Freed-Thrall, *Princeton Society of Fellows*
Dustin Friedman, *National University of Singapore*
Karen Gaffney, *Raritan Valley Community College*
Erica D. Galioto, *Shippensburg University*
Cari Gerriets, *Century College*
Adam Haley, *Pennsylvania State University*
Gina Hausknecht, *Coe College*
Dana Heller, *Old Dominion University*
Astrid Henry, *Grinnell College*
KateLynn Hibbard, *Minneapolis Community and Technical College*
Crag Hill, *University of Oklahoma*

Stefan Höppner, *University of Calgary*
Craig Howes, *University of Hawai'i at Manoa*
Leeann Hunter, *Washington State University*
Mark Allan Jackson, *Middle Tennessee State University*
Phoebe Jackson, *William Paterson University*
Susan Jacobowitz, *Queensborough Community College, City University of New York*
Elisabeth Joyce, *Edinboro University*
Chris Kamerbeek, *University of Minnesota*
Ronak Kapadia, *University of Illinois, Chicago*
Maureen M. Kentoff, *George Washington University*
Soo La Kim, *Northwestern University*
Gabrielle Kirilloff, *University of Nebraska, Lincoln*
Ivan Kreilkamp, *Indiana University*
Peter Kunze, *University at Albany, State University of New York*
Travis Kurowski, *York College of Pennsylvania*
Dinah Lenney, *University of Southern California*
Michael Lewis, *Indiana University*
Jennifer L. Lieberman, *University of North Florida*
Elizabeth Lundberg, *University of Iowa*
Robin Lydenberg, *Boston College*
Linda Macri, *University of Maryland*
David Magill, *Longwood University*
David McGlynn, *Lawrence University*
Alexander McKee, *University of Delaware*
D. Quentin Miller, *Suffolk University*
Deborah M. Mix, *Ball State University*
Jesse Molesworth, *Indiana University*
Patricia Elise Nelson, *University of Southern California*
Kinohi Nishikawa, *University of Notre Dame*
Stella Oh, *Loyola Marymount University*
Tahneer Oksman, *Marymount Manhattan College*
Sarah Panuska, *Michigan State University*
Donna L. Pasternak, *University of Wisconsin, Milwaukee*
Katie Peel, *University of North Carolina, Wilmington*
Klaus Rieser, *University of Graz, Austria*
Candida Rifkind, *University of Winnipeg*
John Paul Riquelme, *Boston University*
Melissa Rogers, *University of Maryland, College Park*
Valerie Rohy, *University of Vermont*
Debra J. Rosenthal, *John Carroll University*
Bonnie Roy, *University of California, Davis*
JoAnne Ruvoli, *Ball State University*
Jennifer D. Ryan, *Buffalo State College, State University of New York*
Sinduja Sathiyaseelan, *University of Nebraska, Lincoln*
Heidi Schlipphacke, *University of Illinois, Chicago*
Megan Schott, *Southern Methodist University*
David Schuman, *Washington University in St. Louis*
David Seelow, *Excelsior College and Rensselaer Polytechnic Institute*

Nhora Serrano, *California State University, Long Beach*
Matthew Sewell, *Minnesota State University, Mankato*
Lauren Shohet, *Villanova University*
Rasmus R. Simonsen, *Copenhagen School of Design and Technology*
Charlee Sterling, *Goucher College*
Gary Stonum, *Case Western Reserve University*
Robert S. Sturges, *Arizona State University*
Louise Sullivan-Blum, *Mansfield University*
Haley Swenson, *Ohio State University*
Kate Thomas, *Bryn Mawr College*
Janine Utell, *Widener University*
Lee Wallace, *University of Sydney, Australia*
Cara Williams, *University of North Carolina, Greensboro*
Elizabeth Williams, *Illinois State University*
Meg Worley, *Colgate University*
Anne Frances Wysocki, *University of Wisconsin, Milwaukee*

WORKS CITED

Abbott, Alysia. "'We Just Sat and Held Each Other': How It Feels to Watch Your Life Story Onstage." *The Atlantic*, 12 Nov. 2013, www.theatlantic.com/entertainment/archive/2013/11/we-just-sat-and-held-each-other-how-it-feels-to-watch-your-life-story-onstage/281369/.

Abbott, H. Porter. *The Cambridge Introduction to Narrative*. 2nd ed., Cambridge UP, 2008.

Abbott, Sidney, and Barbara Love. *Sappho Was a Right-On Woman: A Liberated View of Lesbianism*. 1972. Madison Books, 1979.

Adair, Casey, and Nancy Adair. *Word Is Out: Stories of Some of Our Lives*. Glide Publications, 1978.

Albee, Edward. The American Dream: *A Play*. Coward McCann, 1961.

Alcott, Louisa May. *Little Women*. 1869. Penguin Classics, 1989.

Anderst, Leah. "Feeling with Real Others: Narrative Empathy in the Autobiographies of Doris Lessing and Alison Bechdel." *Narrative*, vol. 23, no. 3, Oct. 2015, pp. 271–90.

Applebee, Arthur N. *Curriculum as Conversation: Transforming Traditions of Teaching and Learning*. U of Chicago P, 1996.

Appleman, Deborah. *Critical Encounters in High School English: Teaching Literary Theory to Adolescents*. 2nd ed., Teachers College P, 2009.

Argyris, Chris, and Donald Schön. *Organization Learning: A Theory of Action Perspective*. Addison-Wesley, 1978.

Aronson, Joseph. "Introduction." *The Cabinet-Maker and Upholsterer's Guide*, by George Hepplewhite, Dover Publications, 1969, pp. i–viii.

Arum, Richard, and Josipa Roksa. *Academically Adrift: Limited Learning on College Campuses*. U of Chicago P, 2011.

Atwell, Nancie. *In the Middle: New Understandings about Writing, Reading, and Learning*. Boynton/Cook, 1998.

Austen, Jane. *Pride and Prejudice*. 1813. Penguin Classics, 2002.

B., David. *Epileptic*. Translated by Kim Thompson, Pantheon, 2005.

Baetens, Jan, and Hugo Frey. *The Graphic Novel: An Introduction*. Cambridge UP, 2015.

Bahr, David. "Labile Lines: Art Spiegelman's 'Prisoner on the Hell Planet,' Darryl Cunningham's *Psychiatric Tales*, and the Graphic Memoir of Mental Illness." *Lifewriting Annual: Biographical and Autobiographical Studies*, vol. 3, no. 1, 2015, pp. 1–34.

———. "No Matter What Happens." *Boys to Men: Gay Men Write about Growing Up*, edited by Ted Gideonse and Rob Williams, Carroll and Graf, 2006, pp. 66–88.

———. "'Outside the Box': Teaching Graphic Narrative in the Multicultural Community College." M. Miller, pp. 51–61.

———. "The Things We Carry: Embodied Truth and Tim O'Brien's Poetics of Despair." *The Melancholic Muse: Affective Disorder and Writing the Academy*, edited by Stephanie Stone Horton, Palgrave Macmillan, 2014, pp. 100–15.

Bannon, Ann. *Odd Girl Out*. Gold Medal Books, 1957.

———. *Women in the Shadows*. Gold Medal Books, 1959.

Barounis, Cynthia. "Alison Bechdel and Crip-Feminist Autobiography." *Journal of Modern Literature*, vol. 39, no. 4, Summer 2016, pp. 139–61.

Barry, Lynda. *One Hundred Demons*. Sasquatch Books, 2002.

Barthes, Roland. *Camera Lucida: Reflections on Photography*. Translated by Richard Howard, Hill and Wang, 1981.

———. *The Pleasure of the Text*. Translated by Richard Miller, Farrar, Straus, and Giroux, 1975.

Bates, Elizabeth Bidwell, and Jonathan L. Fairbanks. *American Furniture, 1620 to the Present*. Richard Marek Publishers, 1981.

Baudrillard, Jean. *Simulacra and Simulation*. Translated by Sheila Glaser, U of Michigan P, 1994.

Bauer, Heike. "Vital Lines Drawn from Books: Difficult Feelings in Alison Bechdel's *Fun Home* and *Are You My Mother?*" *Journal of Lesbian Studies*, vol. 18, no. 3, 2014, pp. 266–81. *Taylor and Francis Online*, dx.doi.org/10.1080/10894160.2014.896614.

Beaton, Cecil. *Self Portrait with Friends: The Selected Diaries of Cecil Beaton, 1926–1974*. Edited by Richard Buckle, Littlehampton, 1979.

Bechdel, Alison. "Alison Bechdel: Creating *Fun Home: A Family Tragicomic*." Mind TV, 10 Mar. 2009. *YouTube*, www.youtube.com/watch?v=cumLU3UpcGY.

———. *Are You My Mother? A Comic Drama*. Houghton Mifflin Harcourt, 2012.

———. *The Essential Dykes to Watch Out For*. Houghton Mifflin Harcourt, 2008.

———. *Fun Home: A Family Tragicomic*. Houghton Mifflin Harcourt, 2006.

———. Interview. *Outside the Box: Interviews with Contemporary Cartoonists*, by Hillary L. Chute, U of Chicago P, 2014, pp. 155–76.

———. "Lesbian Cartoonist Alison Bechdel Countered Dad's Secrecy by Being Out and Open." Interview by Terry Gross, *Fresh Air*, National Public Radio, 29 Aug. 2015, www.npr.org/2015/08/17/432569415/lesbian-cartoonist-alison-bechdel-countered-dads-secrecy-by-being-out-and-open.

———. "OCD." *YouTube*, 18 April 2006, www.youtube.com/watch?v=_CBdhxVFEGc.

———. "On Psychotherapy, LGBT Identity, and Cultural Visibility: In Conversation with Alison Bechdel." Interview with Adam R. Critchfield and Jack Pula, *Journal of Gay and Lesbian Mental Health*, vol. 19, no. 4, 2015, pp. 397–412.

———. Personal interview with Susan Van Dyne. 27 May 2015.

———. "Queers and Comics Keynote: Alison Bechdel." The Graduate Center, City University of New York, 23 June 2015. *YouTube*, www.youtube.com/watch?v=kQrKPmnrZYw.

———. "Re: quick question and big congratulations." Received by JoAnne Ruvoli, 30 June 2006.

———. "Reading and Discussion by Graphic Artist Alison Bechdel." 16 Apr. 2009, Cornell University. *YouTube*, www.youtube.com/watch?v=kKy0yJ_Owi4/.

Bechdel, Alison, and Hillary L. Chute. "Public Conversation: Alison Bechdel and Hillary Chute." *Critical Inquiry*, vol. 40, no. 3, Spring 2014, pp. 203–19.

Bechdel, Alison, et al. "Fun Home." *Theater Talk*, CUNY TV Foundation, 23 May 2015. *CUNY Television*, www.cuny.tv/show/theatertalk/PR2004138.

Bechdel, Helen. "County Home to Many Mine Tragedies, Too." *Centre Daily Times* (State College, PA), 6 Feb. 2006, p. 1.

———. "Remembering a Friend from the Theater." *Centre Daily Times* (State College, PA), 13 July 2009, p. 1.

Bercovitch, Sacvan, and Cyrus R. K. Patell, editors. *The Cambridge History of American Literature: Prose Writing, 1940–1990*. Vol. 7, Cambridge UP, 1994.

Boland, Eavan, and Mark Strand. *The Making of a Poem: A Norton Anthology of Poetic Forms*. W. W. Norton, 2001.

Bona, Mary Jo. "Queer Daughters and Their Mothers: Carole Maso, Mary Cappello, and Alison Bechdel Write Their Way Home." *La Mamma: Interrogating a National Stereotype*, edited by Penny Morris and Perry Willson, Palgrave Macmillan, 2018.

Booth, Wayne C. *The Rhetoric of Fiction*. U of Chicago P, 1961.

Bourdieu, Pierre. *Distinction: A Social Critique of the Judgment of Taste*. Translated by Richard Nice, Harvard UP, 1987.

Bourriaud, Nicolas. *Relational Aesthetics*. Les presses du reel, 1998.

Brady, David. *Beckett:* Waiting for Godot. Cambridge UP, 2001.

Broumas, Olga. *Beginning with O*. Yale UP, 1977. Yale Series of Younger Poets.

Brown, Rita Mae. *Rubyfruit Jungle*. Bantam Doubleday Dell, 1973.

Butler, Judith. *Gender Trouble: Feminism and the Subversion of Identity*. Routledge, 1990.

Camus, Albert. *A Happy Death*. 1972. Vintage International, 1995.

———. *"The Myth of Sisyphus" and Other Essays*. Translated by Justin O'Brien, Alfred A. Knopf, 1955.

Card, Orson Scott. *Ender's Game*. Tor Science Fiction, 1994.

Carter, James B. "Going Graphic: Understanding What Graphic Novels Are—And Aren't—Can Help Teachers Make the Best Use of This Literary Form." *Educational Leadership*, vol. 66, no. 6, 2009, pp. 68–73.

Caruth, Cathy. *Unclaimed Experience: Trauma, Narrative, and History*. Johns Hopkins UP, 1996.

Cauterucci, Christina. "Lesbians and Key Rings: A Cultural Love Story." *Slate*, 21 Dec. 2016, www.slate.com/human-interest/2018/03/women-and-femmes -phrase-in-queer-feminist-activism-makes-no-sense.html.

Cerveris, Michael. "Taking *Fun Home* to Orlando, for a Catharsis Onstage and Off." *The New York Times*, 5 Aug. 2016, www.nytimes.com/2016/08/06/theater/ taking-fun-home-to-orlando-for-a-catharsis-onstage-and-off.html.

Chaney, Michael A. *Graphic Subjects: Critical Essays on Autobiography and Graphic Novels*. U of Wisconsin P, 2011. Wisconsin Studies in Autobiography.

Chute, Hillary L. "Comics as Literature? Reading Graphic Narrative." *PMLA*, vol. 123, no. 2, 2008, pp. 452–65.

———. "Comics Form and Narrating Lives." *Profession*, 2011, pp. 107–17.

———. *Disaster Drawn: Visual Witness, Comics, and Documentary Form*. Belknap Press, 2016.

———. "Gothic Revival." *Village Voice*, 4 July 2006, www.villagevoice.com/2006/07/04/gothic-revival-2.

———. *Graphic Women: Life Narrative and Contemporary Comics*. Columbia UP, 2010.

———. "An Interview with Alison Bechdel." *Modern Fiction Studies*, vol. 52, no. 4, Winter 2006, pp. 1004–13.

———. "Materializing Memory: Lynda Barry's *One Hundred Demons*." Chaney, pp. 282–309.

———. *Why Comics? From Underground to Everywhere*. Harper, 2017.

Chute, Hillary L., and Marianne DeKoven. "Introduction: Graphic Narrative." *Modern Fiction Studies*, vol. 52, no. 4, 2006, pp. 767–82.

Clark, Kenneth. *The Nude: A Study in Ideal Form*. Pantheon Books, 1956.

Clement, Olivia. "Jeanine Tesori Identifies Her Own 'Ring of Keys' Moment." *Playbill*, 7 June 2015, www.playbill.com/news/article/jeanine-tesori-identifies-her-own-ring-of-keys-moment-350790.

Cohn, Neil. *The Visual Language of Comics: Introduction to the Structure and Cognition of Sequential Images*. Bloomsbury, 2013.

Colette. *Earthly Paradise: An Autobiography of Colette Drawn from Her Lifetime Writings*. Edited by Robert Phelps, translated by Herma Briffault, 1966. Farrar, Straus and Giroux, 1975.

Conlogue, Bill. *Here and There: Reading Pennsylvania's Working Landscape*. Penn State P, 2013.

Connor, David J., et al., editors. *DisCrit: Disability Studies and Critical Race Theory in Education*. Teachers College P, 2015.

Conrad, Joseph. *Heart of Darkness*. 1899. Penguin Classics, 2012.

Cooper, H. J. *The Art of Furnishing: On Rational and Aesthetic Principles*. Henry Holt, 1881.

Le Corbusier. *Toward an Architecture*. 1924. Translated by John Goodman, Getty Publications, 2007.

Crowley, Sharon. *Composition in the University: Historical and Polemical Essays*. U of Pittsburgh P, 1998.

Culler, Jonathan. *Literary Theory: A Very Short Introduction*. Oxford UP, 1997.

Cvetkovich, Ann. "Drawing the Archive in Alison Bechdel's *Fun Home*." *Women's Studies Quarterly*, vol. 36, nos. 1–2, 2008, pp. 111–28.

Dahl, Roald. *James and the Giant Peach*. 1961. Puffin Books, 2007.

Dällenbach, Lucien. *The Mirror in the Text*. Translated by Jeremy Whitely, U of Chicago P, 1989.

Daly, Mary. *Gyn/Ecology: The Metaethics of Radical Feminism*. Beacon Press, 1978.

Davidson, Cathy N. *Now You See It: How Technology and Brain Science Will Transform Schools and Business for the Twenty-First Century.* Penguin Books, 2012.

Davis, Diane. *Inessential Solidarity: Rhetoric and Foreigner Relations.* U of Pittsburgh P, 2010.

Dean-Ruzicka, Rachel. "Mourning and Melancholia in Alison Bechdel's *Fun Home: A Family Tragicomic.*" *ImageText: Interdisciplinary Comics Studies,* vol. 7, no. 2, 2013, www.english.ufl.edu/imagetext/archives/v7_2/dean-ruzicka/.

Delgado, Richard, and Jean Stefancic, editors. *Critical White Studies: Looking Behind the Mirror.* Temple UP, 1997.

D'Emilio, John. *Sexual Politics, Sexual Communities: The Making of a Homosexual Minority in the United States, 1940–1970.* U of Chicago P, 1983.

De Rosa, Tina. *Paper Fish.* Feminist Press, 1996.

Derrida, Jacques. *Dissemination.* Translated by Barbara Johnson, U of Chicago P, 1981.

DiMassa, Diane. *Complete Hothead Paisan: Homicidal Lesbian Terrorist.* Cleis Press, 1999.

Dong, Lan, editor. *Teaching Comics and Graphic Narratives: Essays on Theory, Strategy, and Practice.* McFarland, 2012.

Douglas, Kate, et al. "Building Reading Resilience: Re-thinking Reading for the Literary Studies Classroom." *Higher Education Research and Development,* vol. 35, no. 2, 2015, pp. 254–66. *Taylor and Francis Online,* www.tandfonline.com/doi/abs/10.1080/07294360.2015.1087475?journalCode=cher20.

Downing, Andrew Jackson. *Cottage Residences.* Wiley and Putnam, 1842.

Drabble, Margaret. *The Waterfall.* 1969. Houghton Mifflin Harcourt, 2013.

Du Maurier, Daphne. *Rebecca.* 1937. William Morrow, 2006.

Dziemianowicz, Joe. "Five Design Secrets of the *Fun Home* Set on Broadway." *New York Daily News,* 6 Apr. 2015, www.nydailynews.com/entertainment/theater-arts/5-design-secrets-fun-home-set-broadway-article-1.2172882.

Eakin, Paul John. *How Our Lives Become Stories: Making Selves.* Cornell UP, 1999.

Earle, Monalesia. "Does Twenty-First-Century Feminist Fiction Challenge or Uphold Conventional Notions of the Family? A Critique of *A Mercy* and *Fun Home.*" *A Comic of Her Own: Women Writing, Reading and Embodying through Comics,* special issue of *ImageText: Interdisciplinary Comics Studies,* edited by Jeffrey A. Brown and Melissa Loucks, vol. 7, no. 4, 2014, www.english.ufl.edu/imagetext/archives/v7_4/earle/.

Eddison, Eric. *The Worm Ouroboros.* 1922. A&C Boni, 1926.

Edelman, Lee. *No Future: Queer Theory and the Death Drive.* Duke UP, 2004.

Edwards, Clive. *Interior Design: A Critical Introduction.* Berg, 2011.

Eisner, Will. *Comics and Sequential Art: Principles and Practices from the Legendary Cartoonist.* 1985. Rev. ed., W. W. Norton, 2008.

———. *Graphic Storytelling and Visual Narrative.* W. W. Norton, 2008.

El Refaie, Elisabeth. *Autobiographical Comics: Life Writing in Pictures.* UP of Mississippi, 2012.

Enders, Jody. "Rhetoric, Coercion, and the Memory of Violence." *Criticism and Dissent in the Middle Ages,* edited by Rita Copeland, Cambridge UP, 1996, pp. 24–55.

Enterline, Lynn. *Shakespeare's Schoolroom: Rhetoric, Discipline, Emotion.* U of Pennsylvania P, 2011.

Esslin, Martin. *The Theatre of the Absurd.* 3rd ed., Knopf, 2009.

Eveleth, K. W. "A Vast 'Network of Transversals': Labyrinthine Aesthetics in *Fun Home.*" *South Central Review,* vol. 32, no. 3, Fall 2015, pp. 88–109.

Everett, William A., and Paul R. Laird. *The Cambridge Companion to the Musical.* 2nd ed., Cambridge UP, 2008.

Fantasia, Annette. "The Paterian Bildungsroman Reenvisioned: 'Brain-Building' in Alison Bechdel's *Fun Home: A Family Tragicomic.*" *Criticism,* vol. 53, no. 1, Winter 2011, 83–97.

Faulkner, William. *As I Lay Dying.* 1930. Vintage Books, 1985.

Fecho, Bob. *"Is This English?" Race, Language, and Culture in the Classroom.* Teachers College P, 2004.

Felski, Rita. *The Limits of Critique.* U of Chicago P, 2015.

Five Lesbian Brothers. *Brave Smiles . . . Another Lesbian Tragedy.* WOW Café, New York, 1992.

Fleming, J. David. "The Very Idea of a *Progymnasmata.*" *Rhetoric Review,* vol. 22, no. 2, 2003, pp. 105–20. *Taylor and Francis Online,* dx.doi.org/10.1207/S15327981RR2202_1.

Forbes, Esther. *Johnny Tremain.* 1943. Houghton Mifflin Harcourt, 2011.

Forster, E. M. *Maurice.* 1971. W. W. Norton, 2005.

Freedman, Ariela. "Drawing on Modernism in Alison Bechdel's *Fun Home.*" *Journal of Modern Literature,* vol. 32, no. 4, 2009, pp. 125–40.

Freire, Paulo. *Pedagogy of the Oppressed.* Translated by Myra Bergman Ramos, Herder and Herder, 1970.

Freud, Sigmund. *Beyond the Pleasure Principle.* 1920. *The Freud Reader,* edited by Peter Gay, W. W. Norton, 1989, pp. 594–626.

———. "Family Romances." *On Sexuality.* 1909. Edited by Angela Richards, Penguin Books, 1991, pp. 217–25. Penguin Freud Library.

———. "Humour." Freud, *Standard Edition,* vol. 21, pp. 160–66.

———. "Remembering, Repeating, and Working-Through." 1914. Freud, *Standard Edition,* vol. 12, pp. 146–56.

———. *The Standard Edition of the Complete Psychological Works of Sigmund Freud.* Edited and translated by James Strachey, Hogarth, 1953–74. 24 vols.

Friedman, Susan Stanford. *Mappings: Feminism and the Cultural Geographies of Encounter.* Princeton UP, 1998.

"*Fun Home* Performance Tony Awards 2015." *YouTube,* Tony Awards, 18 July 2015, youtu.be/pMAuesRJm1E.

Gaard, Greta. "Toward a Queer Ecofeminism." *Hypatia,* vol. 12, no. 1, Winter 1997, pp. 114–37.

Gardiner, Judith Kegan. "Bechdel's *Dykes to Watch Out For* and Popular Culture." *Queers in American Popular Culture,* edited by Jim Elledge, vol. 2, Praeger, 2010, pp. 81–101.

———. "Queering Genre: Alison Bechdel's *Fun Home: A Family Tragicomic* and *The Essential Dykes to Watch Out For.*" *Contemporary Women's Writing*, vol. 5, no. 3, Nov. 2011, pp. 188–207.

Gardner, Jared. "Autography's Biography." *Biography*, vol. 31, no. 1, Winter 2008, pp. 1–26.

———. "A History of the Narrative Comic Strip." *From Comic Strips to Graphic Novels: Contributions to the Theory and History of Graphic Narrative*, edited by Daniel Stein and Jan-Noël Thon, De Gruyter, 2013, pp. 241–54.

Gaughan, John. *Reinventing English: Teaching in the Contact Zone.* Heinemann, 2001.

Gere, Charlotte. *The House Beautiful: Oscar Wilde and the Aesthetic Interior.* Lund Humphries, 2000.

Gilmore, Leigh. *Autobiographics: A Feminist Theory of Women's Self-Representation.* Cornell UP, 1994.

Giroux, Henry A. *Teachers as Intellectuals: Toward a Critical Pedagogy of Learning.* Bergin and Garvey, 1988.

"Glenn Ligon: Notes on the Margin of a Black Book." *Guggenheim*, The Solomon R. Guggenheim Collection, 2018, www.guggenheim.org/artwork/10382.

Gloeckner, Phoebe. *"A Child's Life" and Other Stories.* Rev. ed., Frog Books, 2000.

———. *The Diary of a Teenage Girl: An Account in Words and Pictures.* Rev. ed., North Atlantic Books, 2015.

Goldsmith, Jenna. "Landing on the Patio: Landscape Ecology and the Architecture of Identity in Alison Bechdel's *Fun Home.*" *DisClosure: A Journal of Social Theory*, vol. 23, no. 1, Jan. 2014, pp. 1–25.

Golub, Jeffrey N. *Making Learning Happen: Strategies for an Interactive Classroom.* Heinemann, 2000.

Graff, Gerald. "Conflict Clarifies: A Response." *Pedagogy*, vol. 3, no. 1, 2003, pp. 266–76.

Graff, Gerald, and Cathy Birkenstein. *They Say / I Say: The Moves That Matter in Academic Writing.* 2nd ed., W. W. Norton, 2012.

Grahame, Kenneth. *The Wind in the Willows.* 1908. Aladdin Paperbacks, 1989.

Grass, Günter. *The Tin Drum.* 1959. Translated by Breon Mitchell, Houghton Mifflin Harcourt, 2010.

Griffiths, Timothy M. "'O'er Pathless Rocks': Wordsworth, Landscape Aesthetics, and Queer Ecology." *Interdisciplinary Studies in Literature and Environment*, vol. 22, no. 2, Spring 2015, pp. 284–302.

Groensteen, Thierry. *The System of Comics.* Translated by Bart Beaty and Nick Nguyen, UP of Mississippi, 2007.

Halberstam, Jack (published as Judith). *In a Queer Time and Place: Transgender Bodies, Subcultural Lives.* New York UP, 2005.

Hall, Justin, editor. *No Straight Lines: Four Decades of Queer Comics.* Fantagraphics, 2013.

Hall, Radclyffe. *The Well of Loneliness.* 1928. Wordsworth Editions, 2014.

Hansberry, Lorraine. *A Raisin in the Sun.* Vintage Books, 1994.

Hatfield, Charles, and Craig Svonkin. "Why Comics Are and Are Not Picture Books: Introduction." *Children's Literature Association Quarterly*, vol. 37, no. 4, Winter 2012, pp. 429–35.

Heller, Marielle, director. *Diary of a Teenage Girl*. Caviar Films, 2015.

Hemingway, Ernest. *The Sun Also Rises*. 1926. Scribner, 2006.

Herman, David, et al., editors. *Routledge Encyclopedia of Narrative Theory*. Routledge, 2005.

Hirsch, Marianne. *Family Frames: Photography, Narrative, and Postmemory*. Harvard UP, 1997.

Hirschfeld, Magnus. *Homosexuality of Men and Women*. 1922. Prometheus Books, 2000.

Homer. *The Odyssey*. Edited by H. Rieu, translated by E. V. Rieu, Penguin Books, 2003.

hooks, bell. *Teaching Community*. Routledge, 2003.

Hughes, Langston. "Theme for English B." *The Collected Poems of Langston Hughes*, edited by Arnold Rampersad and David Roessel, Vintage Classics, 1995, pp. 409–10.

Hume, Margee. "Adopting Organisation Learning Theory in the Classroom: Advancing Learning through the Use of Blogging and Self-Reflection." *International Journal of Learning and Change*, vol. 6, nos. 1–2, 2012, pp. 49–65.

Iuliano, Fiorenzo. "Du côté de *Fun Home*: Alison Bechdel Rewrites Marcel Proust." *Partial Answers: Journal of Literature and the History of Ideas*, vol. 13, no. 2, June 2015, pp. 287–309.

Jakaitis, Jake, and James F. Wurtz, editors. *Crossing Boundaries in Graphic Narrative: Essays on Forms, Series, and Genres*. McFarland, 2012.

James, Henry. *The Portrait of a Lady*. 1881. Penguin Books, 2011.

———. *Washington Square*. 1880. Penguin Books, 2003.

Jay, Karla, and Allen Young. *The Gay Report: Lesbians and Gay Men Speak Out about Sexual Experiences and Lifestyles*. Summit Books, 1979.

———, editors. *Out of the Closets: Voices of Gay Liberation*. Pyramid Books, 1972.

Jennings, Louise B., and Cynthia P. Smith. "Examining the Role of Critical Inquiry for Transformative Practices: Two Joint Case Studies of Multicultural Teacher Education." *Teachers College Record*, vol. 104, no. 3, 2002, pp. 456–81.

Jerke, Bud W. "Queer Ruralism." *Harvard Journal of Law and Gender*, vol. 34, no. 1, 2011, pp. 259–312.

Johnson, Mat, and Warren Pleece. *Incognegro: A Graphic Mystery*. DC Comics, 2008.

Johnston, Jill. *Lesbian Nation: The Feminist Solution*. Simon and Schuster, 1973.

Jones, John Bush. *Our Musicals, Ourselves: A Social History of the American Musical Theatre*. 2nd ed., Brandeis UP, 2004.

Joyce, James. *Dubliners*. 1914. Penguin Books, 1993.

———. *A Portrait of the Artist as a Young Man*. 1916. Viking Books, 1982.

———. *Ulysses*. 1922. Penguin Books, 2015.

Jung, Carl. *The Archetypes and the Collective Unconscious*. Translated by R. F. C. Hull, Bollingen Foundation, 1959.

Kaplan, E. Ann. *Trauma Culture: The Politics of Terror and Loss in Media and Literature*. Rutgers UP, 2005.

Kaufman, George S., and Moss Hart. *You Can't Take It with You*. 1937. Dramatists Play Service, 1998.

Kazyak, Emily. "Disrupting Cultural Selves: Constructing Gay and Lesbian Identities in Rural Locales." *Qualitative Sociology*, vol. 34, no. 4, 2011, pp. 561–81.

Kellogg, Carolyn. "South Carolina Lawmakers OK Funding Cuts over Gay-Themed Books." *Los Angeles Times*, 28 Feb. 2014, articles.latimes.com/2014/feb/28/entertainment/la-et-jc-south-carolina-votes-to-cut-university-funding-over-gay-themed-books-20140228.

Kennedy, George A., translator. *Progymnasmata: Greek Textbooks of Prose Composition and Rhetoric*. Society for Biblical Literature, 2003.

Kennedy, Rosanne, et al. "Reading Resilience Toolkit." *Reading Resilience: A Skills-Based Approach to Literary Studies*, Australian National University, 17 Nov. 2014, chelt.anu.edu.au/sites/default/files/Projects/Reading%20Resilience/Toolkit%20PDF%2026%20April.pdf. PDF.

Kerouac, Jack. *On the Road*. Penguin Books, 1976.

Kierkegaard, Søren. *Søren Kierkegaard's Journals and Papers*. Translated and edited by Howard V. Hong and Edna H. Hong, vol. 4, Indiana UP, 1967.

King-O'Brien, Charissa, director. *The Paper Mirror*. 2012.

Kipling, Rudyard. *Just So Stories*. 1902. Puffin Books, 2008.

Koedt, Anne. *Lesbianism and Feminism*. 1971. *CWLU Herstory Project*, Chicago Women's Liberation Union, www.cwluherstory.org/classic-feminist-writings-articles/lesbianism-and-feminism?rq=koedt.

Konnikova, Maria. "Being a Better Online Reader." *The New Yorker*, 16 July 2014, www.newyorker.com/science/maria-konnikova/being-a-better-online-reader.

Krafft-Ebing, Richard von. *Psychopathia Sexualis: With Special Reference to Contrary Sexual Instinct*. Translated by Charles Gilbert Chaddock, F. A. Davis Company, 1884.

Kristeva, Julia. "Bakthine, le mot, le dialogue, et le roman." *Critique*, no. 239, 1967, pp. 438–65.

Kübler-Ross, Elisabeth. *On Death and Dying*. MacMillan, 1969.

Labio, Catherine. "The Architecture of Comics." *Critical Inquiry*, vol. 41, no. 2, 2015, pp. 312–43.

Lauretis, Teresa de. "Queer Theory: Lesbian and Gay Sexualities: An Introduction." *Differences*, vol. 3, no. 2, 1991, pp. iii–xviii.

Lavery, Bryony. *Her Aching Heart*. *Her Aching Heart, Two Marias, Wicked*, Methuen Drama, 1991.

Lavin, Sylvia. "What Good Is a Bad Object?" *Flash in the Pan*, by Lavin, Architectural Association London, 2015, pp. 45–55.

Lejeune, Philippe. "The Autobiographical Pact." *On Autobiography*, by Lejeune, translated by Katherine Leary, U of Minnesota P, 1989, pp. 3–30.

Lentricchia, Frank, and Thomas McLaughlin, editors. *Critical Terms for Literary Study*. 2nd ed., U of Chicago P, 1995.

Liu, Ziming. "Reading Behavior in the Digital Environment: Changes in Reading Behavior Over the Past Ten Years." *Journal of Documentation*, vol. 61, no. 6, 2005, pp. 700–12.

Long, Helen. *The Edwardian House: The Middle-Class Home in Britain, 1880–1914.* Manchester UP, 1993.

Lutes, Jason. *Berlin, Book One: City of Stones.* Drawn and Quarterly, 2000.

———. *Berlin, Book Two: City of Smoke.* Drawn and Quarterly, 2008.

Lynn, Steven. *Texts and Contexts: Writing about Literature with Critical Theory.* 6th ed., Longman Publishing, 2011.

MacCurdy, Marian M. "From Trauma to Writing: A Theoretical Model for Practical Use." *Writing and Healing: Toward an Informed Practice*, edited by Charles M. Anderson and MacCurdy, NCTE, 2000, pp. 158–200.

Martin, Del, and Phyllis Lyon. *Lesbian/Woman.* Glide Publications, 1972.

Marton, F., and R. Säljö. "On Qualitative Differences in Learning: I. Outcome and Process." *British Journal of Educational Psychology*, vol. 46, 1976, pp. 4–11.

Masters, William H., and Virginia E. Johnson. *Homosexuality in Perspective.* Little, Brown, 1979.

McCloud, Scott. *Making Comics: Storytelling Secrets of Comics, Manga, and Graphic Novels.* William Morrow, 2006.

———. *Understanding Comics: The Invisible Art.* William Morrow, 1994.

McIntosh, Peggy. "White Privilege and Male Privilege: A Personal Account of Coming to See Correspondences through Work in Women's Studies." Delgado and Stefancic, pp. 291–99.

McLane, Maureen Noelle. "Literate Species: Populations, 'Humanities,' and *Frankenstein*." *English Literary History*, vol. 63, no. 4, 1996, pp. 959–83.

Meskin, Aaron. "Comics as Literature?" *British Journal of Aesthetics*, vol. 49, no. 3, July 2009, pp. 219–39.

Metropolitan Museum of Art. *Nineteenth-Century America: Furniture and Other Decorative Arts.* New York Graphic Society, 1970.

Milford, Nancy. *Zelda: A Biography.* 1970. Harper Perennial, 1992.

Miller, J. Hillis. *On Literature.* Routledge, 2002.

Miller, Matthew L., editor. *Class, Please Open Your Comics: Essays on Teaching with Graphic Narratives.* McFarland, 2015.

Millett, Kate. *Flying.* U of Illinois P, 1974.

Milne, A. A. *The World of Pooh.* 1926. Dutton Children's Books, 2010.

Miodrag, Hannah. *Comics and Language: Reimaging Critical Discourse on the Form.* UP of Mississippi, 2013.

Mitchell, Adrielle. "Spectral Memory, Sexuality, and Inversion: An Arthrological Study of Alison Bechdel's *Fun Home: A Family Tragicomic*." *ImageText: Interdisciplinary Comics Studies*, vol. 4, no. 3, 2009, www.english.ufl.edu/imagetext/archives/v4_3/mitchell/.

Mitchell, Diana, and Leila M. Christenbury. *Both Art and Craft: Teaching Ideas that Spark Learning.* NCTE, 2000.

Mitchell, W. J. T. "Comics as Media: Afterword." *Critical Inquiry*, vol. 40, no. 3, 2014, pp. 255–65. *JSTOR*, www.jstor.org/stable/10.1086/677376.

Mizener, Arthur. *The Far Side of Paradise*. 1951. Vintage Books, 1959.

Mortimer-Sandilands, Catriona, and Bruce Erickson, editors. *Queer Ecologies: Sex, Nature, Politics, Desire*. Indiana UP, 2010.

Morton, Timothy. *Hyperobjects: Philosophy and Ecology after the End of the World*. U of Minnesota P, 2013.

———. *Realist Magic: Objects, Ontology, Causality*. Open Humanities Press, 2013.

Murray, Peter, and Linda Murray. *The Oxford Dictionary of Christian Art and Architecture*, edited by Tom Devonshire Jones, Oxford UP, 2013.

Naples, Jessica. "The Uses of Hand-Drawn Photographs in Alison Bechdel's *Fun Home*." 2014. Typescript.

Nelson, Maggie. *The Argonauts*. Graywolf Press, 2015.

Nicholls, Peter. *Modernisms: A Literary Guide*. U of California P, 1995.

Nin, Anaïs. *Delta of Venus*. Harcourt Brace Jovanovich, 1977.

Noddings, Nel. *Critical Lessons: What Our Schools Should Teach*. Cambridge UP, 2006.

O'Brien, Tim. *The Things They Carried*. Houghton Mifflin, 1990.

Osborn, Paul. *Morning's at Seven*. 1939. Samuel French, 1967.

Our Bodies, Ourselves: A Book by and for Women. Boston Women's Health Collective, 1971.

Packard, Robert T. *Encyclopedia of American Architecture*. McGraw-Hill, 1995.

Pasternak, Donna L. "Combat Ready: Teaching Young Adult and Classic Literature about War." *Special Interest Group: A Network on Adolescent Literature*, vol. 34, no. 1, 2011, pp. 34–43.

———. "Poetry and Pop Culture: Exploring America and Norway." *English Journal*, vol. 96, no. 1, 2006, pp. 105–09.

Pasternak, Donna L., and Tom Scott. "Quality Teachers, Critical Teachers: Engaging the Profession." *English Leadership Quarterly*, vol. 29, no. 3, 2007, pp. 2–6.

Paulson, Michael, and Patrick Healy. "Tony Awards: *Fun Home* Wins Best Musical and *Curious Incident of the Dog in the Night-Time* Best Play." *The New York Times*, 8 June 2015, www.nytimes.com/2015/06/08/theater/theaterspecial/curious -incident-captures-the-tony-for-best-play.html?_r=0.

Pearl, Monica B. "Graphic Language: Redrawing the Family (Romance) in Alison Bechdel's *Fun Home*." *Prose Studies*, vol. 30, no. 3, Dec. 2008, pp. 286–304.

Plato. *Theaetetus*. Translated by John McDowell, Oxford UP, 2014.

Poletti, Anna, et al. "The Affects of Not Reading: Hating Characters, Being Bored, Feeling Stupid." *Arts and Humanities in Higher Education*, vol. 15, no. 2, 2016, pp. 231–47.

Portwood, Jerry. "Cast of *Fun Home* Visited South Carolina to Counter Homophobic Controversy." *Out*, 24 Apr. 2014, www.out.com/entertainment/popnography/ 2014/04/24/cast-fun-home-alison-bechdel-visited-south-carolina-counter.

Pratt, Minnie Bruce. *S/he.* 1995. Alyson Books, 2005.

Price, Margaret. "'Her Pronouns Wax and Wane': Psychosocial Disability, Autobiography, and Counter-Diagnosis." *Journal of Literary and Cultural Disability Studies*, vol. 3, no. 1, 2009, pp. 11–33.

Proust, Marcel. *Remembrance of Things Past.* Translated by C. K. Scott Moncrieff and Terence Kilmartin, Random House, 1981.

———. *Remembrance of Things Past.* Translated by C. K. Scott Moncrieff and Sydney Moncrieff, Kindle ed., Centaur, 2013.

"Queer Nation NY History." *Queer Nation NY*, 2016, queernationny.org/history.

Quinan, Christine. "Alison Bechdel and the Queer Graphic Novel." *Doing Gender in Media, Art, and Culture*, edited by Rosemarie Buikema et al., Routledge, 2018, pp. 153–68.

Rainey, Lawrence. *Modernism: An Anthology.* Blackwell, 2005.

Ray, Brian. "A *Progymnasmata* for Our Time: Adapting Classical Exercises to Teach Translingual Style." *Rhetoric Review*, vol. 32, no. 2, 2013, pp. 191–209.

Reid, Louann. "Rationale for Teaching Alison Bechdel's *Fun Home.*" *Rationales for Teaching Graphic Novels*, edited by James B. Carter, Maupin House, 2010. CD-ROM.

Reitz, Charles. *Art, Alienation, and the Humanities: A Critical Engagement with Herbert Marcuse.* State U of New York P, 2000.

Rich, Adrienne. *The Dream of a Common Language.* 1978. W. W. Norton, 2013.

———. "Notes toward a Politics of Location." *Blood, Bread, and Poetry: Selected Prose 1979–1985*, W. W. Norton, 1994, pp. 210–31.

"Robert Rauschenberg, *Erased de Kooning Drawing*, 1953." *San Francisco Museum of Modern Art*, 2018, www.sfmoma.org/artwork/98.298.

Rochlin, Martin. "Heterosexual Questionnaire." Gender and Sexuality Center, University of Texas, Austin, 1972.

Rohy, Valerie. "In the Queer Archive: *Fun Home.*" *GLQ: A Journal of Lesbian and Gay Studies*, vol. 16, no. 3, 2010, pp. 341–61.

Rosie, Anthony. "Online Pedagogies and the Promotion of 'Deep Learning.'" *Information Services and Use*, vol. 20, 2000, pp. 109–16.

Rule, Jane. *Desert of the Heart.* 1964. Bella Books, 2005.

Ruskin, John. *The Stones of Venice.* John W. Lovell, 1885.

Russell, Bertrand. *Principles of Mathematics.* W. W. Norton, 1903.

Ruvoli, JoAnne. Review of *Are You My Mother? A Comic Drama*, by Alison Bechdel. *Packington Review*, vol. 4, 2013, www.packingtownreview.com/issues/4/JoAnne-Ruvoli/Review-of-Alison-Bechdels-Are-You-My-Mother-A-Comic-Drama.html.

Salinger, J. D. *The Catcher in the Rye.* 1951. Back Bay Books, 2001.

Sarton, May. *Mrs. Stevens Hears the Mermaids Singing.* 1965. W. W. Norton, 1993.

Satrapi, Marjane. *Persepolis.* Random House, 2003.

Saussure, Ferdinand de. *Course in General Linguistics.* Translated by Wade Baskin, edited by Perry Meisel and Haun Saussy, Columbia UP, 2011.

Sbicca, Joshua. "Eco-Queer Movement(s): Challenging Heteronormative Space through (Re)imagining Nature and Food." *European Journal of Ecopsychology*, vol. 3, 2012, pp. 33–52.

Scherr, Rebecca. "Teaching 'The Auto-Graphic Novel': Autobiographical Comics and the Ethics of Readership." Syma and Weiner, pp. 134–44.

Scholes, Robert. "The Transition to College Reading." *Pedagogy: Critical Approaches to Teaching Literature, Language, Composition and Culture*, vol. 2, no. 2, 2002, pp. 165–72.

Schwab, Gabriele. *Haunting Legacies: Violent Histories and Transgenerational Trauma*. Columbia UP, 2010.

Scott, Joan W. "Experience." Smith and Watson, *Women*, pp. 57–71.

Sedgwick, Eve Kosofsky. *Epistemology of the Closet*. U of California P, 1990.

Shakespeare, William. *The Taming of the Shrew*. Simon and Schuster, 2004. Folger Shakespeare Library.

Shelley, Mary. *Frankenstein*. Edited by Johanna M. Smith, Bedford/St. Martin's Press, 1992.

Shilts, Randy. *And the Band Played On*. St. Martin's Press, 1987.

Shoolbred, James. *Designs of Furniture: Illustrative of Cabinet Furniture and Interior Decoration*. James Shoolbred and Company, 1874.

Small, David. *Stitches: A Memoir*. W. W. Norton, 2009.

Smith, Sidonie. "Performativity, Autobiographical Practice, Resistance." Smith and Watson, *Women*, pp. 108–15.

Smith, Sidonie, and Julia Watson. *Reading Autobiography: A Guide for Interpreting Life Narratives*. Expanded ed., U of Minnesota P, 2010.

———. "Witness or False Witness? Metrics of Authenticity, I-Formations, and the Ethic of Verification in Testimony." *Biography*, vol. 35, no. 4, Fall 2012, pp. 590–626.

———, editors. *Women, Autobiography, Theory: A Reader*. U of Wisconsin P, 1998.

Solomon, Andrew. *Far from the Tree: Parents, Children, and the Search for Identity*. Scribner, 2012.

Sontag, Susan. "Notes on Camp." *Against Interpretation*, Laurel, 1969, pp. 277–93.

———. *Regarding the Pain of Others*. Picador, 2003.

Soter, Anna O., et al., editors. *Interpretive Play: Using Critical Perspectives to Teach Young Adult Literature*. Christopher-Gordon, 2008.

Sparke, Penny. "The Crafted Interior: Elsie de Wolfe and the Construction of Gendered Identity." *Craft, Space, and Interior Design, 1855–2005*, edited by Sandra Alfoldy and Janice Helland, Ashgate, 2008, pp. 123–138.

Spence, Jo, and Patricia Holland. *Family Snaps: The Meanings of Domestic Photography*. Virago, 1991.

Spiegelman, Art. *Maus: A Survivor's Tale*. Pantheon, 1986.

Spock, Benjamin. *Baby and Child Care*. 1946. Pocket Books, 1967.

State of Arizona, House of Representatives. "House Bill 2281." 49th legislature, 2nd session, 2010, www.azleg.gov/legtext/49leg/2r/bills/hb2281s.pdf.

Stempel, Larry. *Showtime: A History of the Broadway Musical Theater.* W. W. Norton, 2010.

Stevens, Wallace. "Sunday Morning." *Harmonium.* 1923. Faber and Faber Poetry, 2001.

Stevenson, Robert Louis. *A Child's Garden of Verses.* 1885. Simon and Schuster, 1999.

———. *Dr. Jekyll and Mr. Hyde.* 1886. Signet Classics, 2012.

Stolberg, Sheryl Gay. "Peaceful Rally of Thousands in Baltimore Is Followed by Unrest after Curfew." *The New York Times,* 3 May 2015, p. A22.

Sturm, James. *Market Day.* Drawn and Quarterly, 2010.

Styron, William. *Sophie's Choice.* Vintage Books, 1979.

Sweeting, Adam W. *Reading Houses and Building Books: Andrew Jackson Downing and the Architecture of Popular Antebellum Literature, 1835–1855.* UP of New England, 1996.

Sword, Helen. *The Writer's Diet.* 2005. 2nd ed., Auckland UP, 2015.

Syma, Carrye Kay, and Robert G. Weiner, editors. *Graphic Novels and Comics in the Classroom: Essays on the Educational Power of Sequential Art.* McFarland, 2013.

Szalai, Jennifer. "Maggie Nelson's *The Argonauts.*" *The New York Times,* 5 May 2017, www.nytimes.com/2017/05/10/books/review/maggie-nelsons-the-argonauts.html.

Tabachnick, Stephen, editor. *Teaching the Graphic Novel.* Modern Language Association, 2009.

Tesori, Jeanine, and Lisa Kron. *Fun Home.* Samuel French Acting Edition, 2015.

———. *Fun Home: A New Broadway Musical.* P.S. Classics, 2015. Audio CD.

———. *Fun Home Full Soundtrack. YouTube,* uploaded by Isabel Panciera, www.youtube.com/playlist?list=PLsGw3wo0ypeQ_XU-9pS5wkPSlk0XKX72T.

Thompson, Becky. "Way Before the Word: Queer Organizing and Race When Beauty Still Counts." *Feminist Studies,* vol. 39, no. 2, 2013, pp. 526–48.

Thompson, Craig. *Blankets: A Graphic Novel.* Top Shelf, 2003.

Thurman, Judith. "Drawn from Life: The World of Alison Bechdel." *The New Yorker,* 23 Apr. 2012, www.newyorker.com/magazine/2012/04/23/drawn-from-life.

———. "Finish Line." *The New Yorker,* 11 May 2015, www.newyorker.com/magazine/2015/05/11/finish-line-backstage-at-fun-home.

Tison, Hélène. "Loss, Revision, Translation: Re-membering the Father's Fragmented Self in Alison Bechdel's Graphic Memoir *Fun Home: A Family Tragicomic.*" *Studies in the Novel,* vol. 47, no. 3, 2015, pp. 346–64.

Tolkien, J. R. R. *The Fellowship of the Ring.* 1954. Ballantine Books, 1967.

Tolstoy, Leo. *Anna Karenina.* 1878. Random House, 2000.

Tripp, Clarence Arthur. *The Homosexual Matrix.* McGraw-Hill, 1975.

Twain, Mark. *The Adventures of Huckleberry Finn.* 1885. Penguin Classics, 2002.

Twine, France Winddance, and Jonathan Warren, editors. *Racing Research, Researching Race: Methodological Dilemmas in Critical Race Studies.* New York UP, 2000.

Tyldum, Morten, director. *The Imitation Game.* Performance by Benedict Cumberbatch et al., Black Bear Pictures, 2014.

Vida, Ginny, editor. *Our Right to Love: A Lesbian Resource Book.* Prentice-Hall, 1978.

Ware, Chris. *Jimmy Corrigan: The Smartest Kid on Earth.* Pantheon, 2000.

Warhol, Robyn. "The Space Between: A Narrative Approach to Alison Bechdel's *Fun Home.*" *College Literature,* vol. 38, no. 3, 2011, pp. 1–20.

Watson, Julia. "Autographic Disclosures and Genealogies of Desire in Alison Bechdel's *Fun Home.*" *Biography,* vol. 31, no. 1, Winter 2008, pp. 27–58.

Weber, Bruce. "Leslie Feinberg, Writer and Transgender Activist, Dies at 65." *The New York Times,* 24 Nov. 2014, www.nytimes.com/2014/11/25/nyregion/leslie-feinberg-writer-and-transgender-activist-dies-at-65.html.

"What Is Reading Resilience?" *Reading Resilience: A Skills-Based Approach to Literary Studies,* Australian National University, 2014, chelt.anu.edu.au/readingresilience/what-is-reading-resilience.

White, E. B. *The Trumpet of the Swan.* 1970. HarperCollins, 2001.

Whitlock, Gillian. "Autographics: The Seeing 'I' of the Comics." *Modern Fiction Studies,* vol. 52, no. 4, Winter 2006, pp. 965–79.

Whitlock, Gillian, and Anna Poletti. "Self-Regarding Art." *Biography,* vol. 31, no. 1, 2008, pp. v–xxiii.

Wilde, Oscar. *An Ideal Husband.* 1895. Dover Publications, 2001.

———. *The Importance of Being Earnest.* 1895. Dover Publications, 1990.

———. *The Picture of Dorian Gray.* 1891. Dover Publications, 1993.

Wildman, Stephanie M. "Making Systems of Privilege Visible." With Adrienne D. Davis. Delgado and Stefancic, pp. 314–19.

Wimsatt, W. K., and Monroe Beardsley. "The Intentional Fallacy." *Sewanee Review,* vol. 54, 1946, pp. 468–88.

Winnicott, D. W. "Transitional Objects and Transitional Phenomena." *International Journal of Pscyhoanalysis,* vol. 34, 1953, pp. 89–97.

Woods, Marjorie Curry. "Boys Will Be Women: Musings on Classroom Nostalgia and the Chaucerian Audience(s)." *Speaking Images: Essays in Honor of V. A. Kolve,* edited by Robert F. Yeager et al., Pegasus, 2001, pp. 143–66.

Woolf, Virginia. *The Letters of Virginia Woolf.* Edited by Nigel Nicolson and Joanne Trautman, Harcourt Brace Jovanovich, 1975. 6 vols.

———. *Orlando: A Biography.* 1928. Mariner Books, 1973.

Zimmerman, Phillip D., and Charles Thomas Butler. *American Federal Furniture and Decorative Arts from the Watson Collection.* Edited by Catherine E. Hutchins, The Columbus Museum, 2004.

INDEX